Journey into Darkness

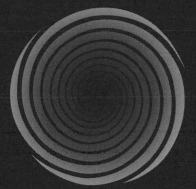

Journey into Darkness

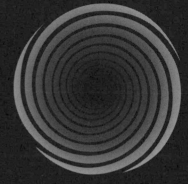

GENOCIDE IN RWANDA

Thomas P. Odom

Foreword by Gen. Dennis J. Reimer

TEXAS A&M UNIVERSITY PRESS · COLLEGE STATION

Library of Congress Cataloging-in-Publication Data

Journey into darkness : genocide in Rwanda / Thomas P. Odom ;
foreword by Dennis J. Reimer.
    p. cm.—(Texas A&M University military history series ; 100)
    Includes bibliographical references (p.) and index.
    ISBN 1-58544-427-8 (clth : alk. paper); ISBN 1-58544-457-X (pbk.)
    1. Genocide—Rwanda—History—20th century.   2. Rwanda—History—
Civil War, 1994—Atrocities.   3. Rwanda—History—Civil War, 1994—
Refugees.   4. Rwanda—History—Civil War, 1994—Personal narratives,
American.   5. Odom, Thomas P. (Thomas Paul), 1953–   6. Americans—
Rwanda—Biography.   7. Diplomats—Rwanda—Biography.   8. Diplomats—
United States—Biography.   9. Refugees—Congo (Democratic Republic)—Goma
(Nord-Kivu)—History—20th century.   10. Goma (Nord-Kivu)—Social
conditions—20th century.   I. Title.   II. Series.
DT450.435.O34   2005
967.57104'31—dc22   2004028031

To Rich Higgins and Peter McCarthy,
who died in the service of peace,
and to all others who risk their lives
in the service of their fellow man

Contents

Foreword

With the fall of the Berlin Wall in December, 1989, the world changed dramatically. The Cold War era that existed for almost fifty years gave way to the New World Order that some have described as "long on new and short on order." The pace of change during the last decade of the twentieth century is unprecedented. The Information Age has brought us closer together in a very real sense, and all institutions were impacted by this change. No institution faced greater change than the U.S. Army.

Built primarily as a threat-based force, designed to defeat the Soviets on the plains of Europe, the U.S. Army found itself involved in new and different situations and in places it, as an institution, knew precious little about. Fortunately, in recognition of its global responsibilities, the army had developed a Foreign Area Officer Program, which quickly became the cornerstone of the effort to adjust to this changing world. Foreign Area Officers, or FAOs as they are commonly referred to, are regional specialists trained in the language, culture, history, and politics of their target area. Typically an FAO undertakes intensive language training, attends a master's degree area studies program, and then spends a year in the area. Many attended foreign military schools during that time, followed by nearly a year of regional travel. They have always been important assets, but with the end of the Cold War they became invaluable, particularly in their role as strategic scouts for the U.S. military.

These soldiers-scholars-warriors provided valuable intelligence to the army and the nation concerning the specific situation in their country. They were soldiers first and foremost, who demonstrated enormous dedication and selfless service. America owes them a great debt of gratitude.

Tom Odom is one of these people. The story of his experience in Africa captures in a larger sense the challenges FAOs faced and the conditions they endured. They were truly on the front lines, often lonely, and we asked a great deal of them. In hindsight, maybe the nation has not always made the right decisions, but Tom and his comrades did not fail us. The dangerous but predictable era of the Cold War was replaced by a complex and unpredictable world filled with the emotions of centuries. These Strategic Scouts reported properly, but it took us a while to figure out this world and adjust the decision-making apparatus. To their credit, these brave soldiers never lost heart.

Tom's experience in bridging the gap between the Department of State and the Department of Defense in foreign countries is illustrative of the story of all FAOs. Tom led troops and served as the intelligence officer for an Airborne Infantry Battalion. He commanded a detachment in Turkey and worked with the NATO headquarters and the U.S. diplomatic mission. He served four months with the Sudanese Army, attending their staff college, and then traveled throughout Africa. Tom taught Middle East military history to U.S. and foreign military officers and wrote two books on Africa as a faculty member and then student at the U.S. Army Command and General Staff College. He served with the United Nations as an unarmed peacekeeper in Lebanon and Egypt.

Austere living conditions, understaffed and unarmed organizations, bureaucratic turf issues, and isolated locations were par for the course. Add to that Mega Death, unprofessional and untrained out-of-control militia, and power-hungry dictators, and you have a truly fascinating story. Colonel Odom deals with all of these issues up close and personal. In so doing, he provides a remarkable glimpse into his life of service to the army and our nation. A careful reading of his story also provides a glimpse into the future. We must learn from his insight or else the road ahead may be very familiar.

I have known and served with Tom since 1990. I was impressed with him from the first time we met, and after having read *Journey into Darkness*, I remain equally impressed. His story is that of a scholar, a Strategic Scout, and, most of all, of a soldier. When you read it you will understand why soldiers are our credentials.[1]

GEN. DENNIS J. REIMER
CHIEF OF STAFF, U.S. ARMY, 1995–99

Preface

Genocide is a purely human experience, for only man is capable of genocide. Yet genocide also brings into question the humanity of man; the poison of genocide kills the souls of the perpetrators, sears the hearts of the survivors, and eliminates another uniquely human attribute, man's capacity for mercy. I hope this memoir will illuminate that horror. It was my fate to wade through the aftermath of genocide, and I, too, felt my humanity at risk. I hope in penning this book I can take you along on my odyssey to the darkness immortalized by Joseph Conrad in *Heart of Darkness* nearly a century ago. In his short story Conrad used the brutality associated with Belgian King Leopold's Congo Free State to symbolize the darkness present in Man. My experience in Zaire (now again the Congo) and Rwanda was no literary metaphor; it culminated my fifteen-year journey as a military specialist on the Middle East and Africa, placing me in two war zones as well as in the nerve center of the U.S. Army during what is now referred to as the First Gulf War.

I also should say up front that this is not intended to be a scholarly history replete with footnotes and sterling prose. For sterling is also cold, and my experiences though sometimes chilling were anything but cold. A soldier's world is filled with people—typically fellow soldiers—and as such is one filled with emotions, mostly humor, thankfully, but sometimes horror. So I will talk to you as a soldier and at times offer some of the experiences that made me and others laugh and some that made us cry. This story is for those—scholars or not—interested in the world of intelligence operations, crisis management inside this nation's military structure, or life abroad in that peculiar fishbowl known as a U.S. embassy.

Journey into Darkness

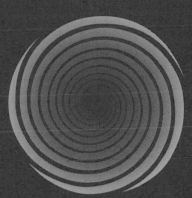

CHAPTER 1

Early Years

I did not pick Africa, much less Zaire or Rwanda. Africa picked me. In March, 1978, I was blissfully unaware the Dark Continent lay in my future. I was doing what I wanted to do, leading men. A junior officer in the 82d Airborne Division at Fort Bragg in North Carolina, I was the acting commander for a newly formed and untried intelligence company. My company commander was away with part of the unit undergoing its initial tests in a major annual exercise. As I looked forward to heading home one day, my battalion operations officer walked into the office.

"We are on a real world alert for Zaire," Luke Taylor announced. "Configure your unit for deployment." The next five days passed in a haze as we scrambled to get ready and then waited. Thanks to the French, the Belgians, and not least of all "Peanuts" Carter, we did not go. But that was not the end of this story, only its beginnings.

I had never even heard of Zaire. A history major with a penchant for stories of brush fire wars, I had read repeatedly *Washing of the Spears* on the Zulu wars in South Africa.[1] *Zulu*, the classic film treatise on Rorke's Drift, was more than a movie to me; it was a model for small unit leadership. I had heard of the Congo and Dr. Livingston. I was also an anthropology minor and had studied Pygmies in the eastern Congo. But aside from wondering what might have happened on the stillborn operation, my interest in Zaire soon faded, though my interest in the Third World did not. It was a taste I had acquired early in life and it stayed with me.

Rednecks, Roughnecks, Cajuns, and Crawfish

I grew up in Port Neches, a small industrial town in Southeast Texas. Our greater community, somewhat grandly called the "Golden

Triangle," was a direct descendant of the Spindletop Oil boom of the early twentieth century. Before World War II, the river- and bayou-laced area just ninety miles east of Houston along the Louisiana border probably had more ducks and certainly more mosquitoes than humans; the few residents ate the ducks and were eaten alive by the "skeeters." It was ideal for the petrochemical industry: cheap land if somewhat given to flooding with ready access to the Gulf of Mexico. Originally founded as Grigsby's Bluff on the Neches River—a small rise of high ground in an area typically at or below sea level—Port Neches and our sister town of Groves became the home to any number of chemical companies during World War II. Once established, the industry thrived. That certainly had its negative side; the "Golden Triangle" was an environmental nightmare, one that made your eyes water and stomach turn. Still, those smelly refineries and the money they brought to the community gave us a first-class education unavailable to many of our contemporary Texans. There was the ever-present infatuation with high school football, but we also had the opportunity to learn and learn well. I did and graduated in 1972 as the class valedictorian. I applied and was accepted into Texas A&M, looking forward to the challenges of the Corps of Cadets.

Texas A&M University

Texas A&M was as much a way of life as it was a school. When I started the school had but fifteen thousand students, about two thousand in the Corps of Cadets. The big news my freshmen year was that the school would now have some one thousand women living in dorms on campus. Women had attended A&M but only in small numbers, and they had never lived on campus. The school actually built two new ultra-modern dormitories just to house them.

Despite its numerical minority status, the Corps of Cadets, and by extension the women who dated members of the Corps of Cadets, ran the campus. Student leadership was largely Corps aside from the representatives of the civilian dorms (called non-regs as in non-regulation). There was some tension between Corps turds (as the non-regs called us) and the civilians. But it was largely swamped in the overall school spirit. We were all Aggies and presented a united front to the outside world.

A lot of Aggies had gone to Viet Nam as soldiers, aviators, and sailors. Some died or were wounded. A few became POWs and got an extended stay. I remember one, a U.S. Air Force captain who spoke at the December, 1973, commissioning. He claimed his fish (freshman) year had prepared him for the experience at the hands of his captors. He was of course exaggerating, but not too much.

The Corps of Cadets made no bones about it: hazing was a revered practice in a school worshipping tradition. There was no preparatory "Beast Barracks" in the service academy mode. The entire fish year was a marathon Beast Barracks. Fish were the lowest rung of the ladder. Seniors were on the top. Every step up cost you. Hazing combined the physical and the mental, worked into a witches brew by the evil minds of the pissheads (sophomores) and their handlers, the sergebutts (juniors) and the zips (seniors).

The only way to get through it was to stick together like the fish we were. We lived and breathed by company. Class divisions ordered everything inside the company. Inside the class structure, it was with your "ole lady," also known as your roommate. You did everything with your ole lady from fall out on the wall for preformation hazing to reporting for more personalized torture at the hands of your sophomore squad leader. Unbeknownst to me as I applied to A&M, my class was to be the Centennial Class for the school, meaning we were scheduled to graduate in 1976, the hundred-year anniversary of A&M's existence. That alone meant we were marked for special treatment. And though we got it, we returned it with a vengeance. As fish we were expected to get back at our tormentors. Some of it was sanctioned.

Our high-water mark for the fish year was dubbed "Hell Week." Tied to the buildup for the Thanksgiving game against the University of Texas, called always by the diminutive "t.u," Hell Week capped the month-long effort to build the annual bonfire just across from the Corps quadrangle. The tradition called for the freshman to do something outlandish to their company commander. In return, the CO would, of course, devise something only four years' experience in Aggieland could foster. It was "Beast Barracks" in reverse; we had already undergone months of hazing. Hell Week was intended to guild the lily; afterwards we would be full-blown fish, no longer viewed as wannabes.

We decided to kidnap the CO. Some of us would take him to Austin and dump him on the t.u. golf course in his underwear with one bent dime for a phone call. The rest of us would strip his room and haul it all out to a classmate's family farm outside Bryan. We thought we could always use his possessions to bribe our way out of the expected retaliation.

Naturally our plan did not unfold as expected. We did get him. We ransacked his room. And we did drop him at the t.u. golf course at 2 A.M. on a cold November morning. But the CO was a resourceful Aggie, and he made it back to College Station in time for the 6 A.M. formation. So our Hell Week was just that, and my roommate decided not to come back the next spring. Still we had made our mark. That weekend we had a beer bust to celebrate, and we all were happy to see it over. But like all who survive such rites of passage, we looked forward to the next year when we would be handing out the grief.

Sophomore year came and went. Let me say that although we dealt a lot of grief to the new fish, we also soon learned our status as sophomores was even more stringent than as freshmen. They were expected to make mistakes and they also were expected to retaliate. As pissheads, we caught all of the same hazing and had none of the fun. But the juniors did call us by our first names while they screwed with us. By year's end we looked forward to the "white belts" of junior status, which was amazing in attracting female companionship. We also underwent junior leadership interviews. I was selected to be my battalion's sergeant major, a position marking me for command of the battalion the next year if I did well as a junior.

In my year as battalion sergeant major, I was responsible for the administration of and discipline for the four companies in the battalion of some two hundred cadets. I was also selected to the Ross Volunteers, the junior and senior honor drill unit for the Corps. The highlight of the year was leading the King Rex parade at Mardi Gras. We also got serious about ROTC; most of our previously free weekends saw us out training. That summer we went for advanced ROTC training camp at Fort Riley, Kansas. I worked hard to make sure I was ready for the course. I had attended the U.S. Army Airborne school the previous summer, and compared to Fort Benning and the airborne instructors, camp was a snap.

Senior year came, and we put on our senior boots and the gold spurs marking us as the Centennial Class. I commanded my battalion, doing well in the Corps and at the university, and emerged as the Top Cadet graduate for 1976 and the top ROTC graduate for Third ROTC Region. I felt especially proud of being selected by my peers on the Ross Volunteers for the firing squad; we provided the honor squad for all Silver Taps ceremonies whenever a fellow Aggie passed away.

After considering law school, I decided to go ahead and join the army. I owed four years for my ROTC scholarship. I picked intelligence as a military career, because I thought that would offer the greatest opportunity to see the world. I reported to the Intelligence School at Fort Huachuca, Arizona, in May, 1976.

Welcome to the *Real* Army!

For the six months at Fort Huachuca, I worked hard on conditioning while training in tactical intelligence. My goal was the U.S. Army's Ranger course at Fort Benning. A number of classmates at A&M had gone, and I wanted that distinctive tab of a black background and gold letters spelling Ranger. I expected I would be headed to the 82d Airborne Division, and Ranger training would better prepare me for that. I succeeded in getting a slot and spent the next nine weeks in misery. Two classmates died in the course, and we graduated with their tabs on the company flag.

My next stop was at long last the real army with real soldiers in a real unit with real missions. I reported to the 82d Airborne Division

Graduation and commissioning with Texas A&M University President Jack Williams.
I had just won the top cadet award for 1976.

in January, 1977. The 82d was considered among the elite of the army since its soldiers had to voluntarily undergo paratroop training. They could at any stage terminate their jump status and transfer out of the unit. The "Deuce," as we referred to the division and its parent headquarters XVIII Airborne Corps, sported maroon berets, which marked us as paratroops.

I spent two years with divisional intelligence units, during which time the alert for Zaire flared and then died. As I said earlier, we did not deploy. A few weeks later I reported in as intelligence officer, or S2, for the 2d Battalion 505th Parachute Infantry Regiment of the division's 3d Brigade. Our brigade commander was Col. Art Stang, who had just come from forming a Ranger battalion. His operations officer was Maj. William Garrison, who later as a major general would direct U.S. Special Operations Forces in Somalia.

As for my unit, the CO was a martinet and not nearly as good as he thought. It made life difficult, but the rest of the staff and the line company leadership were first rate. Jim Warner and Carlos Negrete were lieutenants who had been in my Ranger class; Jim was in my platoon. He and Carlos, along with Randy Mixson, another lieutenant in our unit, would become generals. Our troops were motivated, but we still had a lot of problems. The high point of the year was our jump into Andrews Air Force Base for Armed Forces Day. Typical for the period, the president did not attend such an openly militaristic event. After thirty-five months in the 82d, I signed out and headed west to Fort Huachuca one more time.

CHAPTER 2

Soldier, Scout, Statesman

L ike all intelligence officers in the late 1970s, I lived and breathed the Soviet threat. But it became apparent that the army had enough Soviet experts. I considered myself a student of Israeli military history. So when selected for early graduate schooling, I decided to become a Middle East foreign area officer (FAO), the regional specialist program the army uses to develop expertise about the world at large. I was as ignorant of the FAO program in 1980 as I was of Zaire in 1978, but it sounded exciting. I first heard of FAOs in 1976 when a fellow student at the officer's basic course asked a visiting lecturer about the program. "Don't worry about the FAO program now, lieutenant. You have years of dues to pay before you can even apply," was the response.

Be All an FAO Can Be

So three years later, I put in for training as a Middle East FAO. Based on my cadet record at Texas A&M, the army had guaranteed my graduate schooling. Becoming a FAO would require a year of Arabic language beyond the graduate degree. Then there was what was referred to as "in-country training" to follow later. All of that was in the future. I was exchanging the 82d Airborne for the advanced course at Fort Huachuca. From there I would head to Monterey and the Naval Postgraduate School, followed by the Defense Language Institute. I did not realize at the time that I was leaving the tactical army forever. Or more accurately, the next tactical missions I would be on would not be with U.S. forces.

Two years later I had a master's degree in Middle Eastern Affairs and some proficiency in Arabic. I graduated with honors from both the Naval Postgraduate School and language training. I wrote a thesis on U.S. and Soviet interests in Saudi Arabia. My classmates in the graduate program were a mix of all the services. The navy sent intelligence officers, SEALS, and an occasional aviator to the area studies program. My army companions were to a man foreign area officers like me; I would continue to bump into them over the next fifteen years. Air force officers also attended, mainly those headed to attaché duties. The faculty was largely civilian, and the regional specialists were just that, area experts. A bonus for my group of Middle East area studies students came from an unexpected quarter: Israel had a number of students in various courses at the school. Their senior officer, Col. Ran Goren, attended several of our seminars. Later, Ran would rise to the rank of major general and deputy commander of the Israeli Air Force. He was able to offer us an insider's view on the Israeli military that textbooks could not hope to match.

We soon got to meet the other side of the Middle East equation: the Arabic department at the Presidio of Monterey offered its own type of regional immersion on the shores of Monterey Bay. We had Syrians, Lebanese, Iraqis, and Egyptians, each with their own identity and axe to grind. Classmates were largely army, mainly interpreters or other FAOs. Two would work with me in the 1991 Gulf War. We did have one senior sergeant who was from the secretive Delta Force, recuperating from injuries sustained in the aftermath of the abortive Desert One rescue attempt. There were several air force officers headed to attaché duty and one marine from the Corps' smaller FAO program. One of the air force officers would become the assistant air attaché in Egypt, where I ran into him while traveling. And we had a navy lieutenant commander from the SEALS who would become the admiral in charge of all navy special operations. Other attendees included FBI agents and others from unspecified agencies. A female FBI agent in the course ended up at my twentieth Texas A&M class reunion, married to one of my friends who had left the marines for the FBI Hostage Rescue Teams. In short, it was a diverse and very select group that would maintain contacts long after leaving Monterey.

Two things from the instruction stuck in my mind. The first was an instructor's comment that Lawrence of Arabia was the role model for true FAOs. He meant we should bury ourselves in our regions if we were to be effective. I took that to heart. I knew I had to get an in-country tour as soon as possible, the final stamp on an FAO's training. The army sends you to a country in your region. Typically you go through one of the country's military schools, then you travel through the region. Many of my graduate school companions were headed to their regions.

Second was a fundamental shift in my view of the Middle East. Education is a wonderful thing, and like most Americans I was woefully ignorant of the region before my schooling. I had long read about the Holocaust and the Arab-Israeli Wars. I knew very little about the real history of the region. And I was overwhelmingly sympathetic to the Israeli view. As I studied the region and watched the play on the international scene, my views became more centered. I could understand how terrorism was an attractive option to radicals in the Arab world. The Israelis had themselves used terrorism coupled with guilt over the Holocaust to resurrect their country. I did not condone Arab terror, nor did I condone Israeli air attacks on refugees. Neither side wore a white hat, and trust in the region comes with a very limited warranty. I adhere to that view today.

First Taste of Foreign Air: Turkey

So there I was, a newly birthed "Lawrence" itching to get to the Middle East. The army offered me Korea. After days of phone calls, the personnel center suggested a year in Turkey. Not officially considered the Middle East, Turkey was at least a Muslim country. We had studied the Ottomans as part of the region's rich history. I took the assignment and asked for an in-country training tour afterward. FAO assignments said if I did well in Turkey, I would get a special tour in Sudan. (Still somewhat naïve, I believed "special" equated to something especially good.) I just had to go back to language school for French. Another language was another language. I did not question why.

Turkey started me down the road of small independent operations. My headquarters was in Belgium, a couple of thousand miles away. I was lucky. The job was a major's command and I got it as a junior captain. More importantly, I stayed in command for nearly the entire year until headquarters forced my full colonel boss to replace me with a major. I learned some things. The international flavor of the job supporting two NATO commands and their U.S. components was a different challenge from pushing troops at Fort Bragg.

A large part of that support involved day-to-day contact with U.S. flag officers, a big change for a junior officer, especially giving similar support to the U.S. consul general in Izmir. The initiation into the turf wars was revealing. Part of my job was watching for terrorism warnings and, if such a warning arrived, getting it to the proper decision makers. The chain was clear; such matters went to the consul general for a decision. But when I did get a viable threat warning, that person was unavailable, so I went to my general. He did the right thing and issued restrictions on movements. When the word reached the consul general, he wanted to relieve my general, more for usurping his authority than anything else. That did not happen, but it was an eye-opener. Security was sacrificed for appearance.

Turkey's security situation was not the best; it had just gone through martial law and was again playing with democracy. But even as its internal security improved, Turkey's external setting grew more tenuous. The Middle East was explosive: Israel had again invaded Lebanon. The PLO was being driven out, under U.S.-French military escort, and Israeli Defense Minister Ariel Sharon set the dogs of war loose on Palestinian refugee camps outside Beirut. Given the internal state of Turkish affairs and the regional context, I sought to improve security around my shop, housed in a multistory office building that also contained the base group commander's office. My efforts drew attention, and I had to go explain why as an army captain I was questioning security arrangements as established by an air force colonel. The colonel dismissed my recommendations with, "Captain, you are talking pretty sophisticated terrorists." The Beirut marine barracks bombing and a similar attack against the U.S. embassy would occur just months later. I also learned from a friend that a car bomb had been discovered just outside the door of the American hotel in Izmir the same week the marines in Beirut were attacked. Fortunately it had not gone off.

I found a special kind of joy in living abroad. A boy from a pearly white Southeast Texas refinery town, I inhaled the culture just as I had the fumes from my hometown. The Turks are an intriguing blend of Western secular nationalism, Muslim faith, and Middle Eastern culture. The Turkish military are, in a word, "hard." All said Turkey was but a stepping-stone to my getting that in-country training tour.

Land of the Mahdi, Gordon, and Kitchener: Sudan

Eighteen months after leaving for Turkey, I felt the Swiss Air flight start its descent into Khartoum, Sudan. Finally I was starting my in-country training tour as a Middle East FAO—almost four years ahead of the approved schedule for the career track. I had read up on the country and its fascinating history. As the British governor general in the mid- and late 1800s, Chinese Gordon predated and outshone T. E. Lawrence as a regional influence. The Mahdi as Gordon's nemesis predated Osama Bin Laden by more than a century. Both Gordon and the Mahdi died locked in the bloody conflict between the Arab north and the African south still simmering today. Soon I was over in the Sudanese Staff College in Omdurman, protected by the Mahdi's tomb.

I attended the junior staff course modeled on the British Army's junior command and staff college. The Brits taught the tactical portion, and the Sudanese taught the administrative side of the course. My classmates were divided between northern Muslim Sudanese, three Christian southerners, and four Ugandans. The real education was not in the curriculum but in the interaction between these groups.

Colonel "Tommy" Tucker headed the British Army Training Team. He told me, "You know, Tom, that you will not be the honor graduate of this course." The real trainers were two lieutenant colonels. One was John Byrncs, an infantry officer who had commanded a battalion of the Green Howards. He was Catholic and had an American grandmother. We became good friends and spent quite a bit of time off duty together. The other Brit was a different kettle of fish. He was a tanker, as I recall, whose manner would have made Field Marshall Montgomery proud.

As for the students, the Sudanese Arabs stuck together, but they made me part of their group. We started every day with *futur*, our communal breakfast with all the beans, oil, and whatever else was on the table mashed up in a bowl, peppered to make a mummy weep, and scooped out with bits of bread using the right hand. I took to the red pepper breakfasts quite well. Neatness was considered bad form and I showed very good manners to the Sudanese.

The Sudanese Christians made up the second set of students, and they spent most of their time with the Ugandans as the "African" contingent. There was a definite schism between the two groups. The war down south had flared up again after nearly fourteen years of relative peace, sparked by President Nimeri's declaration of Islamic Law. Soon afterward, the government began to amputate limbs for theft or stone to death those convicted of adultery. And of course there was flogging, a punishment for any number of lesser offenses. All of these hard-line changes made the non-Muslim southerners justifiably nervous.

The spreading war down south reinforced those fears. We studied tactics, and the Brits used their operations in post–World War II Palestine as a case study on combating an insurgency. John Byrnes would offer limited use of force and confidence building as the solution. The Sudanese Arab students saw things differently. They advocated scorched-earth tactics whenever resistance was encountered. You could tell they meant it, and the southern Sudanese believed them. As for the Ugandans, they were all guerrillas just emerged from one bush war and headed to another.

We also went to the field for tactical map exercises. Our main training area was the Omdurman battlefield where Kitchener had destroyed the Khalifa's army in 1898. By Western standards, the exercises were standard military fare. The Sudanese took the exercises as a joke; they made fun of the way I dressed the first time we went out. I wore field gear with two full canteens at first. My companions had briefcases, wooden map boards, and low-quarter shoes to scramble around the hills in the desert. Then the sun started beating them up, and I had to upgrade to four canteens to meet their demands for water. The Ugandans were just baffled by the whole thing. Overall, both Sudanese and Ugandans were ill prepared for anything beyond rudimentary staff work.

The reason for this was the role of their armies, a role common to most militaries in the Third World. They were there as guarantors of the current regime. At the same time they were by definition the greatest threat to their own government. The Sudanese literally could not dispatch a single vehicle without Palace approval. Sudan's President Nimeri had come to power through military coup. Uganda's President Obote had emerged through civil war. Both would ultimately depart the same way they had arrived. As part of the initial welcome, the Brits had offered a block of instruction on the "Role of the Army." They showed a film, offered other insights, and then asked for questions or comments. One of my friends stood and said, "The role of our army is to keep the government in place." That ended that block of instruction.

Other things made life interesting at the junction of the Nile Rivers. One factor was the neighboring countries. Part of the staff course was a visit to all the major commands in Khartoum, established by branch. One Thursday we visited the Air Defense Command in Omdurman. The Sudanese Air Defense was a secondhand copy of the Soviet Air Defense system equipped with third- or fourth-hand equipment. To cap off the visit, they ran an exercise on an intruder from Libya. Of course the bad guy was blasted from the sky.

The next day, when the Sudanese went to Mosque, a single Libyan Tu22 bomber penetrated the country's defenses from the west. Flying at five hundred feet, the strategic bomber flew at slow speed up the White Nile and then attacked the main radio tower at Omdurman. It dropped four or five one-thousand-pound bombs. All but one exploded with little damage, leaving the tower intact. The last was a dud. It skipped thorough one house, a maid's apartment, and two walls before it came to rest in the front wall of Col. Tommy Tucker's Omdurman house. Tucker and his wife were not at home at the time, and the bomb was defused.

That was not the first of the Libyan adventures and it would not be the last. The previous year a Libyan hit team had attempted to assassinate Sudanese President Nimeri but failed. Sudanese guards near key installations remained jumpy after dark. An embassy officer got lost one evening and made a whipping turn into the driveway of the main security headquarters. A stitch of AK47 fire across the front of the vehicle told him he had knocked on the wrong door. Incredibly, he repeated the act two weeks later with similar results. Consequently, we were all very careful when we drove after dark. But Libya was the boogieman of the moment, and Quadafi justified the name by secretly mining the Red Sea. A couple of tankers hit mines and prompted concerns the Red Sea oil routes might be suspended. Egypt dispatched an air defense battalion to reinforce "beleaguered" Khartoum. A classmate's great grandfather had been one of the main Sudanese generals against Kitchener and the Anglo-Egyptian Army of 1898. My classmate told me he would kill as many of the Egyptians as he could, a sentiment echoed by all the other Sudanese students. He was not kidding.

After four months of the Omdurman course, I was ready to start my travel in the Middle East. It was not to be. I soon learned Sudan was an African FAO training base—that was the reason I had been schooled in French. I put in my first travel plan for the Middle East but was directed to travel in Africa. The army personnel center had neglected to tell me this when I signed on the dotted line. Nevertheless I enjoyed Sudan and the people. Life in Khartoum defined the word "rough," and outside the city living conditions only got worse. Finished with the Sudanese Staff College, I had nine months and nine thousand dollars to see Africa.

I did three external trips out of Khartoum. Between those trips I worked on the Sudanese drought relief effort, my first taste of disaster relief operations. I made several trips to the west as well as Port Sudan. I also traveled with my Sudanese Army buddies, visiting all of the eastern garrisons. On one of these trips, I made my boss happy when I stumbled across a full battalion of Ethiopians who had deserted en masse after losing a battle to the Eritreans. And I managed to get south into the war zone when an American oil company base camp at Malakal was struck by southern Sudanese rebels and then "rescued" by the Sudanese Army. Being saved by the Sudanese Army was indeed risky. Based on what I saw at the camp, they adhered to the same "kill it to save it" mentality my companions had displayed in the insurgency course. Again this made my boss happy because it made him look good. As an accredited diplomat he could not travel without permission so I went instead. Using me this way was against policy, but I was having fun and he was getting good information.

But the high points of my travel were the trips abroad. The first trip was forty-five days, and I took in all of Egypt, Somalia, and Kenya. I came back to Khartoum with a case of amoebic dysentery thanks to Egyptian food and a scar on my head courtesy of the rock-throwing Somalis. Zaire was the next destination, with plans to continue on to Liberia. I ended up spending nearly three weeks in Zaire, including a side jaunt to Chad. My final trip out was a one month, six-thousand-mile road trip with the FAO trainee in Malawi. We traveled through Zambia, Botswana, South Africa, Lesotho, Swaziland, and Zimbabwe together. I was growing attached to my new region.

Each posting should teach you something, but Sudan was a graduate school education. Four months of interaction inside a foreign army cannot be duplicated in books. I believe one of the hardest lessons for any American to absorb is that the rest of the world does not necessarily think like we do. Dealing with my Sudanese Army buddies was a crash course in that reality.

Inside the U.S. diplomatic mission, I studied the internal politics. All departments played at this to some degree. We had State, CIA, the U.S. Agency for International Development (USAID), the Security Assistance Mission, and the DAO. The turf fights and the alliances between the players shifted like sands. I thought this game to be a waste of time and talent, but I learned how it is played. I also learned the nuts and bolts of disaster relief, such as how to get several million tons of sorghum from a primitive port to hungry mouths over a

As a foreign area officer trainee, I traveled to several countries, including Egypt, in 1984.

thousand miles away. The worst obstacles were usually the bureaucrats in between. Finally, in all my travels through eighteen different countries I was privileged to meet any number of senior State and military officers. I saw embassies that worked, and I saw embassies that did not. The difference between them was always a question of leadership. If the leaders focused on their mission, the embassy cooked. If they focused on the internal squabbles, the mission suffered. Usually the difference depended on the ambassador.

Unplanned Pregnancy: Combat Studies Institute

It was at this stage that the foreign area officer branch completed its conquest of me. The courtship was soon over, and I certainly did not get kissed. I had lined up a company command in the newly formed Military Intelligence Group that supported U.S. Central Command, the regional headquarters for the Middle East. Military Intelligence branch declared I did not need the tour with tactical MI even though I had been away for almost five years. Foreign area officer branch chimed in with the plea they were critically short of African FAOs. My new assignment orders soon arrived. I was headed to Fort Leavenworth, Kansas, to teach African studies at the Command and General Staff College. At least that's what FAO branch told me. When I got to Leavenworth I learned the college had a standing policy that in order to teach core subjects like African studies, you had to be a course graduate and be promotable to major. I was neither.

In a way I was lucky. Since I had a bachelor's degree in history, the Combat Studies Institute, the history department of the college, took me. I ended up writing on Africa and teaching an elective on Middle East military history over the next three years. Again Zaire seemed to find me. I was looking for a major research topic and picked the 1964 Congo Crisis. Col. Fred Wagoner, another African FAO, had written a geopolitical analysis on the crisis, published in 1980 by the National Defense University.[1] I read the book and was intrigued. The subject begged for more research. Soon I was enmeshed in the history of the Congo. Guiding me in this process was the man who became my longtime teacher and friend, Dr. Roger Spiller. Roger was a senior historian in the department. His real gift was the ability to coach officers on the use of history, especially how to write history in a way that was interesting.

Researching the 1964 Congo Crisis was a lifetime opportunity. Most of the participants were still alive, retired, and therefore willing to talk. I ended up interviewing many of the key Americans as well as fellow authors such as Fred Wagoner and David Reed, who had written *111 Days in Stanleyville*.[2] The capstone for the project came with the opportunity to go to Belgium and France. Our counterparts in the Belgian military history department granted me full access to their files on the operation. They also set up interviews with the key Belgians from the Paracommando Regiment and from the colonial military.

I interviewed nearly twenty Belgian officers, and all provided superb insights on the operation and on the Congo. Two really stood out. The first was Maj. Gen. Charles Laurent, commander of the Paracommando Regiment in 1964. Laurent and I spent hours discussing how the operation to rescue western hostages had evolved. He made it clear that political guidance had restricted his tactical options and thereby dictated certain results. He had spent years in the Congo and had a large repertoire of stories. His agreement to meet me opened the door to the remainder of his officers. Like Laurent, all were old Congo hands with stories to tell.

The real find, however, was Col. Frederic J. L. A. Vandewalle. VdW, as he signed his name, had been the last security chief for the Belgian Congo. He became a hated symbol of "imperialism" to Western liberals in 1960 when he directed the Belgian attempt to set up an independent Katanga under Moise Tshombé. When Tshombé returned in 1964 to save the Congo, Vandewalle came back and set up the mercenary operation. I spent two days interviewing him and it was an experience. If you wanted to know about the Congo, VdW was the man.[3] I ultimately found that what these men told me about the 1960s Congo remained just as true in 1994.

The other half of my Leavenworth tour was teaching Middle Eastern military history. I tag-teamed a seminar with Dr. George Gawrych in the spring quarters. We taught a blend of Israeli, Arab, and U.S. students. The discussions were intentionally lively, and it was an instructive exercise in diplomacy that sometimes resembled professional wrestling without makeup. My final year Israeli Col. Itimar Chezik—formerly the Israeli security boss for southern Lebanon—said to me, "Tom, you are doing a good job in there. You make everybody angry, so that means you are being fair."

Thirty months later I had finished the draft for *Leavenworth Paper #14: The Dragon Operations, Hostage Rescues in the Congo, 1964–1965* and taught three CGSC classes on the Middle East.[4] Then Brig. Gen. Fred Franks was kind enough to let me go, so I headed to the Middle East as a U.N. military observer in southern Lebanon. When Colonel Chezik heard, he grabbed me and pulled me into the hall outside our class. "You be careful. Our army likes to shoot at blue berets," he warned. It was a fair warning.

Go to War but Don't Take a Gun: Lebanon

So off I went to duty with the United Nations Truce Supervisory Organization (UNTSO) in June of 1987. As a Middle East FAO, I understood what we were in for better than most of my companions. UNTSO had been in existence since 1948 as an observer organization drawn from a broad spectrum of countries including the United States and the USSR. I was headed to Observer Group Lebanon (OGL), made up of officers from sixteen countries, officially called U.N. Military Observers or UNMOs. OGL command rotated between the United States and Australia. At the time of my arrival, Australian Lt. Col. Ewen Cameron was two weeks from assuming command.

In 1987 Lebanon was a dangerous place for Americans. There were a number of hostages rotting up in Beirut as proof. We learned that as U.S. military observers, we were worth five hundred thousand dollars each to Hizballah, not a reassuring welcome message. Due to the threat against us, American observers were restricted to duties inside the Israeli occupied security zone. We manned the permanent observation posts (O.P.s) that mainly looked south into Israel. Our duties were captured in the logo for the OGL T-shirt, which showed a U.N. observer peering through binoculars over a frying pan. "Cooking and Looking" was a shared role. We teamed with a partner, and one cooked while the other had the daily patrol. The observer on patrol went to a partner O.P., picked another observer, and then completed a designated patrol route. The patrols lasted all day long and were exhausting given the summer heat, rough roads, mountainous terrain, and security conditions. We usually logged around two hundred kilometers on a patrol day and our vehicles showed it. They were beat

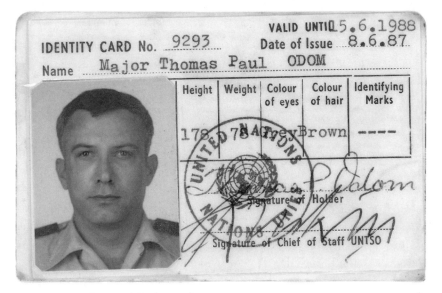

Here is my UNTSO identification card.

An Israeli Armored Personnel Carrier rumbles past a U.N. observation post in Lebanon in 1987.

up and most had their frames repeatedly broken and welded. They were also not air conditioned, hence our moniker as "dirty, dusty UNMOs." Picking up our patrol mate for the day was the only time we went outside our O.P.s alone.

The French had already drastically reduced their manning in Lebanon. The UNIFIL (U.N. Interim Force in Lebanon) reaction force was French, but it stayed in Naquora base camp unless called out. There was but one Frenchman in OGL, a Foreign Legionnaire unhappily serving as the recreation house manager. Even having the wrong name could be dangerous. A Canadian para named Steve France found that out. Up above the security zone on a negotiating team, Captain France had drawn special attention from local Hizballah members. One approached.

"*Vous etês* Français?" Steve spoke French but was smart enough to wait until the question was repeated in broken English. Then he pointed at the Maple Leaf flag on his shoulder and repeated "Canada, Canada, Canada" until the questioner was satisfied. From then on Steve wore a Canada nametape over both pockets on his field blouse and a Canadian flag T-shirt underneath. We called him "Captain

Canada." The other nationalities served on liaison teams farther north in the area occupied by UNIFIL, the armed U.N. peacekeepers in Lebanon. Many of the Americans groused at this slight to their honor, especially the marines. That said, the "security zone" had its own set of challenges and risks.

The new commander of all U.S. military in UNTSO, Lt. Col. William R. (Rich) Higgins, had been tasked by the secretary of defense to determine whether Americans should be on the U.N. liaison teams. Discussing it at my apartment that July, Rich asked me the same question. My response surprised him.

"Not only should we not be on the teams, you should not be coming here as the next OGL commander. The other nationalities don't want us out there with them. They are more likely to get blown away or taken hostage if an American is riding with them. The reason you should not come here as OGL commander is simple. You cannot safely do all the things the OGL commander should do. The last American who commanded the group had to use his operations officer, a Canadian, to do what he should have been doing." Rich listened to me, agreed I had a point, but he said he would have to see for himself.

I had already had the test all soldiers ponder; my first evening in southern Lebanon we drew light machinegun fire from an Israeli Defense Force (IDF) patrol looking to say hello. It was like having time slow down at the same time your senses are heightened. You are

U.S. Military Observer Group commander, Lt. Col. William Rich Higgins and Maj. Steve Piccarilli at the 1987 U.S. Marine Corps Birthday Ball.

not scared because you do not have time to get scared or even stay that way. But you see and hear everything in heightened detail. We were on O.P. Mar overlooking a permanent Israeli position inside the Lebanese border. Manned by an infantry-tank team, the IDF ran daily patrols out of the position every evening. You could set your watch by them. I was on the observation deck with my counterpart and the liaison team that shared the compound. I watched the patrol come out and go through their pre-combat preparations. Through the 20X "Big Eyes" telescope, you could almost read nametags. The machine gun and sniper team set up on the road. Then I felt time slow as the gunner aimed directly at me. I called a warning. I saw the flash and heard the crack of rounds past my head. We all hit the deck. The IDF did not necessarily want to hit us. Then again, they did not care if they did. My Israeli student Colonel Chezik had been right: his army did like to shoot at U.N. berets.

Many of my companions also came under fire of one form or another. Fortunately most did well. My greatest fear—shared by many—was being taken hostage. Four of my friends were hijacked on their training tour, their very first sortie into Lebanon. American Capt. Vic McCloud was directing the half-day jaunt through the area. Quite the professional, Vic was the group assistant operations officer. Four officers—two Americans, one Swede, and one Canadian—were the trainees. The roads in southern Lebanon were largely tank-crushed asphalt, potholes, and serpentine turns. You could tell a vehicle a mile away was coming by the dust plume, but you could rarely see more than one hundred yards in front of you. Vic's Wagoneer had just rounded a bend when an AK47-armed Lebanese appeared in the middle of the road. As they stopped, a second gunman stuck an AK47 in their faces and waved them off the road.

Canadian Maj. Vern McKeen remarked, "Vic, this is really realistic training!"

Vic shot back, "Vern, this is NOT training."

The second gunman had them dismount and lay side-by-side face down in the dirt. U.S. Air Force Maj. Roy Lauer later told me the three Americans tried to hide the U.S. flags sewn to the right sleeves of their tunics. Fortunately it was a straight robbery, not a hostage seizure; all five UNMOs made it to happy hour that evening for a well-deserved drink. I took one of the five out with me the next day on his first O.P. He was most alert on the drive out. Vern was right. It did make for a good training mission.

Others had problems dealing with the danger. Some of them avoided it by seeking safer jobs. Some acted as if it was not there until it nearly killed them. One U.S. observer almost got his privates shot off the same evening I was baptized by fire. He too was on his first O.P., one with a record of near misses. Earlier that month an American on duty at that O.P. had been having dinner one evening when a rifle round hit the wall a foot from his head. This harassing fire was almost routine; you just minimized use of the generator at night and you did not profile yourself. This particular evening the team had shut down for the night. The generator was off and the O.P. dark. He heard a noise in the emergency shelter. His superior told him not to do anything; remember U.N. observers are unarmed. He ignored his senior and went to investigate. Walking up to the bunker waving a flashlight, he saw the lock was cut on the steel gate and the door was open. Hearing voices, he shone his torch inside and challenged two intruders, both armed with AK47s. One swung and fired a low burst that stitched a path between his legs, convincing him a speedy return to the sleeping caravan was in order. He spent the rest of the night inside but did not sleep. According to his senior, he kept the generator on every evening from then on.

Two weeks later his nightmare escalated. This time he was on O.P. Mar where I had been shot at, and I was on the O.P. where he had accosted the gunmen. Remember that O.P. Mar shared its compound with an observer team attached to one of the UNIFIL battalions. The two men on the O.P. lived in the main building; the UNIFIL team had a small caravan as its quarters. That night they had come in late and gone to their trailer. As they entered, an IDF patrol went by and fired several rounds at a dog. Already permanently nervous and almost a eunuch, our guy inside the O.P. cut the master light switch, thinking, he told me later, that the position was under attack.

Next door, the UNIFIL team was surprised. The generator was still running but no lights? One team member walked over to the main O.P. and banged loudly on the locked door, hoping to be heard over the generator. He was; his thumping convinced our man bad guys were at the door, and he ordered his companion to stay low. To his credit, he risked crawling up the stairs to the observation tower and radioed out a "Mayday" message his position was under attack. I was lying in the rack at my O.P. when the net call alarm sounded on our radio. OGL rear warned everyone something bad was happening. Every U.N. observer on duty in the security zone tuned in on the radio.

Meanwhile the team outside the O.P. could not get the U.N. observers inside the O.P. to come to the door or even answer. Nonplussed, they walked back to their caravan and called headquarters. Back in the rear, alarms were screaming; UNIFIL's reaction forces had mounted up to save the O.P. some twenty miles away. Then we heard the voice of the team leader asking if there was a problem and the O.P. Headquarters immediately asked where he was. "I am outside the bloody O.P.," he answered, and the situation dissolved into comedy. A sheepish American soon opened the door and greeted his attackers. He had had a rough night. He would have an even rougher time at the next happy hour.

My other nightmare was mines. Getting shot was not something one wanted, but you generally could anticipate that risk. Even artillery fire—and we got that too—gave some warning. But mines just blew. They had issued us Viet Nam–era flak jackets when we arrived and then proscribed our wearing them. Doing so supposedly made us unarmed observers look "nervous," as one U.N. staffer sitting comfortably in the rear base camp explained. Anyone who was not nervous in southern Lebanon was stupid, dead, or both. So we could either sit on the jackets or drape them over our seatbacks. You could tell who feared what by where their flak vest was placed. Family jewels are family jewels. I sat on my vest.

Southern Lebanon offered other insights as well. There were two separate U.N. peacekeeping organizations operating in close cooperation with each other. It was a time-tested arrangement. The United Nations Truce Supervisory Organization (UNTSO) and the United Nations Interim Force in Lebanon (UNIFIL) had been in southern Lebanon since 1978. UNTSO effectively served as the scouts for the more conventional UNIFIL. Yet each battalion or contingent brought its own way of doing things into the larger organization. Some, like the Irish, the Finns, and the Norwegians, were quite effective. Others like the Fijians were there for the money. The factions and the Israeli Defense Forces singled out the weaker units for special attention. Sometimes the attention was funny. Sweden fielded a new hospital company every six months. Its nickname was "SwedeBcdCoy." Replete with blonde buxom nurses, the new trainees attracted everyone, and they generally welcomed the attention. One of our marines, bachelor Capt. Ron Johnson was nicknamed the "BedCoy" boy. We joked that he had his own O.P. set up with the Swedish nurses. On one occasion, a new South Lebanese Army platoon was passing the compound, and the nurses were outside sunning. Some of the Viking blondes were topless. The platoon of Lebanese militia dissolved and stormed the wire. UNIFIL's reaction force—a French light cavalry troop—charged in to "restore" order. As Frenchmen, they also got a good look at the ladies while they were running off the Lebanese.

Supporting the military side, the U.N. fielded a large contingent of field service workers, the bureaucrats and blue-collar workers inside any U.N. peacekeeping operation. They too sometimes pursued their own agendas. But without their cooperation and support, the logistics machine ground to a halt. The salient point was that the U.N. force commander did not command in the conventional sense. He influenced, cajoled, and sometimes blustered—even in a long-term operation like UNIFIL. In a place like Lebanon, that made the job even harder.

The complexity of the social, political, and military situation in Lebanon was staggering. The Lebanese were as diverse a population as you might find in the Middle East. Christian and Muslim sects, each subdivided, worked with and against each other. Alliances changed without notice. The Muslims had multiple militias, the most notable being Amal and Hizballah. Both Shia, they fought each other as much as they contested the Israelis or their clients, the South Lebanese Army, a nominally Christian militia. The Sunni too had their armed wings. And the Israeli military was right in the middle of it all. My friend Colonel Chezik was back again as the Israeli intelligence officer for the area. I saw his men cross into the zone several times. They were easy to spot. They always drove top-of-the-line sedans festooned with antennas, and they dressed like punk rockers with Uzis. Later, after finishing my tour, I got word to Chezik, and he sent his bodyguards to pick me up for dinner. My Israeli neighbors were quite intrigued by the sight of these Uzi-draped, gold-chain-wearing soldiers picking up a U.N. soldier.

There were incidents everyday. Shootings were common. Full-fledged firefights broke out from time to time, especially in the areas on the northern fringe of UNIFIL's area. On the seventh of August I was out on a patrol with Vern McKeen when we ran off the road to dodge Israeli reinforcements headed north to a firefight being watched by our mates at Beaufort Castle. Mines as I have mentioned were a constant threat. So were unexploded air munitions left from uncounted Israeli air raids. Those raids were fairly rare, at least those that dropped bombs or fired rockets. Overflights by fighters, helicopters, and drones were common. Artillery fire punctured the ground on occasion. Katusha rockets served as the militias' choice response. One of my friends, marine Maj. George Solly, was on duty at O.P. Hin one afternoon when two Katusha rockets slammed into the ground just outside the O.P. wire. Luckily the wall of the O.P. caught the fragments, not George. The Nepalese Battalion in UNIFIL was not so lucky on August 19 when two RPG7s hit one of their positions and wounded four soldiers. Those were the most blatant forms of attack. Occasionally we got a car bomb. One of the teams discovered a roadside bomb inside the Israeli secure zone on August 10, and a car bomb blew up inside the Ghanaian Battalion zone August 16, killing three men in the car and a nearby eight-year-old boy.

Intimidation was another common occurrence, one the Israelis practiced daily. My first experience of hostile fire was just such a tactic. Every time an Israeli patrol set out, they used test fires to announce they were coming. And they really did not care where the rounds went. After the shooting incident at my first O.P. and another at a sister O.P., headquarters actually issued us flares as part of an agreement with the Israelis' local command. Supposedly the agreement was that if the IDF happened to shoot at a U.N. O.P., firing off the flares would get them to stop, assuming the IDF's firing at O.P.s painted white with ten-foot letters "U.N." painted on all sides under a U.N. blue flag was a mistake. Most Israeli patrols included armored personnel carriers, infantry, and an occasional tank. At times, they would surge an artillery battery into the zone and practice rapid-fire missions while on the move. As the patrols moved farther north, they became less restrained. There was a U.N. observation post at the base of Chateau Beaufort, an old Crusader castle that looked north and down into the fifteen-hundred-foot-deep Litani River Valley. O.P. Beaufort was outside the security zone, and Americans could not be assigned there. We could, however, visit, and it was a favorite stop on our daily patrols.

The Israelis had taken Chateau Beaufort from the Palestine Liberation Organization (PLO) and put almost a company of infantry with tanks inside the position. The IDF outpost literally looked down at the U.N. O.P. on the lower slope. The Israelis loved to set the U.N. post on fire with tracer rounds. They were less gentle with the adjacent village of Arnun. The village was empty of military-age men. Women, children, and the elderly were the sole inhabitants. But they were PLO or Hizballah or Amal or someone else's sympathizers and the Israelis wanted them gone. I was at the O.P. one morning when an Israeli tank drove through the village and fired several main gun rounds through the houses, a sort of peace through cannon-rounds.

The United Nations got much the same treatment. On one occasion, an Israeli artillery battery bulled its way inside the Norwegian Battalion compound and set up to fire north. They refused to move and the deputy UNIFIL force commander—a French brigadier—arrived with the quick reaction force to eject them. The Norwegian commander defused the situation by bringing out a video camera. Once the Israeli commander saw he was being filmed, he ordered his unit out. Israeli radio made special efforts to deny the incident had occurred. Anytime we encountered an Israeli patrol we backed off: one of my friends had the front end of his Wagoneer flattened by an Israeli tank. I narrowly escaped the same treatment while out on patrol when an Israeli tank came barreling out of one of their positions and charged across the road. I stomped on the brakes and slid into a berm. They did not hesitate to fire, and the first round going past was all the warning you got. An Arab American visiting his family in the area was shot one afternoon when he went too fast through an Israeli and Lebanese militia position just outside my O.P. When the Israelis discovered he was American, they called in a helicopter and evacuated him to Israel. We later learned he had died.

They also encouraged the Southern Lebanese Army (SLA) to play the intimidation game. One SLA position protected the Middle East TV retransmission antenna inside the zone. It had been blown up more than once. A Christian fundamentalist group in the United States funded Middle East TV. It offered a varied fare mixing evangelism, professional wrestling, and Monday Night Football dubbed in Arabic. I often wondered who thought such programming was needed in a war-torn country. The retrans station was just around the corner from one of our O.P.s. We had to go by there using a protocol established by gunfire. If we drove too fast or too slow, we drew fire. If we did not wave hello, we drew fire. If we did not get the speed right and wave, we drew fire. Or if the guard was just in the mood, we drew fire. None of this fire was aimed directly at us. But it was close enough to hear the crack of the rounds and the ricochets. Often the shooter was fifteen or sixteen, and the recoil from the assault rifles walked them all over the place. The same was true at O.P. Khiam, immediately adjacent to Khiam Prison. The prison was nominally SLA-run, so it made an excellent place for the Israelis to work over hard cases away from prying media eyes. From time to time the United Nations would request access to inspect the conditions, a request rarely granted. For the Palestinians and Lebanese prisoners it was grim. If you listened at night when the generator was off, you could hear their screams. If you showed too much interest in the place, driving by or just looking from the O.P. roof one hundred yards away, you drew fire. The bottom line was you could get shot in Lebanon for lots of reasons or no reason at all.

One of the things that made Lebanon truly bizarre was that life went on with a sense of near normalcy. When you talk to Lebanese, the purists among them will tell you they are not Arabs. They are Phoenicians, traders of ancient lore. They may be stretching things, but they are traders. That was what made Beirut the Paris of the Middle East before the 1975 civil war broke out, and it remains the greatest hope for a resurrected Lebanon. In 1987, that trading instinct played out as smuggling. Unlike Sudan, where you could not buy anything, Lebanon was a place where you could buy everything. And the prices were cheap. Naquora was the village outside the U.N. base camp. The main street ran north along the edge of the sea. Lined by shops, it reminded me of the main bazaar in Izmir, Turkey—only with a much more eclectic selection. I went in one store and found a selection of Barbie dolls adjacent to the rack of rip-off XXX videos and vibrators. Do Arab women use vibrators? Ah, the issues one ponders as an FAO.

The other disconnect was that the Lebanese were as a people quite nice. But villages were quilted with religious factions. I would visit one side of the street and talk to Shia elders. Cross the road and the leaders would be Sunni. They would be equally friendly to me. We would often stop in these places and have tea. Their neighbors across the road could have been a thousand miles away. Fifteen feet of road was as effective as the Berlin Wall. Each stayed on their side of the street; the penalty for ignoring that barrier was death. Christian villages appeared almost Western at times. Every three months, the Southern Lebanese Army and Israelis would bring down new recruits from Beirut and the Bekka Valley. They marked these occasions with parades through the main burgs. I remember seeing a column move through Marjayoun cheered by the Christians. Extremely good-looking young women in tight short shorts and crop tops lined the upper balcony of a large building. The girls strutted, flirted, and teased the recruits as they marched by. The males of the family watched like attack dogs. Any other male touching the prancing girls would of course set off a blood feud. A similar display in a nearby Shia village would have gotten the women stoned and beaten. Women there remained largely out of sight or wrapped in yards of black cloth. But there were Shia men watching this display of Christian women, and that was what it was all about. It challenged the local Muslims and backed the challenge with muscle. My patrol partner and I were watching from the outskirts of the town as the columns formed up. A local eased up beside us and tapped on my window. Pointing at the passing SLA troops, he grinned and said, "Car bomb good!" As he bent laughing, overcome by his own humor, I got us out of there.

Lebanon had been very interesting work but nearing the end of six months, I was ready to go. I took several lessons with me. I could function when gun smoke was in the air. I also saw some could not, and you really could not tell until the shooting started. The six months was an education on how the United Nations works, especially in peacekeeping. I also got a firsthand look at low-intensity combat between a relatively modern force and a mixed guerrilla force. All combat is intense when the shooting starts and you are the target. Values placed on human life—much less humane behavior—erode very quickly. Israeli soldiers shot dogs and Lebanese with equanimity. The Lebanese could be equally bloody. Both would go home and kiss their kids. Finally, the surreal atmosphere in Lebanon allowed tranquility to turn to terror in a heartbeat. All said, I was proud to have served but glad to move on. I was especially grateful we had not lost anyone. The last casualties in Observer Group Lebanon had been in 1982, something to be proud of. I marked my departure by taking two weeks in Turkey.

Leaving Lebanon, Losing Friends

I celebrated too early. In January, I had just completed a week in Sinai when I passed through the U.N. recreation house in Cairo. I expected word from a friend still in Lebanon, Peter McCarthy of the Australian Army. Peter was a favorite in OGL; he got along with everyone, and that's not easy to do in such an organization. Peter had promised to visit for a couple of nights before heading to Luxor. There was a telegram for all hands posted on the message board. It announced that Capt. Peter McCarthy had been killed while on duty in southern Lebanon on January 12, 1988. The cable also said Canadian Maj.

Gil Coté had been seriously wounded in the same incident but was expected to recover.

The word was that Peter and Gil had been inside the security zone headed north in a Jeep. The road was broken asphalt with long stretches of dirt; I had been on it many times and knew it well. They struck what appeared to have been two stacked anti-tank mines. The focused blast blew the engine out of the small truck; the block was found 150 feet away. The same blast killed Peter in the driver's seat. Gil was more fortunate. Because anti-tank mines are shaped charges, the directed explosion only grazed him. Still, it shredded his left shoulder and blew him out the side of the Jeep. We always operated on checkpoints and time hacks in the zone. When there was no word from Peter and Gil, the base dispatched a patrol to look for them. They found Gil incoherent, staggering along the road a few hundred yards from the destroyed Jeep. Investigators found that a six-foot man could stand in the hole blown in the road with only the top of his head showing. The mines could have been placed recently or they could have been there for years. Chance had ruled that the Jeep's wheel would trigger them.

Certainly the loss came as a shock.[5] But it was hardly a surprise. The armed U.N. troops we supported sustained at least ten dead in the six months I was in southern Lebanon. As unarmed observers, we had been lucky and we had gotten used to it. Colonel Higgins and I had talked many times since our initial discussions. We often mused about what was happening and about the Middle East in general. Rich and I became friends. The night before I went to O.P. Khiam on my final jaunt into Lebanon, he threw an impromptu party on top of the Marine House for me. Millions of brain cells and a large bottle of Jack Daniels expired that night. I certainly felt like death on the two-hour trip to Khiam the next morning. Rich and I next saw each other at the New Year's party in Cairo and he was itching to take over as OGL commander. He intended to tighten things up and improve training.

The Abduction of Rich Higgins

In mid-February we got another shock. For the Americans it was much more personal. One evening after dinner, I was on duty in Sinai with another American when our Cairo headquarters called all its stations on the radio. The voice was very weak and distorted but we understood. Rich Higgins had been taken hostage that day in southern

Lebanon. Headquarters announced the United Nations was making all possible efforts to find him and get him back. My O.P. mate and I looked at each other, stunned by the news. I poured us each a very stiff drink, and we toasted Rich.

Rich had been headed back from a meeting in Tyre with the Shia Amal militia. He drove his own vehicle alone trailed by another vehicle with two U.N. observers. Later I would become friends with one of the two following Rich, Lt. Col. Don Zedler. The area was outside the zone normally traveled by UNTSO, and parts were outside UNIFIL's control. Rich had outpaced his trail car and, rounding a curve, was stopped and snatched by Hizballah. The trail team found his empty vehicle when they caught up. There was an international appeal for his release and acrimony between the United Nations and his family. His wife, Robin, was a marine corps major in the Department of Defense public affairs shop at the time. Robin tried every thing a wife could do for a missing spouse but to no avail. My assessment was and still is that Rich was trying to do what could not be done. As an American, he could not fully perform as OGL commander without excessive risk to himself and those around him. As he had told me five months earlier, he set out to do just that. I believe that is why he was in the vehicle alone.[6]

Sinai: Magical Wasteland

The remainder of my U.N. duty was in Sinai. A week out in the desert earned a week in garrison. To a military historian and Mid-East FAO, it was fascinating. Sinai breathed history. When you took a step in Sinai you took a step in time. We often bought Roman coins in the coastal villages. I gave battlefield lectures to my U.N. comrades. We shared the area with the orange berets of the Multinational Force and Observers (MFO) and their "Men from Mars" civilian observers in flame orange jumpers. The United Nations had been asked to stay even after the Camp David Accords created the Multinational Force and Organization in 1978. Our mission was presence. The MFO had infantry battalions occupying permanent positions. One was American. Another was Fijian. The Fijians would do a tour in Sinai then go north to UNIFIL in southern Lebanon. As in Lebanon, we operated from a handful of two- or three-man O.P.s in Sinai. Unlike in Lebanon, we patrolled alone. The only risks were getting lost, break downs, or straying into minefields.

I relax after a trip up Mount Sinai in 1988.

The Soviets: Comrades and Clowns

Another element made the U.N. tour in Egypt unique in the U.S. military. In 1988 Observer Group Egypt (OGE) was the only place U.S. officers worked and lived with Soviet officers. The Soviets operated under strict guidance from Moscow, and the watchers among them were easy to spot. All spoke English and some spoke American. At the beginning of my tour, they were restricted to Cairo and to the support O.P. at Ismalaiya on the west side of the Suez Canal. Moscow had not recognized the Camp David Accords, so the Soviets could not go into Sinai. I spent one week on O.P with them and it was interesting to hear their views on the world. Midway through my tour, the political atmosphere changed, and they were released to go into Sinai. For the first time they were allowed to go out paired with other nationalities.

All of the restraints of living a monitored life fell away, and the Russians went wild. They talked freely, offering cultural insights not evidenced by studying Soviet tactics. One was that they truly longed for freedom but were at the same time terrified of the idea. The socialist state was a massive baby blanket that made them feel secure against the violence of the world. They considered us—the Americans—to be very dangerous. To them, we seemed to worship violence. More than one brought up the subject of American films. We alternated showing movies at the rec house each week. One week I offered Sam Peckinpah's *The Wild Bunch* as the ultimate American Western. The Russians were more bewildered by our behavior in watching the film than they were by the film itself. We oohed and laughed and cheered when the slow motion gunfights began. They cringed. They did not get how we could support Peckinpah's antiheroes. But when the Soviets started going out on O.P., they requested we bring "action" films to watch. *The Wild Bunch* remained a favorite.

They did their best to imitate those outlaws. Drinking was second nature, but they did not just drink. They swam in the stuff. One got drunk for a solid week and was soon sent home. They also drove like maniacs. For many, U.N. duty was the first time in their lives they got the keys to a truck and were free to go off on their own. Several wrecks resulted. They also could not read a map to save their lives. Sinai was fairly easy to navigate, but in some of the patrols you had to "wadi bash." That meant reading a topographic map and driving in hub deep sand. More than a couple of the comrades were late coming back from their patrols. The group commander finally declared that no Soviet would be allowed to go out on patrol alone until trained by senior U.N. observers. That slap in the face brought them up short, and the mishaps grew more rare.

The French: La Legion Etrangère!

Before moving on from U.N. duty in Egypt I should also mention the French. A French officer always commanded OGE. Ours was Lieutenant Colonel Gasche, late of the Foreign Legion. Rumor had it Gasche had been cashiered for losing a battalion payroll in a robbery; the large chip on his shoulder lent credence to this gossip. French and Soviet officers occupied all but one staff position in the group headquarters. It often seemed that the Soviets liked us Americans better than the French did, especially our French commander. Colonel Gasche's welcome aboard speech focused on the 1956 Suez War when the United States stood against the British-French-Israeli grab to take the Suez Canal from Nasser. Gasche spoke at great lengths describing how we—and he looked at us as if we had been there—had sold out our allies in that war. He gave this same talk to all incoming U.N. observers, Soviet and Americans alike. For the "dirt" observers who went on Sinai O.P.s, wisdom held that we stayed out of headquarters.

As for the remainder of the French officers, we generally got along. There was friction but nothing like back in Cairo. I learned rapidly there were two French armies that did not like each other. One was the conventional military inside France, including the navy and the air force. This group hung together and stayed away from Gasche the Legionnaire. The other was the exterior army of France, dedicated to maintaining and policing France's former colonial empire. The Foreign Legion and the Naval Infantry (formerly the Colonial Infantry) were the main players, along with France's Special Operations forces. Most of the French in OGE were from the exterior forces. All of them had served in one capacity or another in Africa.

Just as the six months in Southern Lebanon had offered valuable lessons, so did my time in Egypt. U.N. organizations act like their major national components. OGE functioned with the discipline of the Legion and the social structure of the USSR. The French, in particular the French exterior forces, would do anything to further what they saw as French interests in the Third World. They also saw the United States as at least a rival if not an adversary in those regions.

All in all, the tour with the United Nations was both enlightening and frustrating. That year, U.N. peacekeeping won the Nobel Peace prize and all of us were collective recipients.[7] One of the Americans drafted a request that we be awarded an expeditionary medal as a standing U.S. Military Observer Group. All who served in Lebanon had drawn the $110 imminent-danger pay, an amount unchanged since before Viet Nam. We were not authorized a "combat" patch though we had lost comrades, including our commander. The expeditionary medal would have marked our collective experience as outside the norm. It was not to be; we got a unit citation instead. Our efficiency reports read that our rater was currently hostage, and the substitute could not evaluate us. That sentence alone encapsulated the unreal experience of duty in Lebanon. Still, we survived.

Shaba II: Zaire Revisited at Leavenworth

Finished with the United Nations, I returned to Leavenworth as a student. The course had its challenging moments, but that is not its true purpose. The Command and General Staff Officers Course really serves to indoctrinate field grade officers in the ethos of staff work. We were broken down into fifteen-person groups for instruction. Mine was much like all the others. We had one foreign officer, Colonel Hegab from Egypt, one air force officer from the special ops world, Maj. David Scott, and the rest of us were army. Two of the army guys came from the Reserves and the Guard. We all shared our backgrounds. I had finished telling mine when one of my contemporaries remarked, "Well, you haven't been in the real army." When I asked the last time he or any of the others had been shot at it, he backed off.

Aside from the main course, I used my spare time to do a second master's degree. As the thesis subject, I picked the Shaba II War in 1978 in Zaire. My first book, *Leavenworth Paper #14* on the Congo Crisis of 1964, came out in print that fall. In researching the 1964 Congo, I had already uncovered quite a bit of material on the Shaba II War, so I went to see my friend, Dr. Roger Spiller. Roger agreed to chair the committee for me. My other main advisor was Dr. Gerald Linderman, a visiting professor in the history department. As a young foreign service officer, Linderman had served in the Congo in the 1960s. He had attracted my attention in a presentation he made at the U.S. Army Command and General Staff College. It was 1988, the USSR remained intact, but the Cold War seemed to be dying out. I had just served with our long-standing enemies. One could see the cracks in the Soviet military. Linderman talked about the future of the U.S. military. He foresaw a period of Pax Americana coming just like the earlier Pax Britannica of Queen Victoria. He predicted that a smaller American military would be called to fight small wars and conduct other operations across the globe, out of sight and largely out of mind of the American public. Just back from a small war in Lebanon, I understood what he meant. His speech fifteen years ago remains just as relevant today.

With Spiller's backing, but at my own expense, I returned to Brussels over Thanksgiving to conduct research. The Belgians had played a major part in the Shaba II crisis, but their role was drummed out by the French Foreign Legion's public relations fanfare. Once again I had a chance to talk with the officers involved. I took copies of *LP#14*, and the paracommandos made me a member of their mess. The high point of the trip was a chance to see my old friend VdW. Now in his late seventies, he was still going strong.

Thesis done and, with Spiller's guiding hand, on the way to becoming my second book, I was soon ready to graduate.[8] Branch had come out to see us. The Military Intelligence guy looked at my file and told me I really needed to get back to "real MI," that is, the tactical army. There I was with two—not one—two foreign area designators, two languages, and three unaccompanied tours in my regions. All of that stemmed from MIs deciding in 1984 I did not need to go back to troops after being away from them for four years. Now after more than five years this guy was telling me to go tactical again. He was correct in the check-the-block approach to getting ahead in MI. The branch focuses on grooming officers for promotion via troop leading because it sells on promotion boards. It does not, therefore, focus on its mission of providing intelligence to commanders. Had I gone back to troops in 1984, I would have agreed with him. But in 1989, it made no sense for me or for the good of the army. As he spoke, I could see what would happen to me as a major going back to a tactical battalion. With a lot of work I could do it. But I wanted to best use my talents and training. I told him I wanted Washington and got it.

The Pentagon: Ground Zero

Years before, I had sworn I would never serve in the Pentagon, and yet there I was headed to the Office of the Deputy Chief of Staff for Intelligence (ODCSINT), specifically to the Directorate for Foreign Intelligence. I learned via letter that my first job would be in the Anti-Terrorist Intelligence and Operations Cell. It sounded sexy but proved less interesting than I hoped. It was a year of night shifts doing little more than watching an empty in-box.

Still, that initial year was good preparation for coming events. To begin with, it offered me insights into the maze of interagency cooperation. I made contacts throughout the intelligence and foreign policy community. It was like embassy life on a mega scale; all the agencies had their own agendas. Some were players, and some were mere observers. I also got to see what a full-blown Crisis Action Team was like with Operation Just Cause, the U.S. operation to rid Panama of El Jefé Noriega. Sadly the single terrorism-related event of the year dealt with Rich Higgins. I was on duty when we learned the Israelis had snatched a Shia sheikh in southern Lebanon. I penned a short piece predicting Hizballah would not allow the act to go unpunished. The next day we saw the CNN footage of Rich supposedly being hung in retaliation. I did not want it to be him, but I knew it was. I also knew the United States would probably be unable to strike back. For me, as an army analyst in the Army Operations Center, it was a sidebar, a sad one to be sure, but a sidebar nonetheless.

In June, 1990, I was overjoyed to get out of the dungeon and off night shift. I had served my year, and my reward was the current intelligence desk on the Middle East. I was on a more normal schedule. We had to be at our desks by 0430 but we got off by 1400. The work was interesting. We scanned stacks of traffic and picked out the pearls to write on. Fast-breaking events required fast writing. Our articles went into the army's Black Book as well as the Joint Intelligence production system under the Defense Intelligence Agency. We briefed the DCSINT and his deputy on our regions. Once I got to brief the chairman, Gen. Colin Powell. We also sent down briefing items to the Army Operations Center. Occasionally we wrote and briefed special topics on Friday. That was the day the Deputy Chief of Staff Operations (DCSOPS) and DCSINT attended the morning brief.

I immersed myself in the Middle East. Daily I scanned the traffic from over fifteen countries to get a feel for the region. I was very lucky in my fellow analysts. One was Maj. Eric Kramer, a fellow intelligence FAO who had studied Arabic with me in 1981. The other was Dr. Norman Cigar, a civilian analyst with an encyclopedic knowledge of the region. They were the long-term analysts for the region; they looked out several months to several years. My focus was the immediate. Naturally we cooperated in our analyses. It helped that we soon became friends. They had to accept a degree of "hip shooting" from me, and I had to accept their more measured approach. We got along.

Quivers in the Middle East Spiderweb

Way back when I was doing my thesis on Saudi Arabia, I compared the Middle East to a spider web. Linked by language and religion but divided into subsections, events in one area could be felt in another. A purely political change in Syria might not cause any repercussions in Egypt. But if it were designed to control the Sunni majority, it might. Accusations once made were hard to retract. Arabs look on words as actions. Normally there was a certain level of verbal attacks directed at Israel, usually from the hard-liners who tended to be safely far away from Tel Aviv. Verbal attacks from one Arab state on another were rarer. Iraq might not like Egypt's relations with Israel, but public criticism was muted. Cairo had backed Baghdad in the war with Iran. There was a sort of peace now, but tensions remained. Iraq still wanted Egypt in its corner if the war resumed.

As I tracked the tensions, I became more and more concerned. Norm Cigar had the front-line states, so we huddled every day on what was happening. Public attacks were matched by underlying actions. Iraq threatened to "burn Israel" and was building up its ballistic missile arsenal. That was just one element of the tension. Israel rebuffed a major terrorist attack on the beach at Tel Aviv. It was linked to Libyan support. Egypt was having its own fundamentalist problems. Several tourists had been killed and fingers pointed at Iran. Norm and I agreed the tensions in the region resembled those of the early 1970s on the eve of the October War. I wrote a longer analytical piece called "Rumors of War" laying out our concerns. A senior intelligence officer called me to task about it. He said he could not see any prospect for war in the region. I told him we could not point to a coming conflict, but we could tell the region was explosive. He disagreed.

Storm in the Desert: Saddam Invades

Mid-July clarified matters. Saddam Hussein's posturing against Israel slipped into context as he reopened an old grievance against Kuwait to leverage relief on his war debts. His claim on Kuwait as Iraqi territory enjoyed some historical support. But the same argument could be made that Iraq belonged to Turkey. Kuwait had backed Saddam in the Iran-Iraq War. The Sheikhs had bankrolled the Iraqi military and shipped Iraqi oil when Iraq's main port at Basra was closed. Iraq was cash starved after eight years of war. Saddam had oil, but he needed money to jump-start his economy and his oil production. Leaning on the Kuwaitis was a way to get it. Suddenly all the regional chatter focused on the bad boy in the Middle East playground. Still the consensus was that Kuwait, perhaps with some under-the-table assistance from the Saudis, would buy off Saddam.

I was just getting back from shopping on a Sunday afternoon when my phone rang, It was the watch officer notifying me that a critical message I needed to see had come in on the Middle East.

I reported to the Army Operations Center (AOC) and grabbed the watch officer. He briefed me, and I read the traffic as I evaluated the situation in the Middle East. The salient change was that Saddam had ordered almost the entire Republican Guard corps south toward the Kuwaiti border. These were the regime's guardian units and the "victors" of the Iran-Iraq War. Three heavy armored divisions and their support equated to an armored corps. You do not just move such formations on a whim. It costs money and equipment. You do not send the main bulwark of your regime away from the capital unless you are betting on a sure thing. I was sure Saddam planned to invade Kuwait.

That analysis on a July Sunday affected my life for the next two years. For the next eleven days I went to a near-war footing. Every morning I was in by 0330 to scan the Iraqi traffic and write it up for the morning's Black Book. I also updated the AOC morning brief. Norm, Eric, and I huddled daily to review the situation. Norm was the first to agree Saddam was going to invade. Eric followed but gave the caveat that Saddam "probably" would attack. I briefed the DC-SINT—a three star—at least every other day. He had been the Central Command J2 and had a fair understanding of the region. But he was not a regional specialist. Earlier that year he had offered his annual view of the world to the army staff, and Iraq was not on the hotspot list, a suggestion that angered General Schwartzkopf, commander of the new Central Command. The DCSINT continued to adhere to that position. When the subject was the Kuwaiti crisis, he always came back with "Saddam is bluffing."

Saddam was not bluffing, and he proved it on August 2, 1990. Around 0200 that morning I again got a call from the watch. The caller said "he went south," and I knew my fears had come true. I checked the clock and grabbed another hour's sleep. Again I was at my desk at 0330 writing a summation of what we knew about the invasion. There was some minor fighting, but it was really all over when the first Iraqi tank crossed into Kuwait.

On that Friday morning, I was down in the AOC waiting to give a special topic brief as the watch officer briefed my words on the Iraqi invasion. The DCSOPS Lt. Gen. Dennis Reimer was there, as was the DCSINT, who kept saying, "We thought it was a bluff." Reimer asked some questions, and I answered from the balcony side of the seating arc. I had been on sixteen-hour days since Saddam started moving tanks. Now I shifted to twenty-hour days for the next three weeks. Between August 2 and August 7, when President Bush signed the mobilization order, it was just me and whoever was on watch. On one day alone I briefed eleven times to audiences wearing at least one star. I lived on Capitol Hill, so on my four-hour breaks I could get home and crash for a couple of hours.

With the deployment order signed, a full-scale Crisis Action Team stood up in the Army Operations Center. The chief of staff of the army, Gen. Carl Vuono, inaugurated the first of the daily briefings in the AOC. It had its moments of humor. Secretary of the Army Stone was also there. Stone, once the USAID Mission director in Cairo, spoke a smattering of Arabic. The initial operations briefer was a really nice lieutenant colonel from the South who just could not wrap his southern accent around the Arabic place names. Kafji came out in southern cracker drawl as "caaaaaaaaalf gee." It was his first and last brief in the AOC. Stone stopped him at every gaffe and corrected him, something that just could not be countenanced on the front balcony.

At the conclusion Vuono issued guidance to the staff. Vuono is a brilliant man and a devastating task masker. We called him Darth Vader for good reasons. He had a mercurial temper that once elevated was slow to recede. It came out in many of those briefings. The audience consisted of the staff principals along the front of the balcony and their deputies in the penny seats behind them. To even get a seat, you had to be a promotable full colonel. The remainder of us clustered in a mass like bait fish, praying our bosses would not have to field a Vuono question. We concentrated on the Big Points. Unanswered questions and issues were noted and soon hit the Pentagon hallways as "Chief's taskers." Even when all the questions were answered, Darth might utter, "Turn up the lights." Those became feared words. They meant "stop the brief and switch on the overhead lights; Vader had something to say." A "good brief" meant there were no pauses. A "bad brief" stopped and started repeatedly. Vuono was merciless when something sparked his ire.

Let me make one thing clear here. General Vuono was hard, but he was hardest on senior officers. He was sending his army almost en masse to a desert war, its first since World War II. Vuono to be sure drove the staff hard. But he drove himself as well. He underwent a hip replacement in the early part of Desert Shield and was partially office bound. The staff rigged a four-star plate to an electric cart that carried him down to the Army Operations Center. Vuono's guidance to the staff was, like him, brilliant. He urged the staff to "coordinate, anticipate, and verify—make sure of your information, make sure you have the complete picture, and keep the forces in the field informed."[9] I briefed him deskside on more than one occasion. He listened and asked pertinent questions. The friction came from those who interpreted the questions and the answers. Staff principals and their minions studied the chief as much as they studied the Middle East situation. When they got it wrong there was hell to pay, and the bill always arrived at the action officer level.

On the ODCSINT side, that tendency was painful until Brig. Gen. John Stewart took the lead. Stewart was the Deputy DCSINT, "dual-hatted" as the commander of the Army Intelligence Agency. Under that title he supervised the work of the army's Intelligence and Threat Analysis Center (ITAC) over in the Washington Navy Yard. Armed with the DCSINT's authority and his own control over ITAC, Stewart pushed forward within the staff to become the main intelligence spokesman. Beneath the front office was the Directorate for Foreign Intelligence under Col. James Pardew. An excellent analyst in his own right, Jim became the lead U.S envoy in the Balkans after he retired from the army. He is now the U.S. ambassador in Bulgaria. Col. James Solomon, commander of ITAC, soon joined him in dealing with the Iraq crisis. As we were regional analysts, Pardew was our boss. Solomon's outfit provided the detailed analysis of military capabilities we could not do in the Pentagon. Thank God the two colonels got along. It was painful enough as it was.

Peeling the Onion

As we established the Crisis Action Team, I stood up the ODCSINT-ITAC component aided by my immediate boss, Lt. Col. Jake Almborg. Jake acted as a buffer for us. He stoically took any heat without passing it down to us. But intelligence is like peeling an onion. Senior officers need a certain level of information. The chief needed to know the number, type, and quality of the Iraqi divisions. His deputies needed an understanding of how many brigades were in those divisions. Those two echelons would be the first two layers of the Iraqi military "onion." But needs aside, they always wanted to know more. They would continue with the questioning, peeling another layer off the onion, until the questions could not be answered. The briefer left holding the onion was the one who cried. That was me.

Developing and then delivering intelligence was a mental version of full contact football without pads. I was the guy defending the goal for the first quarter of this game. Mornings were the hardest and that meant night shifts. We were still undermanned in the AOC. I took the night shift every afternoon at 1800 and worked till whenever. On more than one occasion I never went home. The focus was the morning briefs. The big briefing in the AOC required a written briefing. We wrote it the day before. But the DCSOPS wanted an update every morning before the 0800 brief. Typically Jake Almborg would check in with me around 0430 to see how I was doing. He and I game-planned the brief, but he left me alone to get on with it. Colonel Pardew showed at 0530, and I went through it for real. I took the goal line and Pardew ran at me with the first level of spin control. Comments like "Don't say that. Say this" rattled off my helmet. Usually this took fifteen minutes or so; Pardew was thorough, and he did his best to punch through my defenses. The second round was over, and I was already getting sore. Then General Stewart would come in, and we would start all over again.

Stewart's motto was "never brief negativity," meaning never say you did not know something. Spin the negative into a positive. For example, we monitored the theater with satellites, and satellites are not perfect. In 1990 they offered either broad area coverage or detailed coverage of a very small target. You could not watch everything all the time if you were going to analyze specific targets. Iraqi units moved around, and if they did when the satellites were not on them, we lost them, sometimes for weeks. Rather than admit such a problem, we were told to say, "We know where they are; we just can't put our fingers on them." Spin was not my style. I was not a politician and tended to take attackers head on. Stewart was devastating. In essence, he was defending himself, so the morning attacks on the briefer—yours truly—were merciless. So I would go through the brief, and Stewart would knock me on my butt, tweaking the words, none of which I had time to write down. This final session always took longer—sometimes as long as an hour. By the time it was all done, I had gone through two conflicting rehearsals. Coupled with sleep deprivation, I was often left wondering not only what I was supposed to say but also how I was supposed to say it.

Life in the Pentagon is Orwellian, especially among the general officers. Some pigs are most definitely more equal than others. And of all the staff principals, the DCSOPS is the crown prince; selection as DCSOPS means you are headed for four stars. There is an enormous gap in prestige and power between three stars and four stars. Lt. Gen. Dennis Reimer was on that track. The DCSOPS at times peeled the intelligence onion, but he would accept a negative response that could be answered later. In the eyes of our intelligence seniors that was briefing negativity; giving Reimer a negative response was like giving a negative response to Vuono, who by the way took such responses as natural. So every morning I would finish with General Reimer and then all the generals would head upstairs. After the AOC brief, Stewart would come back down and let us know how we had done. When it did not go well, we got more blocking drills.

Interservice Collisions and Cooperation

Still we did good work. This was not an exhibition game. We played for the lives of thousands of American soldiers. Losers would not be back for the next game or even the next season. They would be dead. In one case, I helped derail an early attempt by the air force to preempt the buildup to war with a strategic takedown of Iraq. Col. Tom Leavitt was the pit boss for the Army Operations Center; he ran the Crisis Action Team. He called in Maj. Dan Farley, an Apache attack helicopter pilot, and me. He told us the planners at Checkmate, the targeting section in the Air Staff, had a plan they wanted the army to look at. I was on one of those never-ending shifts that marked August, 1990. I had already been there over twenty hours when Dan and I walked down the hall to Checkmate.

Inside we were soon treated to the sight of an air force brigadier in his flight rompers complete with squadron scarf. There was also an A-10 ground attack fighter pilot from the Central Command staff who joined Farley and me in the audience. We were the audience; the brigadier had a plan he wanted to sell us. Like any good salesman, he pitched the good parts first. The air force had enough assets in place in the Gulf and in adjacent theaters to take down Iraq. The attack would supposedly behead Iraqi command and control and eliminate the Iraqi Air Force. The attack would then turn on high value targets like Iraqi chemical facilities, known ballistic missile locations, and troop concentrations. This pounding would be so severe, Saddam would be forced to withdraw his forces from the Saudi border. The game would be over without our ground forces even taking to the field.

There was a major flaw in the plan. Our ground forces were already on the field, and they were vulnerable. Still the first part of August, U.S. troops on the ground were spread mightily thin. So were tank killers like Apache helicopters or A-10s. Overall, American commanders were short on antitank munitions to arm those platforms. That would remain true for weeks, a subject of great anxiety in the theater and in the Pentagon. On the other hand, there were five Iraqi heavy divisions still poised on the Saudi border. They had the fuel and the weapons to take and hold the Saudi oil fields. When I pointed this out to the briefer, he waved away my concerns. I then told him his plan was not only overly optimistic in its effects on Iraq, it was criminally stupid to ignore the threat to northern Saudi Arabia. The A-10 driver, also a major, echoed my comments to the general. Dan and I were ushered out soon afterward. Later I learned the Central Command staff also trashed this initial air force plan, so fraught as it was with risks. Done with Checkmate, I briefed my bosses on what had been said and just hoped for the best.

Our other major contribution was to start the detailed analysis of Iraqi forces on the ground. Every day we watched and waited to see what the Iraqis would do. I tasked two civilian intelligence analysts detailed to me in the watch to template the Iraqi units. We needed to answer the magic question: were the Iraqis poised to attack, or were they shifting to defense? The two civilian analysts were quick and good. Their templates on a 1:100,000 scale suggested the Iraqis were in a hasty defense. We breathed easier. But the templates did not stop there. Colonel Pardew had us brief them to Major General Clapper, the senior intelligence general for the air force, as a targeting tool. General Stewart took them even further. He ordered Colonel Solomon's outfit to template the entire theater at a scale of 1:50,000—the standard for tactical military maps. That effort paid enormous dividends months later.

Still, the grind continued for several weeks and it was telling. Finally one morning when things had been rough, General Stewart literally stuck his finger in Colonel Pardew's chest, "Tom is like a one-armed paper-hanger down here. Get him some help! Now!" He left. But we got more support, and we set up a schedule to keep from burning out. I was near the edge. Stewart saved me. From that point on my little five-person crisis cell grew to nearly forty people. We did a submarine crew changeover every four days. I had the day shift on one crew. My permanent counterpart was Maj. Eric Kramer. The other crew was set up the same way. Dr. Norm Cigar floated between the crews as the designated hitter for Vuono questions about Saddam. A reservist, Maj. Andrew Terrill, joined him for the duration. Like Norm, Andy was an academic who did excellent analytical work. From Old Dominion University, he came to us with the gentle style of the southern university lecturer. And he was somewhat taken aback by my own pit bull manners. He soon learned. By the end, Andy was actually telling operations guys to get lost—and making it stick. Norm and I laughed at this transformation. I often wonder how Andy did in his first faculty meeting after the war.

Laughter was important and so was rest. When on shift, we worked as long as it took to get the job done, knowing we would stand down after four days for four days of rest. That schedule did two things. First, it kept us from physical burnout. Most importantly, it allowed us mental rest. We stayed sharp as a result. Still the next five months were a blur.

The same thing was happening across the intelligence community. The theater demand for tactical intelligence grew faster than the troop list. The Defense Intelligence Agency (DIA) was not up to the strain. The J2 (intelligence) section in the Joint Staff was much like us in ODCSINT. They just were not staffed to produce tactical intelligence. The answer was to take elements from the service intelligence agencies and create a Joint Intelligence Center (JIC). The army component came from Colonel Solomon and the ITAC. Lt. Col. Paul Barb headed the team. I had gone to graduate school with Paul in the early 1980s. He was an extremely smart guy who was also a deft politician. Barb did a great job getting the JIC going.

Other intelligence agencies were having a rough go as well. The CIA was no exception. They made a poor showing in tactical analysis and even worse in the geostrategic field. This all really came to a head in the National Intelligence Estimate (NIE) process. Chaired by the National Intelligence Officer for the Middle East, the main intelligence agencies sent representatives to draft special estimates on the situation. State, the CIA, and the DIA nominally were the main players.

I sat in on several of these sessions. It was enlightening and disappointing. The principle representatives all knew each other and "groupthink" was in play. They worried more about syntax than substance—and the results showed. One of the most important estimates dealt with the future of Iraq if war did occur. The "groupthink" position stated that any military action taken to liberate Kuwait would plunge the region into chaos, a prediction that stood to tie our military hands. I nonconcurred as the army representative. Our position was Saddam had offered up his forces on a plate. We could cut them off and destroy them. This same issue became a major argument in the Military Intelligence Board, the council of all the service intelligence chiefs. The DIA had gone with the National Intelligence Board position that destroying the Iraqis in Kuwait risked regional chaos. General Stewart managed to convince the service intelligence chiefs that that doomsday prophecy was not true. He pointed out the Iraqi military was in fact exposed. Stewart sold them on the army position, and that is what the military intelligence chiefs sent forward to undercut the National Intelligence stance. The army position eventually became the basis for General Powell's "We're gonna cut 'em off and kill them" briefing. Nevertheless these NIEs deserved General Schwarzkopf's barbs after the war; they stood to tie everyone's hands.

So we continued on until December. Calls from the theater about poor intelligence had us shaking our heads in the Pentagon. I had seen the templates Colonel Solomon's folks were making. They were targeting quality down to crew-served weapons. The Iraqis had stabilized their defenses by then, and they rarely moved. Still something was wrong. General Vuono dispatched Stewart to the theater to become the Army Component of Central Command (ARCENT) G2 (intelligence officer). In theater, Stewart proved very effective in unblocking the dissemination problem. The intelligence was there, but the means to get it in the right hands were not. Stewart fixed that through force of will. He also asked me several times to come over as a specialist for the reconstruction of Kuwait. The DCSINT denied each request.

Meanwhile ODCSINT fixed other theater problems. One was the lack of a theater reconnaissance platform to track the Iraqis after the shooting started. Satellites were not real time, and the SR71 strategic reconnaissance aircraft was gone, retired earlier that year. The Unmanned Aerial Vehicles (UAVs) common to us today were not available. That left pilots' eyeballs and tactical drones, and neither fit the need. The answer was the prototype for the Joint Surveillance and Tactical Airborne Radar System (J-STARS). Essentially a 707 with a huge radar, J-STARS was the ground surveillance soul mate of AWACS, the airborne radar used to control the air battle. The J-STARS system could track hundreds of moving ground targets for over a hundred miles, regardless of weather or visibility. The air force did not want to risk the prototype, but the army pushed it through.

The other stand-out success for ODCSINT came from recruiting Kuwaiti students. The army could not possibly provide the Arabic speakers required in the Gulf. The numbers simply were not there, and the really good linguists were already committed. ODCSINT floated the idea to recruit Kuwaiti students in the United States as linguists. Approved and executed, it was a resourceful measure that provided excellent results, especially when dealing with hundreds of thousands of Iraqi prisoners.

Desert Storm: The Bat Cave

As January, 1991, arrived, we knew the war was coming. The opening of the air campaign changed our operations in the AOC. General Vuono wanted a separate briefing room just for the staff principals. It was for restricted intelligence and matters considered too sensitive for the main AOC brief. We promptly named it the "Bat Cave." Entrance was by invitation only. You walked in. If lucky, you walked out. If not, there were replacements available.

One especially explosive topic in the Bat Cave was bomb damage assessment (BDA), one that became an albatross around ODCSINT's collective neck. Despite all our smart bombs and our sophistication, BDA remained one portion science and two portions guess work. How you guessed was often influenced by the color of your uniform. If you talked to pilots, they never missed, and they never killed the same thing twice. Our main source was Checkmate, the air force targeteers, who were quite conservative in accepting pilot claims of total destruction. I was there twice daily to see what targets were being hit and the results. Briefing those results could get the messenger killed. There was a sense of real frustration with the senior officers in the Bat Cave; the air force had promised to seal off the theater and paralyze the Iraqis. Once that happened more strikes would go against Iraqi units arrayed along the Saudi border to shape the battlefield in advance of the ground offensive. That was not happening; the theater was not sealed, and the Air Staff at Checkmate said so. The shift in strikes was not happening either, not something the senior army generals liked hearing. As the messenger, I was under their guns.

Added to that risk was the fluidity of the situation. The Iraqis attempted to capitalize on that friction with the division-sized probe at Kafji. I was on deck as the intelligence briefer less than fifteen minutes before the scheduled brief when Paul Barb walked in and started relating what was known. Then my bosses told me to brief "an emerging situation" that was underway and move on to the next topic. I might as well have told the chief the building was on fire and ask him to stay seated and burn. That was my last Bat Cave brief for Desert Storm. Less than two weeks later, the ground war was over. As it turned out, I went off shift as it started. It was all over by the time I came back. Relief was the main feeling I think we all shared. And gratitude that very few soldiers had died. Elation over the scale and speed of the victory came later. Still it was a victory shared by all of us. The army had come a long way along a very painful road from Viet Nam. The nation rejoiced and we breathed a sigh of relief.

Things did not stop with the end of the war. There was the follow-up of Operation Provide Comfort in northern Iraq to protect the Kurds; no-fly zones and demilitarized zones to monitor; and estimates of remaining Iraqi forces to write, argue, and rewrite. We stayed busy. Soon however I found myself alone. Andy Terrill returned to teaching with a harder persona. Norm Cigar had worked harder than most during the crisis. Vuono was not comfortable unless Norm was there to tell him what Saddam was thinking. Norm did a fantastic job—better by far than the folks up the river. He was also burnt out. Norm turned down a promotion and took a pay cut to accept a teaching job at Quantico. Eric retired that spring as a major, another FAO promotion casualty. He was gone nearly four months before returning to his old job as a civilian. That left me holding the Middle East "bag." I did what I had been trained to do way back in Ranger school: put your head down and keep putting one foot in front of the other. I also developed a permanent intolerance for stupidity. Thank goodness I got little of that inside the AOC. I made it through the period until Eric came back.

That December I closed the final UNTSO chapter in my life. As a result of the new atmosphere in the Middle East, all the American hostages in Lebanon were released. Col. William R. Higgins was the last to come home. The air force flew Rich's body back to Andrews Air Force Base to be received by the national and military leadership on December 30.[10] Robin Higgins was there of course and so were others. Four of us were from Observer Group Lebanon. Ron Johnson and Steve Piccarilli came as members of the old Marine House gang. Steve France, AKA Captain Canada, flew down from Ottawa to represent the Canadians. We all saluted and we all cried as Rich's body again reached American soil. He was buried in Quantico among his beloved corps. In 1997, a new Aegis class frigate joined the navy as DDG-76, USS *Higgins*. I wear the ship's cap to honor a good man who did his best and paid the ultimate price.

Fort Monroe: The Mail House Gang

At the end of the year, my boss, Col. Jake Almborg, called me and said I was to participate in a study on the Gulf War at Fort Monroe. I arrived the evening of January 1, wondering what this was all about.

The air force had announced it intended to produce a multimillion dollar study of the Gulf air war. General McPeak, the air force Chief of Staff, was behind the study. The Air Force History Center took on the mission to document how the air force won the war. They had several million dollars to produce a multivolume history. An unclassified summary volume would be the flagship for the study. By now General Vuono had retired and General Sullivan was the chief of staff of the army. Reimer had stepped up as the four-star vice chief. The new DCSOPS was Lt. Gen. Binnie Peay after his brilliant command of the 101st Airborne in the war. In a typically army fashion, the chief gave Peay the mission to put together an ad hoc Desert Storm Special Study Project. Brig. Gen. Robert Scales Jr.—widely recognized as a military historian—was at the army's Training and Doctrine Command (TRADOC) at Fort Monroe. He would head a team of eight to ten officers to produce an army study of the war. The budget was a couple of hundred thousand dollars.

After several months of fits and starts the team assembled at Fort Monroe. I was one of the last arrivals. Most had been in the theater. The others like me had been associated with the war from the states. General Scales set the tone for the project. Scales was an artilleryman. If you watch the film *Hamburger Hill*, Bobby Scales is "Cold Steel 6." But Scales was also part of the army's intelligentsia. We would be a familial group, not a hidebound military unit. Scales had convinced the

DCSOPS to broaden the project to become a proper history. Our goal was a book that would find itself on the nightstands of young soldiers. That meant excellent research and even better writing. Everyone had assigned areas. Mine started as intelligence then broadened into the air war. As the intel guy assigned, I fought a running gun battle with my counterparts, including General Scales. To them dissemination problems equaled bad intelligence. I had to educate them over and over again. We eventually arrived at a hard-fought consensus. Part of that was due to my work on the air war, another controversial issue. Taking on those two subjects was like holding two lightning rods. You got hit. Working for someone like Bobby Scales made that both possible and rewarding despite the occasional jolts.

General Scales, Lt. Col. Terry Johnson, and I wrote the book once the research was complete. Terry was an aviator who had been with the 11th Aviation Brigade in the war. We worked well together. The research team had done a good job drafting the ground war chapter, but it needed a major overhaul. General Scales asked me to fix it, and I had it ready four days later. It pretty much stood unchanged. Eight months after starting we held an editorial board at the War College chaired by General Peay. Roger Spiller was there along with General Stoft from the War College and General Chrisman from the army staff. So were three other division commanders from the war. We argued out the changes, and the manuscript passed. I had just coauthored my third book, *Certain Victory: The U.S. Army in the Gulf War*.[11]

The book was done. I headed back to the Pentagon, but now I was promotable to lieutenant colonel. The staff had changed as well. Colonel Pardew had moved over to the Joint Staff. Colonel Solomon now headed the Foreign Intelligence Directorate. Although Jake Almborg was still the boss of the current intelligence side, there were several new analysts. The front office was also changed. Lt. Gen. Ira C. Owens was now the DCSINT. General Owens had a quality prized among analysts: he would listen. General Vuono had retired. General Sullivan became the chief and General Reimer the vice. With Lieutenant General Peay as DCSOPS, the staff had a different style.

Getting the Horn in Africa: Somalia

Somalia soon tested that command style. Less than two weeks after getting back from Monroe, I was back down in the Army Operations Center as a shift leader in another intelligence Crisis Action Team.

The video camera was proving to be a major influence on U.S. international relations. When I was in Sudan in 1984, thousands of Ethiopians, Eritreans, and Sudanese had died in the drought and famine. But the world focused on Ethiopia because the cameras were there. The same thing was happening in Somalia, home to one of the most xenophobic people on earth. Daily programs highlighted suffering in Somalia brought on by drought, famine, and civil war, especially the tragedy of the Somali children, championed by Aubrey Hepburn. A weeping Somali woman holding a dead child would be shown. She would be pregnant and would have her other children beside her. The pitch delivered by the program said the world owed her and her children a chance. It was effective and ultimately misleading. Only the Somalis could change Somalia. Lobbying by NGOs and others soon put pressure on the Bush administration to "do something" about Somalia.

The result was Operation Restore Hope, an intervention to help secure feeding sites and food distribution against the interference by the various Somali warlords. The United States would act in concert with other countries and the United Nations but not as a unified force. The mission was murky; it was not a peacekeeping mission in the classic sense. It was more a stability operation to allow the NGOs and international agencies to get the food out. By now ODC-SINT had a full-time African FAO, Capt. Jeff Taylor. He was bright, dedicated—and fresh meat for the Army Operations Center grinder. I backed him up as an Africanist and showed him the pitfalls of the operations center. We both had been to Somalia. I had a scar on my head from my trip there in 1984. Our problem was conveying the reality of Somalia to the army's leadership.

One morning we were sitting around talking about the operation. Lieutenant General Owens and Colonel Solomon were there along with Jeff and me. Owens encouraged open discussions. The subject was Rules of Engagement (ROE), the guidelines soldiers are forced to live with and sometimes die following. Owens remarked that someone over in the Joint Staff had suggested, "If they have a gun, shoot 'em. If someone else picks up the gun, shoot him too. Keep shooting until no one picks up the gun."

I jumped on that. "Sir, that is exactly what needs to happen," I began. Somalia is an isolated country, and the region likes it that way. I showed the map to General Owens.

"Sir, there are no major roads into Somalia from the surrounding countries. The reason is simple. No one likes the Somalis, and the

Somalis don't like anyone. They spend their lives fighting each other as clans and their neighbors as bandits. Boys are raised as expendable warriors for the clan. The clans work on intimidation. Any sign of weakness is an opportunity to them. Gentleness is a weakness. They will turn on anyone who tries gentle persuasion. If we are going to send troops, they have to be able to shoot." Owens listened and I think he probably agreed, but that decision would be made over in the White House.

The other area of discussion was force structure. Those of us who had been in Somalia suggested an armored cavalry regiment, a blend of tanks, armored infantry carriers, and artillery. An ACR was a miniature heavy division. The Somalis had ample heavy machine guns, RPGs and some armor. They would fight if presented the opportunity. The operations side of the house pushed light infantry, because they could get over there quickly and they could move around using helicopters. Given the context of the initial mission, the light advocates won.

I also did my best to educate the army leadership by having Andrew Natsios, the president's disaster relief coordinator, come brief the leadership. Natsios spent nearly two hours with Sullivan, Reimer, Peay, and Owens. They had a better understanding of the situation when he left. Unfortunately Natsios and the rest of the first Bush administration were on the way out. That was probably the genesis of the bloody end to Operation Restore Hope. It began at the worst possible moment in the American political system, the transition from a losing administration to a new one with a dramatically different flavor.

I was reaching the end of my tenure in the Pentagon. I continued on with Restore Hope almost to the end. I watched as the mission got muddled and expanded and changed and altered under the new administration. One of my final days was when Secretary of Defense Les Aspin denied the ground commander's request for M1A2 tanks. I had but two days to sign out when Colonel Solomon called me at home.

"Tom, I know you are almost gone but I needed to tell you this. The Chief has a very short list of names as nominees for the J2 of UNISOM. Your name tops the list. What do you want?"

I told him that if the chief really wanted me to go I would. But that I had prepared for years for my next assignment, and my family's plans were built around it. He called me back the next day.

"The Chief said you are right. Go on to Zaire."

CHAPTER 3

Return to Zaire

G oing back to Zaire was a decision that evolved over my last two years in the Pentagon. Part of it was professional and the other personal. The professional interest stemmed from my long association with the place. I knew the country and wanted to live there. I had watched recent events fulfill Belgian prophecies about its inevitable collapse. The Zairian Armed Forces (FAZ) had mutinied in 1991, destroying much of the capital city and prompting a major evacuation of westerners. The U.S. embassy had shrunk like a dried-up sponge. In the case of the Defense Attaché Office (DAO), it had gone from a twenty-five-person staff to a two-man show. The security assistance office was gone altogether. USAID reduced its staff, and the Peace Corps closed its doors. In 1993 the Zairian Army again took to the streets. The rioting was less severe this time, largely because there was hardly anything left to steal.

So why go to Zaire? As a foreign area officer—especially an intelligence background FAO—you went where the action was likely to occur. At the time I volunteered for Zaire, I expected to make lieutenant colonel, and the defense attaché position in Kinshasa had been downgraded to that rank. Being a defense attaché for an FAO was the equivalent of getting command of a line battalion—at least as far as I was concerned. I had researched and written about operations in the country. I had been around good defense attachés and others who did not measure up. Instinct told me Zaire was headed for more trouble, and I wanted to be there. Zaire was the long pole in the tent for central Africa. Now the pole was cracked and likely to fall. Troubles surrounded the country. Angola remained locked in a civil war. Rwanda was on the edge of the abyss. Congo-Brazzaville was also torn internally. No way could I resist such a tempting assignment. The posting to Zaire also resolved what came next for my family. My wife was a USAID officer, and she would be returning overseas. Events were lining up to make Haiti her probable posting. That defense attaché slot was filled but would open when I was due out of Zaire, so Zaire it was.

Hello Again, K-Town

Anticipation best described my mood walking down the steps at Ndjili International Airport, Zaire's official gateway to the world. It was like going back to see an old girlfriend. Kinshasa had not been the prettiest girl in 1984, but she did have her charms. In 1993 Kin La Belle was an old whore whose beauty and health were long gone. She needed far more than cosmetics to resurrect her. "Oh well," I thought, "I did a year in Khartoum. I can do a year here."

My predecessor, Maj. Dean Shultz, greeted me at the foot of the stairs. We went through the *salle d'honneur* reserved for diplomats and, on the way into town, a trip down memory lane. Ndjili is about ten miles outside Kinshasa in what had been the emerging industrial sector of the city. In 1984, the road had been a four-lane avenue with a broad center divider marked with painted concrete blocks. Now it was a four-lane mudslide. The center divider had sunk in the middle, becoming a marginally effective speed bump ignored by most. As we drove, I saw the General Motors plant to the right of the road, built in the early 1980s to assemble Chevrolet Citations and light trucks. Now it looked like a carcass picked over by vultures, its steel ribs rusting in the African climate. Dean explained it had been one of the first sites pillaged by the 31st Paras, the unit that sparked the full military mutiny as they headed into town. They only took what was portable and marketable. The local population then stripped the plant to its bones.

That was the overall impression of the drive into town. You could just make out what had been if you used your imagination, almost like paleontologists looking at fossilized bones can picture the animals they once supported. Otherwise it was just a montage of decay and filth. Closer to town I saw something I remembered. At one stage, Mobutu had embarked on a scheme to make Kinshasa the sports capital of the continent with the highest rotating restaurant in Africa as a centerpiece. Perched on a steel and concrete needle, diners would enjoy a 360-degree vista as they ate their meals in a five-star restaurant. The project had been well underway when I arrived in September, 1984. The base was already centered in an intricate traffic circle composed of ramps and underpasses. The circle was laid out but the ramps were not yet complete. The needle rose out of the center for a couple of hundred feet capped by the concrete saucer of the restaurant. Two construction cranes perched on the saucer lifted concrete and steel to complete the restaurant and its spire.

In October, 1993, the same two cranes were frozen in rust on the top of the never-to-spin saucer. No longer bright "Caterpillar" yellow, only a small patch of yellow colored the cabs. The base looked like a madman's garden. The ramps still led to nowhere, but the African jungle always challenges inactivity. Thirty-foot trees and other greenery engulfed the entire structure. I noticed a few squatter huts tucked in among the trees and off ramps. Once sucked in, the investors soon learned the fundamental rule of Zairian business under Uncle Mobutu and his family of thugs. You must always have a local partner—handpicked by Mobutu—as part of doing business in Zaire. These developers had not heeded that rule. It was cheaper just to walk away from those cranes than to recover them.

We went on to my house. It was a large colonial style two-story house all but hidden behind an eight-foot wall. Topped by broken soda bottles, the formidable frontal barrier was something of a façade. The other walls around the yard were only six feet tall. The house had lots of French-style windows and doors, protected by lots of steel bars and gates, and lots of locks to close them; the main key ring to the house weighed almost two pounds. The master bed and bath were on the top floor. It was the house's final redoubt, deliberately reinforced for that defensive role. The bedroom door was armored with steel, and a steel gate denied entrance through a side door. With the bathroom inside as a source of water, it provided a semi-adequate final retreat for the occupants. It also made a dandy mousetrap. I soon added a bootleg M16 and some grenades to the defenses. Dean handed me the keys and went to the embassy while I grabbed a needed couple of hours of sleep.

Puzzle Palace on the Congo: The U.S. Embassy

At 1300 Dean came back, and we headed to the office. The U.S. embassy looked the same as it had in 1984. It was hardly the imposing structure seen so often in Hollywood movies. Rather it resembled a 1950s hotel, held together by decades of whitewash. Most of the

American embassies in Africa were the same. But here there was a singular difference. We had our own gendarme company on semi-permanent lease from Zaire's Ministry of Defense. The Regional Security Office (RSO) paid and trained them to keep undesirables away from the building and the U.S. personnel. One entered the embassy through an exterior door into a small lobby under the watchful eye of the marine on duty. Enclosed in ballistic plastic, the marine controlled the electric locks on the doors into the main building. My new office occupied the first floor of the rear section. Our office was the same as in 1984 when it held twenty-five people. Inside there was a small lobby used to control access to the hallway. The defense attaché had the first office; I would use it as a meeting room for my contacts. Continuing on was the DAO vault with our communications terminals and computers. It was a classified working area, protected by a massive steel door. This would be my main office for the next year. Once a beehive of activity in earlier decades, the remainder of the office was strangely empty except for that of the operations coordinator (OpsCo). In 1984, the OpsCo had been a warrant officer with a staff of three. Mine would be an army sergeant first class who had come to Zaire that year as a young buck sergeant.

Sgt. 1st Class Stan Reber was truly one of the best NCOs you could hope to have anywhere. That I had him as my OpsCo in Zaire was a masterstroke of good fortune. A thin little guy with the hyper energy so typical of the physiology, Stan stood about five foot seven inches and may have weighed 135 pounds soaking wet. In his mid-thirties, he was already completely bald on top. His remaining hair was blonde. He was fluent in French and semi-fluent in self-taught Lingala. Stan introduced himself, and we shook hands. At that point he had been in country for more than nine years straight—almost unheard-of for an NCO, even in the defense attaché system. But as I was to learn so well over the next year, Stan Reber was an exceptional man.

As a young NCO, Stan had come to Zaire on a Mobile Training Team to teach the Zairians generator maintenance the same year I had visited as an FAO trainee. His team had stayed almost six months as an extension of ZAMISH (the security assistance mission). This was in the mid-1980s and Kinshasa was still Kin La Belle. There was a large expatriate population to interact with, and the cost-of-living allowance made life good for a young sergeant. As a bachelor Stan would get an apartment far better than the barracks he was used to. He wangled an assignment with ZAMISH and stayed when the training team left. After a tour in the security assistance mission, he transferred to the Defense Attaché Office, first as an operations and administrative sergeant and then as the operations coordinator. By the time I arrived in Kinshasa, Stan's love of the place was long gone, killed by the two pillages. He planned to leave after his tour was complete. His relationship with Major Shultz was good. Dean was a hard charger and another hyper personality. He had done well during the second pillage and the two had had their adventures together.

The soldiers' opposition to the new 10-million-Zaire notes sparked the second pillage. Back in 1984, I had thought the exchange rate was bad when it was several hundred to a single U.S. dollar. Then the standard Zaire note was the 50Z or the 100Z. There was a 500Z note but they were rare. In less than ten years the exchange rate had rocketed beyond ten million Zaires to the dollar. Before the second pillage the government had tried to hold the currency line with a 5-millionZ note and failed. They decided to print the 10-millionZ note even though it was widely considered worthless. The 31st Para rebelled against its acceptance, and the mutiny against the currency grew into a full-scale pillage. After several days, the pillage fizzled out, because there simply was not as much to steal anymore. The first pillage in 1991 had seen to that. And the FAZ chief of staff, General Mahele, took the Division Speciale du President (DSP) into the streets and started shooting soldiers. Mahele, hero of the 31st Para operation against Kolwezi in 1978, was sacked soon afterward.[1]

Stan and Dean's role in all this was to monitor the situation and keep the ambassador informed. Not surprisingly, the two were among the very few who actually stepped outside the embassy walls. The ambassador noted their roles during the pillage in cables back to the States. Her praise, however, meant little to the folks at headquarters above the level of the reports officer. In contrast, the State Department hurried to issue citations for bravery to their officers, who mainly stayed inside the compound. Stan laughed about giving the "prevailing direction of incoming gunfire" at country team meetings like a weatherman discussing the winds. While the ambassador was still there, this "can do" attitude worked to the DAO's favor. They were the "fix it" guys. The ambassador also backed their reporting and kept the other players in check. Her departure had left a serious vacuum in the leadership of the mission.

Earlier on my travels through Africa, I noted some missions ran well and others did not. The embassy in Kinshasa was one of the latter. The United States decided not to replace the ambassador, a signal to Mobutu that his time as a favorite African ruler was long gone. That left the embassy in a caretaker status with little function other than telling Mobutu he needed to leave. That is, when they could see him; the president of Zaire no longer lived in Kinshasa. One thousand miles away in Gbadolité, he had built his own gilded sanctuary and ran the country on a whim through his minions, primarily the various factions in the country's military and security services. That left the embassy with an empty portfolio or perhaps a "wish list" stating the U.S. government wished Mobutu would go away. Officially stated, the embassy goal was to bring democracy to Zaire; encouraging various voices of the opposition was the method of choice in achieving it. Unfortunately, there were virtually no opposition figures that had not been tainted by Mobutu. Even those like Tshisekedi, Mobutu's most serious challenger, had been part of the inner circle at one time. Mobutu had more than three decades of practice at manipulating and undermining his opponents. Now in 1993, he was able to do so quite effectively at long distance, making the Kinshasa political stage nothing more than a cheap burlesque. Since the State Department and the embassy could not affect the political scene, their frustration had a convenient target in the Zairian military (FAZ), an institution that served as a daily reminder of Mobutu's rampant corruption. "Doing something about the FAZ" became a favored tactic in the embassy's voodoo policy: sticking enough pins in the FAZ might make Mobutu quit.

Accompanied by Dean, I went up the stairs to the chargé's office that afternoon. As the head of the embassy, he was charged with the dubious task of convincing Mobutu to go. A senior Foreign Service Officer on the threshold of ambassadorial rank, his welcome included the announcement he had "done a Clinton" and avoided all military service. And he was given to equating all military with the local mob. Soldiers were by definition suspect members of a sometimes necessary but never trusted evil. That pretty much set the tone for our relationship over the next year. I soon met the other sections in the embassy.

The main focus for any embassy is the political section. Ours was given to jousting at the political windmills that stirred the ever-muggy airs of Kinshasa. We were sitting in a meeting one morning, and as usual discussions centered on the Zairian military. We had a guest from the African Bureau whose stated portfolio was to "bring democracy" to the continent. She asked all of us and me in particular what we were going to "do about the FAZ?" Her thesis ran if the Zairian military was out of the way, Mobutu would have to leave, which would allow the natural goodness and light of the Zairian people to flower into democracy. Downsizing the Zairian military apparently was the key to Zaire's future. We were war gaming ways to do that. I could not help it; I started laughing. When called to explain myself, I pointed out that reducing and improving the Zairian military had been the consistent goal of the Western powers in Zaire since the 1960s, one that consistently failed. My added comments that the Zairian military had only grown bigger over the years gave no pause to their brainstorming. Still, no one could decide how to hand out the RIF (Reduction in Force) notices. It was rather like the mice deciding to "bell the cat."

Similar fruitless maneuvering marked the role of the CIA section in the embassy. From the 1960s, the CIA had played a large and heavy role in the Congo.[2] Much effort had gone into supporting Mobutu as a main bastion against the Soviets, and the agency had done well. By law, the Director of Central Intelligence (DCI) is the senior intelligence officer in the U.S. government. The DCI also heads the CIA, and some of that authority is transferred to the agency. Yet the agency's management infers much of that transference. It takes as much power as the other players allow it. In Washington, that tendency plays out in turf fights and maneuvering for advantage. I had seen it up close in the National Intelligence Estimate process in the Gulf War.

In embassies like in Kinshasa, the station chief was the senior intelligence officer. That meant he had supervisory control of intelligence operations, quite a portfolio in the 1960s and 1970s, one much reduced in the 1990s. For all practical purposes, the agency's role as the key player in Zaire had ended with the first pillage. Mobutu was in permanent residence up country at Gbadolité, and the Zairian military and security structures were broken. Still the CIA section seemed to go its own way, in many ways in conflict with the embassy. On one hand, the station was tied into the old structure, a relationship validating that structure's continued role in the society and undermining embassy policy dedicated to that same society's demise. On the other, the station looked for possible replacements for Mobutu among the gang running the country, rather like a football scout who never strayed from his own organization's locker room. Nevertheless, the station was there, and I had to deal with its boss. We got along on the surface, but I watched my back. I had seen the same attitude in Khartoum and in D.C., namely "we are the professionals and you are amateurs."

So that pretty well accounted for the major operational players in the embassy. There was also an economics section under a former academic who had decided relatively late in the game to join the State Department. His hopeless task was to make sense out of the Zairian economy. With his newly arrived assistant, he struggled to understand what was keeping the country running. Consider the currency situation. I have already mentioned the 10-millionZ note. The day I arrived in country, Mobutu issued a "New Zaire" note reportedly pegged at four New Zaires to the dollar. Supposedly those holding the old notes had a set period to turn in the old notes before they became worthless.

Well, worthless is a relative term. There were no upheavals in Kinshasa over the new note. The inevitable inflationary spiral began soon afterward. But it was a different story up country where "New Zaire" or "Old Zaire" were often fighting words. Kasai province was the heart of the Zairian diamond industry, and the men who controlled it did their best to minimize ties with Kinshasa. That meant refusing the New Zaires, prompting the Zairian military to pillage two towns in reprisal. Elsewhere the story took a different twist. Soldiers in Kisangani did not like the New Zaire either. Apparently the logic of trading in ten million of an "old something" to get four of a "new something" escaped them. They poisoned three officers to mark their displeasure, an honored and well-practiced tradition in Zaire. Two colonels and a general bit the dust, no great loss since the Zairian military had too many colonels and generals anyway.

Nevertheless the flag officer received a state military funeral in Kinshasa complete with a twenty-one-gun salute. Since the death had been associated with military discontent, there was a Division Speciale du President (DSP) security force nervously watching the proceedings. The crash of the salute must have scared somebody, because the DSP opened up and started a brisk but short "firefight." I have to put firefight in quotes because a Zairian firefight is not the same as a firefight in, say, Viet Nam. In a Zairian firefight, decibels, not accuracy, count. Opponents fire up in the air while looking mean at each other. Rarely do they shoot at anyone who is also armed. In this case, a lot of noise and very serious scowls were exchanged over the new graves.

The bottom line was the New Zaire was not worth any more than the old Zaire. The economics officer had to explain how this worked, and it often left him confused. Stan and I routinely talked to him; he was one of the two State types who actually came down to our offices. I told him to throw Western economic models out the window. Zaire was a kleptocracy, and Mobutu was the head robber baron. Currency old or new was eyewash. What counted was goods, be they diamonds, gold, or chickens. A standard accepted currency is one of the hallmarks of a nation state. Zaire had two currencies, and regardless of who accepted which, they were useless. The economy was broke, and the military was broken.

Les Forces Armées Zairoise

In many ways I was just like the economics officer. My main role in life was to watch and analyze Les Forces Armées Zairoise (FAZ), something I had done as a historian in two books, for Washington. This time I would not enjoy a scholarly buffer zone separating me from the unpleasantry of the FAZ. Now I was in amongst them, and the view was dramatically less academic.

I soon learned how different. Dean had set up a program of introductions with the Zairians and my foreign counterparts. The first included formalities at the Ministry of Defense. Typically, attachés abroad operate with the acceptance and accreditation of the host country military's Foreign Liaison Office. Dean had contacted the Zairian Foreign Liaison Office (FLO) months before when I was first nominated to replace him. As I got closer to my arrival date, the liaison office set up a formal reception as the Ministry's welcome for me.

I do not remember the exact date, but it was within days of my arrival in the country. Dean and I went to the Zairian Army officers club where a TV camera crew tracked us into the main reception. There I met my counterparts from the attaché corps. The senior attaché was a brigadier from Chad who was living in virtual exile from N'djamena. Dominique Bon was a French Naval Infantry colonel who soon became a close contact. Colonel Pettieaux was the Belgian attaché; he too became quite a partner once he learned of my books about the 1964 and 1978 interventions in Zaire. Lieutenant Colonel Koh was the South Korean attaché. He and I became natural friends, given the longstanding relationship between our countries. Finally, the other player in the attaché corps was Colonel Nasr, a remnant of the Egyptian relationship with the Zairian Guarde Civile. My time in Egypt made our relationship easy to establish. Strangely, there were hardly any Zairians present. One was a U.S.-trained Zairian Air Force major from the liaison office. He was the only Zairian who talked to me at the party. Dean made a going-away speech, and I offered the obligatory "I am so happy to be here" bit. As we began to leave a Zairian brigadier who was introduced as the new director of Foreign Liaison shook my hand and said, "We'll talk later."

We never had that talk. The new FLO director was none other than the former Zairian defense attaché in Washington, then Colonel now Brigadier General Loleki. I had tried calling him repeatedly without success during my training. I learned he had left unexpectedly toward the end of my preparations. The day after I attended the reception he sent a formal note stating it was the official position of the Zairian Ministry of Defense not to issue me full accreditation as the U.S. defense attaché. That rebuff would remain in place until Washington issued a visa to the newly nominated Zairian military attaché, still waiting in Kinshasa. In the meantime, I could stay in the country, and I received a residential visa without a problem. But as a non-accredited attaché, I would have no official access to the Zairian military. I would in other words be a non-diplomat in the eyes of the Zairian government.

I was an unwitting pawn in a diplomatic chess game between the Zairians and the U.S. Department of State. Foggy Bottom had been under increasing criticism from the District of Columbia, Virginia, and Maryland over deadbeat diplomats. Usually the gripes dealt with unpaid parking fines and other esoteric matters. But the Zairian embassy had set new standards in scofflaw behavior. None of the embassy staff had been paid on a regular basis. They had all signed contracts on mortgages or rents or car payments that they simply ignored. Even the embassy was behind on its utility and rent bills. As fate would have it, Colonel Loleki became a test case. He owed more than fifty thousand dollars in past-due bills. When it became apparent the U.S. government was going to pressure him to pay, he skipped. Normally diplomats announce their departure dates, allowing the host government to mark the occasion and to clear their records. Not Loleki. He not only skipped, leaving the fifty thousand dollars unpaid; he also took five financed luxury cars back with him to Zaire. With a diplomatic passport, he managed to get them all shipped before anyone was the wiser.

The U.S. State Department's response to this latest Zairian larceny was to refuse a visa to Loleki's replacement. The U.S. position was the Zairians would have to make good on all debts before the new Zairian attaché got his passport stamped. No one at my headquarters or State had bothered telling me about all this before I arrived in Kinshasa. Back in Zaire, Loleki did just fine. With five new cars to bargain with, he got himself promoted to brigadier and named as the new director of Foreign Liaison. He was the one who had decided I would not be accepted as an accredited defense attaché.

Perhaps it would help to understand exactly what military attachés actually do. We are first and foremost intelligence officers dispatched to the country in question to study its military or political-military environment. In other words we are openly declared spies; the host country accepts our presence for a variety of purposes. They know we are collecting information on their military, and they attempt to control what we see. The United States does the very same thing with foreign military attachés. Generally speaking, U.S. military attachés are not involved in clandestine intelligence operations. Frankly we do not need to be; the attaché system produces more hard intelligence than our more exotic counterparts. Our secondary mission is to serve as a diplomat; we represent the U.S. military abroad. In some cases, defense attachés serve as the U.S. senior military representative in the country. I held that position as European Command's SenMilRep in Zaire.

That is the attaché system in broad brush. Underneath that overall system there are two separate and quite different worlds. The first is the modern state attaché whose social skills on the cocktail and dinner circuit are often more important than abilities as an intelligence officer. Typically, attachés in countries like France, Germany, and the United Kingdom get reams of material released to them directly from the host government. Some countries have intelligence-sharing agreements that go back to WWII. Attachés on such duty play an important role in the symbolism of such common history. Mess dress, dress blues, and tuxedoes are part of the kitbag. Then there is the Third World attaché, my world in Zaire. Formality is not a prime consideration in places like Zaire or Angola. The United States does not really care about the Zairian military as a military factor in the world. We do care about its influence within Zaire as a country. We also care about the security ramifications of a collapsing Zaire in the heart of Africa. As a Third Worlder, my main focus was intelligence, not passing the canapés at the behest of the chargé.

So getting semi-PNG'd before I had even gotten started was a setback. Being PNG'd, or declared persona non grata, is diplospeak for getting thrown out of the country. I had not been thrown out, but I was not fully accepted either. I had a residential visa, so they had agreed I could stay, probably in the forlorn hope the debt problem would go away. That left me facing several operational obstacles. First of all I would not be on the Zairian Ministry of Defense's normal invitation list. Technically I would not be allowed into the Ministry of Defense headquarters. I had already snuck in there with Stan. The building dated back to the late 1970s. Set on one of the main hills overlooking the city and Stanley's Pool, it was quite impressive back in 1984 when I first saw it. It even had its own miniature zoo on the grounds with antelope and sable walking among the trees. A most luckless lion prowled a small cage adjacent to the main entrance.

That forlorn feline was still there in 1993, prowling that same small cage. "Leo the Luckless Lion" looked much the worse for wear. So did the Ministry building. It was a fairly simple building design: four floors with stairwells in the center and both ends of the hallways. Maybe 150 feet in length and 50 feet in width, this nerve center of the Zairian military was brain dead. The communications gear installed by—well, pick a donor—no longer worked. The phone system, like the standard phone system in Kinshasa, was gone. Long-haul communications to places like Kasai or Shaba had to rely on mail. The one thing the Ministry had plenty of was senior officers; the general officer list for the Zairian military included more than one hundred generals and one admiral for a paper force of fifty thousand. Many wore multiple stars. There was a four-star chief of staff for the army as well as a four-star chief for the Guarde Civile. There was a four-star general in charge of an air force with a single operational helicopter. A lone admiral wore four stars as commander of the Zairian Navy, a sad collection of river patrol craft sitting in the mud along Zaire's waterways.

Of course, beneath this mantle of stars, there were succeedingly larger levels of subordinate officers. Many of these officers occupied the Ministry offices, where they nominally worked. Unfortunately, they had long overloaded the building's capacity. Naturally no one was going to volunteer for duty elsewhere. The Ministry offered the best access to bribes. The offices were packed, and so were the toilets. The solution was typical Zairian: use the end stairwells as toilets and keep the central stairwell relatively clean. So in a way the Ministry was symbolic. The Zairian military was as deaf, blind, and toothless as Leo the Luckless Lion. The bloated officer corps produced enough crap to flood the stairwells but never got anything done. Both stunk to high heaven.

Consequently, being cut off from the halls of the Ministry of Defense was less a blow than it seemed. Our focus in monitoring the Zairian military was stability. In short form: when would the army again pillage the city? The answer to that question would not come from the Ministry. First of all they would never announce it to the attaché corps. More to the point, no one inside the Ministry would even know rebellion was imminent. Most would not even care.

The key to tracking the mood of the Zairian military was monitoring the sergeants and junior officers on the streets. There were no privates to speak of beyond the ghost soldiers on the payrolls. I had two sergeants in my employ at Ndjili and a number of established contacts that would stay in touch. They had to if they wanted something to eat. Below the Mobutu crony level, basic survival was the focus of day-to-day life. The New Zaire issued in October at four New Zaires to the dollar was at ninety-three New Zaires to the dollar by Christmas. By March it would jump to five hundred New Zaires. Troops received thirty New Zaires a month—if they actually got paid. A single beer cost 130 New Zaires. I did a slice-of-life examination of two junior officers—both relatively well educated and U.S.-trained—just to see how they got by. The answer was beg, borrow, steal, and trade. We kept a larder stocked with rice and chickens to hand out as "gifts." Our contacts kept coming.

I could also maintain contacts with the international community. Prodded by the French and Belgian attachés, the Chadian brigadier who chaired the Attaché Corps allowed me to remain part of the circle. Bon kept the Chadian general afloat with food and money. Without help from the Frenchman, the Chadian would have starved on his salary from N'djamena. Membership proved useful later on but for the most part was a social circle. If a counterpart wanted to share, they called or we met at one of our offices. I looked to the civilian international community for much of my information. Even after two major riots in three years, many diehards remained in the country. Many had been there so long they were more Zairian than Western.

I also had my local employees. Those included two drivers and the two thugs at the airport. Stan ran the drivers. Each morning he held formation in the embassy courtyard for the office staff. He checked them for presentability and then handed out work assignments. My driver was a mild mannered mouse who was generally fairly good as a driver. Stan's was the office scrounger; if we needed something he would get it. That sometimes included information.

As for my airport thugs, what can I say? They were thugs but they were our thugs. As the senior military representative, I was the Air Mobility Command liaison officer. In the 1970s and 1980s the U.S. security assistance mission had an entire section devoted to this task. I had Stan and our thugs. Stan handled the scheduling and landing clearances as well as maintained our equipment at the airport. We had a C141/C5-capable power cart, a tow car, and a forklift. All of this was stored in a medium-sized hangar on the edge of the old military side of the airfield. The two thugs had two main jobs. One was making sure nothing walked away from the hangar. The senior man was a sergeant major (warrant officer) who was quiet and thorough. Not exactly the brightest bulb on the Christmas tree, he did his work conscientiously. The other was a senior sergeant. Bubbly and always friendly, he was the brain of the two-man outfit. Their reward in working for us was steady pay and occasional bonuses like Christmas chickens. The sergeant major was married but lived close by the airport. "Bubbly" lived in the hangar in relative luxury. Their second job was to keep other Zairians away from U.S. aircraft and us when they landed. They had differing techniques. "Bubbly" started friendly and then escalated if you were stupid enough to go too far. The sergeant major did not bother with escalation. He held up a warning hand and if someone came on, he lowered the boom. I saw him butt stroke a Zairian TV reporter cold. We never had any problems at the airport with these two around.

The other half of monitoring the security situation was simply getting out and looking. The U.S. embassy was in the Gombé district of Kinshasa. It was the central heart of the city and extended from the river port inward maybe three miles. Outside that border, the real Kinshasa started springing up: shantytowns and dilapidated markets were the norm. Most of the reporting officers in the embassy had never been outside Gombé. They certainly did not venture into the markets and the shantytowns. Just as I had done in Lebanon, I began regular morning patrols around the city with Stan. You cannot say something is abnormal if you do not know what is normal, especially in an abnormal place like Zaire. When violence was imminent in Lebanon, normal patterns of social intercourse changed. Markets emptied or never opened. Buses did not run. Children were not on the street on their way to school in the morning. That same pattern held for Africa and especially Zaire. Veterans from the 1964 crisis had told me the locals often knew when something was going to happen long before it did. When servants stopped showing up for work, trouble was on the way. That was what Stan and I looked for: a standard by which to judge the mood of the day.

So even without the status of an accredited attaché, I figured I would be able to do my job. Dean Schultz soon left after a week's transition. I had the con and was ready to get on with it. But first I had to make a two-week trip to South Africa for an African attaché conference called by headquarters. The meeting lasted only four days, but getting there and back meant a two-week absence. I tried to get out of going but headquarters said no dice. I enjoyed the stay in Pretoria, and it was nice to meet my counterparts, most of whom I knew. As for the conference, it was notable on two points. First, my boss had not heard of my non-status in Zaire, and his first response was "close the shop." The second was I turned off my boss's knee-jerk reaction by seeing Maj. Gen. John Leide. Leide was the Defense HUMINT Service director and an FAO icon. He was a China FAO and had been in Beijing for the Tienanmen crisis. He went on to become the Central Command intelligence officer for the Gulf War. I told him what had happened, but I also told him we were getting on with the job. I believe my saying the post was a regional watchtower did the trick. Neither my boss nor my bureau made further mention of closing the post.

Back in Kinshasa after Pretoria, Stan and I had become an effective team. We settled into a routine. Each morning Stan picked me up in his truck, and we would pick a section of the city to tour for an hour. You never knew what you might see. It was not all driving. Stan knew the city better than anyone. He knew where all the garrisons were and what units were nominally there. I use the word "nominally" because Zairian units were filled with ghost soldiers. Either they had gone AWOL or died or never even existed, but their commanders kept them on the payroll to claim their salaries, on the rare occasion a payday actually took place. We would study the garrisons and attempt to determine what unit was there and its condition. The Division Speciale du President was the easiest because its troops were relatively well off. Their uniforms were almost uniform. In contrast, regular unit garrisons looked like squatters' villages. Very few uniforms around and lots of civilians. I began to paint a word picture of the Zairian military in my mind.

Our primary mission remained monitoring the security situation vis à vis the FAZ. We did our daily trips and talked to people out on the streets. That included our own Zairian soldiers. The others in the embassy stayed inside or at least inside Gombé, as though the district had an invisible force field to protect them. Embassy reporting and to a certain extent DAO reporting had become too fixated on the FAZ payday as a potential spark for unrest. I told Stan we were going to back away from that standard. The old Zaire and now the New Zaire were relatively worthless. Even at their beginning value of four New Zaires to the dollar, a FAZ soldier could not feed a family on thirty New Zaires a month. They had become used to a worthless salary; those who stayed in uniform had a hidden means of making money. For most that meant open extortion or outright robbery. Payday was therefore becoming a nonevent.

That did not mean violence was not occurring. It certainly was. Currency exchange was considered a woman's industry in the local culture. As soon as one drew a salary in New Zaires, one hurried to the currency mamas to change it into U.S. dollars or French francs. The mamas leaned on the exchange by charging a mid rate; then they turned the money in at a more favorable rate to themselves. Virtually all of the currency mamas were officer wives; this is how many FAZ officers kept their families going. That fall the currency mamas started getting robbed and killed less than five hundred meters from the front door of the embassy. And the murderers were other military. I drew criticism from the embassy over my reporting. The reason was simple: after two pillages, the State had not allowed the embassy to bring back dependents to Kinshasa. A senior member of the embassy wanted his children and did not like seeing outgoing cables on continued military violence.

Still, other incidents took place, and I reported them. In one, the same Guarde Civile troops who had been killing the currency mamas robbed a member of the embassy security office at gunpoint when this security expert decided to walk his dog after midnight. Again the report was dismissed because it was after midnight and therefore of no concern. Then an embassy vehicle carrying the chargé's cook home was shot up one evening. The car was outside Gombé but on the main route up to the Gulf compound in Binza. In another case, the relatively well off DSP started hijacking cars for ransom. One of their more audacious actions was to take the South Korean attaché's vehicle in broad daylight directly in front of the American school.

We still had some payday-associated tension spikes. The DSP tak-ing the Korean attaché's vehicle and another diplomatic-plated car was payday related. By then the New Zaire was at five hundred to the dollar in just six months. The same thing happened upcountry. The only armor unit in the Zairian military rioted and pillaged the local town. Not with their tracks, of course; none of those relics ran. The 31st Para did the same out by the airport; they broke into the arms room and threw grenades and fired at shadows all night. The government played along when this happened and doubled salaries after the value of the New Zaire declined more than a thousand percent. To the embassy leadership, the military remained the cause of all Zaire's ills. To me, the military violence was a symptom of a larger malady.

Zaire: A Country That Never Was

The macro problem facing Zaire was not the Zairian military or even the doyen of the military, Mobutu. The problem was there was no Zaire. Conquest of the Congo basin had been done at the tip of a bayonet. Belgian economic development of the colony had used the same bayonet, and Mobutu depended on it to keep it together as an independent country. There were no Congolese people. There were only ethnic groups lashed together in the patchwork entity—colony or country—once called the Congo and now named Zaire. Independence only weakened the lashings. Mobutu's bayonet got steadily duller over the next thirty years despite billions in western aid. He had been able to hold the country together because Cold War–driven assistance gave him large sums of cash to maintain his kleptocracy and prod any opposition with that same bayonet. By 1994 the Cold War had been over for nearly five years, Western aid monies were gone, and Mobutu had moved up country. The FAZ—as the traditional bayonet used to herd the Congolese—was broken, an assessment I penned in a long cable back to D.C. Zaire as a nation was equally shattered.

You could see the cracks in the masonry inside Kinshasa and out-side in the country. In Kinshasa, private armies were springing up. Most notable was a security company built around junior officers of the DSP. Yigal was an Israeli colonel who had retired after a final tour in Kinshasa heading the Israeli military mission to build the DSP. He had returned and started a security company (SOZAIS) in partnership with Lieutenant General Nzimbi, commander of the DSP.

Nzimbi could release officers to work for SOZAIS, quite a deal for those selected. Salaries were good and the pay steady. They guarded homes and businesses. Yigal had a modern central monitoring station and everyone who was on contract received a security alarm. A react squad responded to all alarms. The squad of four to ten guards was armed with Uzis and grenades. They had heavier hardware at their disposal as well.

Off course there were customers and then there were *customers*. The latter had full-time SOZAIS troops on their doorsteps round the clock. One was my neighbor, a Lebanese diamond dealer who had a steady stream of visitors at strange hours. His SOZAIS squad included a team of ten men equipped with light machine guns. I liked having them as neighbors; they did keep more troublesome elements away. One afternoon I was home from work and heard a crash outside my front wall. The road was always busy, and everyone drove like maniacs. A SOZAIS mobile patrol had gotten into a fender bender with a Guarde Civile vehicle, and the aftermath got intense. By the time it was over, the SOZAIS thugs had taken the Guarde Civile troops prisoner and seized their car.

Others had their private armies, or they leased them from the Ministry of Defense. The money of course went into senior officers' pockets. The leased troops were lucky just to get steady meals. As I have mentioned before, the embassy had its own company from the gendarmes. Later that year, the gendarme commander attempted to up the costs, and when the embassy refused to pay, he replaced the trained troops with a ragbags collection of misfits. Remember also that I had my own mini-militia out at the airport. I had no doubt they would shoot someone if a simple beating did not do the job.

Phone Wars: Telecels and Terror

Such privateering was not a new development. The Zairian military had lived off the land in this manner long before independence. But privateering had grown both comic and tragic in its proportions. One of the more interesting stories developed out of competition for the cellular phone market, controlled by an expatriate whose ties to Mobutu went back to the late 1960s. After the first pillage had destroyed the phone system, this entrepreneur had swung the financing to bring a huge satellite antenna into Kinshasa. Similar systems were emplaced in Goma and Lubumbashi. His direct backer was Yigal's colleague, Lieutent General Nzimbi of the DSP. Even with that type of support, the only way the company could get underway was offering courtesy telephones to all the elite in Zaire's power structure, perhaps the first unlimited minutes program in the world. Someone had to pay for those minutes and phones, so the costs were shifted to the less fortunate consumers.

As a result, cellular service in Kinshasa was expensive. Start up costs ran around seven thousand dollars per phone, and local calls cost more than a dollar a minute. International calls ranged between four to six dollars depending on the caller's location. Incoming international calls cost the receiver two dollars a minute. But everyone who was anyone had a cellular. The embassy had converted over almost entirely to phones. The cellular phones were so pervasive that the powerful—known as Les Grandes Legumes—had bearers who carried the boss's phone and screened all calls. One could even buy fake phones to keep up with the Joneses. The bottom line was the cellular market was big money, and only one company had control of it. Backed by Mobutu and Nzimbi, the original cellular company seemed secure.

But this was Zaire and predators roamed. One of the biggest was Bemba, the model Zairian crook writ large. Big in the diamonds and gold market, Bemba quietly arranged to bring in another cellular base station using second-hand equipment. He had the backing of the Guarde Civile, rival to both Nzimbi's DSP and the private company SOZAIS. Once the new system was ready to go, he announced there was a competitor for Zaire's cellular users. And, of course, he undercut prices to lure away his competitor's customers.

Natural competition, you say? Maybe in the States but not in Zaire. The phone wars soon erupted in Kinshasa. The friction point was satellite access; the two companies would have to share time on a common communications bird that serviced Africa. Soon there were a series of minor gun battles between the competitor's armies. After the Guarde Civile bombed the main base station for the original company, the DSP encamped a full company of troops around the dish to protect it. Naturally the Guarde Civile did the same around Bemba's station. At the height of the tensions, we lost cellular comms for hours and sometimes days.

Outside the capital city, Zaire was similarly fractured. Kasai was evolving into an independent state fueled by diamonds and gold. The province had refused to accept the New Zaire as the standard currency even in the face of military reprisals. Local air carriers moved the diamonds, gold, and money along a pipeline exempt from any taxation. Here was a state that had refused the national currency, avoided virtually all taxes, and defied the national military—all with impunity. I tried to get this across to embassy officers as they focused on the political opera in Kinshasa. One bright star appeared in the political section in the form of Peter Whaley. Though he looked the part of the State Department officer complete with hand-knotted bow ties, Peter was his own man intellectually. We both agreed Mobutu was still in charge; that he was able to maintain that control while living nearly a thousand miles away in Gbadolité was proof that nothing was going to change.

Comic opera also took place out in the bush. Shaba had long been a breakaway province. In 1960 it was called Katanga, then the heart of the Congo's mineral production. The Belgians had sponsored its bid for independence, led by Moise Tshombé. My old friend, Vandewalle, had been the architect of the failed secession. He had established and led the Katangan gendarmes in defying the Western world's efforts to bring Katanga to heel. In 1977 and again in 1978, the remnants of the Katangan gendarmes almost retook the region, now renamed Shaba. Again massive international reaction kept the province as part of Zaire. As a 1993 Christmas present to Kinshasa, the Shaba governor declared Katanga was now a semi-independent nation. That was really no more than a statement of long-term fact, but the presence of the Zairian Defense Minister Nguz Karl I Bond beside the governor made the proclamation notable. Nguz Karl I Bond had been condemned to death for cowardice during the Shaba II war fighting the Katangan secessionists. As was the case with many Zairian failures, he was later rehabilitated and resurrected. Now to mark the rebirth of Katanga, Nguz as defense minister and the governor of Shaba Province drove to the ceremony in Moise Tshombé's old car. You could not sell a script like that in Hollywood: too improbable, they would say. But in Zaire, the improbable ruled.

That was where Zaire was in 1994. Mobutu still had the reins on his team of thugs and through them manipulated what was left of the false state established by King Leopold as a colony. The overt economy was in shambles, and an undeclared economy cooked along under the surface. The Zairian military was similarly a ghost of what years of foreign assistance had tried to make it. Never competent as a national military force, it was now divided and loyal to those who had the money to pay for its doubtful services. The Zairian people did not exist. There were Kinshasans who lived in the capital city. Then there were Kasaians, Katangans, and Kisanganians, but they were not peoples unified by any real provincial identity. Ethnic divisions tore them apart as well. Zaire simply did not exist beyond the efforts of the international community to treat it as a country.

Flames along the Borders: Brazzaville Fireworks

The same situation was developing along many of Zaire's borders. Congo-Brazzaville had plunged into a civil war centered on the capital city. Angola had been in the grip of a twenty-year war. Rwanda and Burundi bubbled with ethnic tensions. All of these conflicts impinged on our day-to-day life in Kinshasa.

Certainly Congo-Brazzaville had the most immediate effect on us. There was an interesting relationship between the two countries. The Congo that became Zaire had been a Belgian colony. Congo-Brazzaville had been a French possession. During the Cold War–fueled rush to independence, the Congo-Zaire remained in the Western camp under Mobutu but only at the cost of years of war and decades of foreign aid that enriched Mobutu. Congo-Brazzaville tilted toward Marxism, though it never went completely under the Soviets' banner. The French managed, as only the French could, to maintain a degree of influence in Brazzaville. At the same time, the French sought to replace the Belgians as the dominant European influence in Zaire. They succeeded. In contrast, the United States had little to do with Brazzaville beyond normal diplomatic representation. Washington pinned its Cold War hopes on Mobutu.

The result of this Cold War chess game was that two African capital cities less than five miles apart acted like the Zaire River was the Berlin Wall. There was intercourse between the two, both economic and social. But military tensions were falsely high. I say falsely because there was never any question of the Zairians invading the Congolese or vice versa. Neither had a military capable of such an attack.

Yet the Cold War did have certain benefits for the African countries that took sides. Those exterior tensions dampened interior tensions. The Congolese in Brazzaville were no exception. Like the Zairians, they were now having their independence problems all over again. But in Brazzaville, those problems were immediate. That fall they erupted into a shooting war. Artillery, mortars, and tank fire supported the ground clashes, and Brazzaville divided itself into two camps with an occupied no-man's-land between them. The fighting was not continuous, because mediators, foreign and domestic, attempted to defuse the tensions. But at times it would erupt into major battles. Our sister embassy issued reports on what was happening, and we read them like the script to a movie being filmed next door.

When the fighting peaked so did the artillery, mortars, and tank fire. Kinshasa got plenty of overshoots, and it could be nerve-wracking. I had a mortar round rattle my bedroom one evening. Whenever the shooting cranked up across the river, the Guarde Civile unit down by the ferry port responded by shooting in the air. The fighting in Brazzaville had serious ramifications. In January, 1994, fighting expanded, and the U.S. ambassador's residence in Brazzaville got in the way. State ordered an evacuation of all dependents and nonessential personnel. That put us in a funny position across the river. We were still on reduced staff after the second pillage. Brazzaville had been our primary escape route. That closed for us, and we became Brazzaville's main escape route because their airport was now Indian country. But even that was somewhat doubtful, because the river was no longer necessarily safe.

Holocaust in the East: Rwanda

Nearly one thousand air miles due east lay the postage stamp country of Rwanda. For the vast majority of Americans, Rwanda was unknown. A few might have heard of Tutsis or Hutus, perhaps even be able to connect those groups with Rwanda and its southern neighbor Burundi. As an African FAO I knew Rwanda in general terms and something of its history. In studying the 1964 Simba rebellion, I had examined Rwanda and Burundi as possible support bases for what was purported to be a communist-inspired and communist-supported insurgency. I also noted with professional interest when the French and Belgians both responded to the initial Rwandan Patriotic Front—the Tutsi-led rebel movement—threat to Kigali in 1991 with a combined intervention. I told my fellow Africa watchers the two forces would never get along. They had separate agendas. I was correct. The French wanted to get into the fight. The Belgians wanted to keep their citizens in Kigali safe.

By the time I arrived in Zaire, the struggle between the Rwandan Patriotic Front (RPF) and the Hutu government was somewhat stalemated. Negotiations at Arusha, Tanzania, had produced signed accords that August. The trick was implementing that power-sharing agreement, one that would allow the Tutsi exiles to come home. Around the first of the year, the United Nations deployed a peacekeeping force, the United Nations Assistance Mission in Rwanda (UNAMIR) to monitor the Arusha accords. It seemed fairly standard stuff, though I was surprised the Belgians sent the paracommandos. Neither side would see them as neutral; both sides would see them as allies to the other, a dangerous equation for any peacekeeping contingent. Still it all seemed on track as we moved into spring. It also seemed remote to our concerns in Kinshasa.

On April 6, 1994, the process ran decidedly off the track. Or perhaps better said, crashed with the plane carrying the Rwandan and Burundian presidents as they returned to Kigali with an implementation plan. A shoulder-fired missile swatted the aircraft out of the sky as it came in for its final approach; ironically its wreckage landed in the president's yard. There have been ethnic slaughters in Africa before, and there will be more. There have been political slaughters, and they too will be repeated. But what happened in Rwanda combined the ethnic with the political forces to create genocide. In the next three months, the Hutu majority, indoctrinated, motivated, and guided by political extremists, slaughtered at least eight hundred thousand of their fellow countrymen, largely Tutsi but with some Hutu moderates added to broaden the texture of the massacre. That figure—and I believe it was actually more than a million—meant at least one in every seven Rwandans died.

In Kinshasa we of course knew of the war, and we read the cable traffic. That made us privy to the State Department's adherence to the position that the killing in Rwanda was not genocide. In fact we were directed not to refer to the slaughter as genocide in our daily contacts. We also got news cables, and it was apparent the non-genocide position was going to cost us. Meanwhile we watched as UNAMIR disintegrated contingent by contingent. One of the first to go were the Belgians, but not before the Rwandan Presidential Guard slaughtered several Belgian paras who guarded the Hutu prime minister, a woman. She was also killed.

Of course, the war was big news in attaché circles, boosted by the French attaché's announcement that Paris was mounting Operation Turquoise to "protect the Rwandans from slaughter." That drew raised eyebrows from all of us, especially the Belgian attaché. Exactly which

Rwandans were to be protected? Suspicions remained high that the French planned a repeat of their 1991 intervention to prop up the old government. That government was now headless, and its army was in the field slaughtering Tutsis and moderate Hutus willing to share power with the Tutsis. It was also being outfought by a lesser-armed RPF. The U.S. position waffled on the French operation, just as we had done on the question of genocide. Washington seemed to pin all its hopes on getting the two sides back to the bargaining table. Meanwhile pressure built in the United Nations to do something after the failure of UNAMIR. Leading the call to action was the UNAMIR force commander Canadian Maj. Gen. Romeo Dallaire. He revealed that months before the genocide began, he had warned the U.N. Security Council that genocide was being planned. He further stated he had been prohibited from taking any preemptive action against the planners. That revelation played havoc with the U.S. stance on nongenocide. The United States had been at least partially responsible for tying Dallaire's hands in stopping the genocide before it started. Now our position that no genocide was taking place looked at best to be ill informed. Part of it stemmed from the disaster in Somalia. No one in Washington wanted another Mogadishu. We were still trying to extract ourselves from that mess. By equating Rwanda to Somalia, Washington tied itself and the U.N. Security Council in knots.

So rightly or wrongly, the French moved. Roughly a brigade-sized force with light armor and a logistical tail, Operation Turquoise soon stretched French expeditionary capabilities to their limits. The French have never developed the strategic lift the United States has in Air Mobility Command. Their medium-range lift is built around their fleet of C160 Transalls and C130s, capable aircraft but not designed for inter-theater deployments. The solution only became possible with the end of the Cold War. The French leased a fleet of Russian IL76s and AN124s, copies of the C141 and C5. Bon was soon hip deep in supporting these flights as they transited Ndjili headed east to Goma. He called me one evening asking to borrow our tractor and power-start unit to support an AN124 he had stuck at Ndjili. I would have helped, but the tow bar would not fit and the starter did not have the necessary hook-ups. Other problems plagued the French, but the biggest was fuel. The Russian jets guzzled it, and the French had drained stores all over central and northern Africa. Operation Turquoise as a rapid deployment slowed to Operation Tortoise.

None So Blind As Those Who Refuse to See

Meanwhile life continued in Kinshasa, and it was more or less business as usual in the embassy. Security remained a source of constant debate between the front office and the DAO. For me the memories of a calm street in southern Lebanon came to mind; it looked safe but things changed in a flash. Even as things were going to hell across the river, we had two inspections that should have reinforced security preparations in the minds of everyone. The first was from the State Department inspector general. As State inspectors they naturally concentrated on the State sections in the embassy. But I was happy to have them in the DAO. I operated on a less-is-best policy. I had run destruction drills as a detachment commander in Turkey. Destroying files takes more time than you think, even with pyrotechnic devices as destruction aids. We had a zero-burn-time office, because we had a single classified document on paper. The rest was on the computer hard drive, and we kept an axe beside the desk. The inspector loved us.

The embassy had a rougher time. Even after two military pillages in Kinshasa and a civil war just across the river, the political section still had thirteen classified safes in their area. The embassy defended the practice by saying they just could not do their jobs without them. The IG slammed them and hit the other sections in a country team meeting. The safes stayed.

The next inspector was from the DIA. He had originally been scheduled to fly into Brazzaville, inspect the DAO there and then cross over to see us. The ordered departure across the river in Congo-Brazza stopped that leg, so he changed his flights around and came in a day early without telling us. Arriving on an early evening flight without an embassy expediter to assist, he got the full treatment from airport security. Like the State inspector, he maxed us on our security, both inside the embassy and our operational procedures outside. We took him along on a daily city tour to give him a taste of life in Kinshasa.

Ultimately the embassy succeeded in convincing State that families should return, a step that would put other families at risk. They would take the embassy reports at face value. The irony was that while the embassy minimized criminal violence, it inflated political unrest. When Tshisekedi had first emerged as an opposition figure, one of his movement's favorite tactics was to call a Ville Morte or a general strike. The idea was no one was to go to work, and Mobutu would be shocked into democracy. There had been two Ville Mortes called in as many months when a third was announced. Nothing happened at all in the first two but the embassy used words like "tense streets" and "anxious moments." Sleepy Hollow was a better description. Stan read our staff the riot act; if they did not show, they had better be bleeding when they did make it to work. Our guys always showed.

We had been doing the morning city tour for months, so we knew what the streets looked like. The third Ville Morte proved equally stillborn. That morning we were out and about in the traditional riot areas out by the main native market. Many shops were open, although the morning crowds were thinner than usual. We saw a couple of platoon-sized patrols around the area, but aside from a single burning tire, that was about it for this strike. I said so in my report and sent it up stairs for approval.

Minutes later the phone rang. It was the front office. Stan and I went up to read a cable by the econ and political sections. It touted the Ville Morte and associated "demonstrations." I scanned it and handed it to Stan. He did the same and started shaking his head. I sensed we were expected to do a rewrite. I preempted.

"That is our report based on first-hand observations. We were out there. Who was out there from the embassy?" I asked.

Stan could not hold back any longer. "It says the trains didn't run. Who said so? Our drivers rode that train to work this morning!"

I did not wait for an answer to put my cards on the table. "My report is first hand. It goes like that or you can put an embassy comment on the bottom."

As it turned out, a local employee for the econ section had provided the drama in the embassy cable. I could not blame the officer who had penned it. He had done what the rest of the embassy did: ask their local hires to go outside and look around. The locals were not stupid. They went outside and returned to report the strike was effective, just what their masters wanted to hear. The front office should have just torn up the embassy report and then canned a couple of local hires. Instead, an embassy comment that their "sources" suggested the strike had been effective went on the cable Stan and I had written. Then the front office released the embassy cable complete with the "no trains ran" business without allowing us to comment. Looking back, I can see that little episode captured perfectly the tenor of life in U.S. embassy Kinshasa: ignore what does not fit; embellish what does when it serves to do so.

CHAPTER 4

A Little Town, a Little Hell

Goma

The Rwandan genocide had begun with the downing of the president's plane on its return from Arusha on April 6, 1994. We—the international community in Zaire—watched the events and pondered their implications. Soon the French were drawn into Operation Turquoise, nominally a humanitarian operation to limit the killing until the new U.N. military mission UNAMIR II could deploy to Rwanda after the first UNAMIR had collapsed. My counterpart in the French embassy, Col. Dominique Bon, was heavily involved in supporting French and French contract-air missions through Ndjili International Airport. But for most of us in Zaire the Rwandan war really began as the new Rwandan military concluded its conquest of the country. We knew horror was occurring, but that was all second-hand. On July 14, it started getting personal.

Initial Warnings, Initial Horrors

I was swimming laps at the American club at 8:30 in the morning when my cellular phone rang at the side of the pool. It was the DCM of the American embassy. He had heard five hundred thousand Rwandan refugees were crossing the border into eastern Zaire and wanted me to confirm the reports with my contacts. "Roger that," I answered. "I will get back to you."

I called Colonel Bon and asked for an update. He confirmed the numbers and added French forces had taken over Goma air traffic control. It was French National Day so I wished Dominique "Happy Independence Day" and said I would see him that evening at the French reception. Another quick call, this one to my Belgian coun-

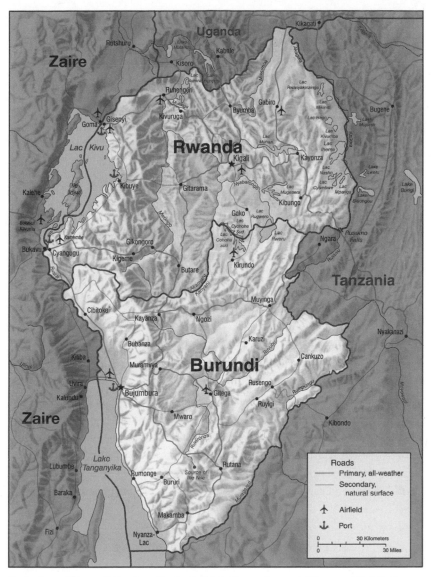

Rwanda and Burundi. **Courtesy the Central Intelligence Agency's Maps and Publications Released to the Public, 740960.**

terpart, confirmed the numbers. I headed to the U.S. embassy and the DCM's office. He and I went in to see the chargé.

It soon became apparent the chargé regarded the refugee crisis as a sidebar to the embassy's business in Kinshasa. The chargé asked what I thought the U.S. military response might be. I told him that would depend on the mission, but airlift was the most likely. I added we might put security forces on the ground, but the numbers would not be large. The chargé then announced he did not think any operation would last more than a couple of weeks. I told him if we went so far as to react, it would be for more than two weeks.

He soon decided to send me as leader of the embassy team, probably to leave July 16 via SHABAIR, the sole surviving Zairian-run civil airline. Kate Crawford as a representative of the Office of Disaster Assistance (OFDA)-USAID and an officer from the embassy political section would accompany me. I went back to the office and dialed U.S. European Command (USEUCOM) and the U.S. Transportation Command (USTRANSCOM) to see what they had on their screens. USTRANSCOM said there were a number of relief flights queuing up, but they were contract flights funded by the office in the Department of Defense concerned with special operations and small conflicts (OSD-SOLIC). I told Stan I was going to Goma—but I wanted headquarters approval ahead of time. I wanted them to know I was going out there without Zairian approval in case I got "nabbed." If U.S. military air became involved, I wanted Stan with me, because he knew how to work airlift better than anyone I had ever met. If the airlift remained civilian contract, Stan would handle the office. I had him get on to our contacts in Foreign Liaison at the Defense Ministry about the probable need for a blanket landing clearance for relief flights, regardless of who flew them. Because I was not formally accredited and could not ask for official clearance to travel to Goma, I told Stan not to raise the subject of our personal travel. That evening before I went to the French reception, the Joint Staff intelligence watch officer called from Washington to relate their intelligence concerns.

The French party was the scene of nervous chatter on Rwanda. No one really had any new information, but that did not slow down the speculation. I did talk with Colonel Bon, and he said he would forward my name to the Operation Turquoise commander, Major General LaFourcade. Bon, a French Naval infantryman, said he knew the general from operations in Chad. To the uninitiated it may sound strange to use Naval Infantry in central Africa, but French Naval Infantry had nothing to do with the French Navy. They were instead the old Colonial Infantry renamed to make them politically correct. France used the Naval Infantry interchangeably or in concert with the Foreign Legion. I had worked with officers from both in Lebanon and

Egypt. Bon's introduction would help get me into what was usually a very closed community.

The next day was prep day, and as always Stan was on top of things. Headquarters approved my deployment and acknowledged my warning that things were likely to escalate. Stan dropped the blanket clearance request at the Foreign Liaison office and drew advance pay and tickets from the embassy. After writing two books on operations in Africa, I knew how important communications were going to be. We were extremely lucky in that Goma had a cellular phone base station, one of three in the country. I told Stan to make me up a speed dial list with all key Washington and other military command numbers. He went several steps farther. Stan contacted the expatriates who ran the Kinshasa cellular phone company to insure I would be able to get my phone switched over in Goma. He had them call Goma to expect my arrival and to get the Goma phone numbers. Finally and most importantly, Stan converted my phone over so I could use satellite communications (SATCOM) long-duration batteries to power it. Like all good sergeants, Stan was a pack rat. When a Special Operations survey team had visited the embassy earlier that year, Stan talked them into leaving all their excess batteries behind. He had nearly two cases of the things. Most of the cellular phones had at best forty-five minutes of transmission power. With the SATCOM batteries wired to a cigarette lighter adaptor, I would get close to five days' use out of a single battery. That single improvement was critical. Stan carefully talked me through the wiring process necessary to replace them once they were dead.

"Don't put the wire in the wrong hole, Colonel, or you won't want to be holding this thing."

You remember NCO advice like that.

By the close of business, I was ready. Tickets in hand, U.S. dollars in my pocket, and reliable comms—I had rigged the cellular/SATCOM battery in a backpack. Hopefully Zairian airport security would be up to its usual low standards. The batteries looked like bombs and the jerry-rigged wires really made it look suspicious. Still with the backpack slung over a shoulder and a journalist's vest on, I looked like any one of a thousand disaster groupies, exactly the look I wanted. The only worry was a sidearm. I never went anywhere in Zaire without a piece. Now I was headed to Goma unarmed. I told Stan to start working on that problem. I called the States that evening to let family know I was headed to Goma the next day. I was keyed up.

I did not even get out of the house the next morning before the cellular rang. The DCM told me the chargé was going with us. Apparently State Operations had called the previous evening and directed he too go to Goma. The USAID director Brian Atwood and the Office of Foreign Disaster Assistance (OFDA) director Nan Borton were due to reach Goma on July 18, and State Operations expected the chargé to be there when they arrived. At the embassy, we convened another planning group with the entire party. One gap in our plans had been where we were going to stay. Kate Crawford came through for us with her contacts and arranged for a house. The landlord would pick us up at the airport. Kate was an Irish American who had been in Zaire for six years. She had first come as a Peace Corps volunteer. She stayed on working various contracts and was at this time a contractor with OFDA. She would become one of my best friends. We had a junior political officer, relatively new to the embassy, along because the chargé did not want to commit his best, Peter Whaley, to the Goma problem. We all headed to the airport around mid-morning.

Our SHABAIR flight took off at 1330 hours headed for Goma via Kisangani. As I expected, no one asked for a travel authorization. Goma sits on the northern tip of Lake Kivu with its Rwandan sister city Gisenyi less than two kilometers across the border. Goma has long been the traditional air hub for the region and has a single eleven-thousand-foot hardened runway. Most of the air traffic through the hub had been commercial cargo—in Zaire, read smuggling. The strip runs almost north to south, and most approaches come in from the lake to pick up the foot of the runway less than a kilometer from the shore. Until the French assumed airspace management control, the airport was strictly visual flight rules, and planes approaching circled the airport before lining up for landing. Our 737 did the same, and we all gathered at the windows to stare down at the town less than fifteen hundred feet below us. The town—that is the Belgian-designed heart of the town—was centered along the main east-west road toward the airport with a series of roundabouts allowing connections to the main north-south route. The main roundabout was less than two kilometers from the border crossing to Rwanda. Goma was in sum a border town of about nine square kilometers fringed, like all African towns, with villages.

On July 16 from fifteen hundred feet, Goma appeared to be the world's largest ant bed. We could see the road along the north shore of Lake Kivu all the way through the town center to the airport. It roiled with black-skinned humanity packed in like worker ants all struggling to push their way into Goma. When we flew low over the airport that day, there were already more than five hundred thousand Rwandans packing the streets with another five hundred thousand on the way to join them. The SHABAIR pilot warned us to all take our seats as we headed out over the lake to make our final approach. The ride got bumpy, and we were happy to feel the 737 fly onto the runway and reverse thrust.

The airport tarmac was strangely quiet. The arrival of the SHABAIR flight drew a few stares and not much more. I could see the French airport operations compound with clustered green tents, vehicles, and razor wire. French soldiers in form-fitting jump suits and berets with bull pup rifles eyed us with that special disdain only the Legion could offer. We trudged to the terminal for the usual niceties. Kate's main contact, Saleem, met her on the tarmac and introduced his driver, Paluku, who would take us into town. Zairian customs and border control officers looked eager to serve us until they realized we were all diplomats; there went their day's worth of bribes. Kate remained a bit nervous because as a contractor she had no diplomatic status. And she was carrying a wad of cash guaranteed to brighten any Zairian's day. She blended with us, and we had no difficulties. As we moved out of the airport, the usual crowd of taxi drivers and other hucksters competed for our attention. But Kate's contacts came through, and two vehicles from our landlord's office were waiting with drivers.

Leaving the airport we left all pretense of a rational world. We had seen the road from the air, but you cannot smell a road from fifteen hundred feet in a jet. The refugees flowed along our vehicles like rapids around two very slow moving rocks. Many were already half-dead, and more than a few had gone insane. Smells of feces and urine filled the air. Just getting the two kilometers into town took an hour. Our guide took us along the lake road to our house for the next forty days, just two hundred meters from Mobutu's Goma resort. That was good news security-wise. Also, one of the two decent hotel restaurants in Goma was just three hundred meters farther. The house itself sat across the road from Lake Kivu, its source of water via a two-pump system. We could stand on our porch and look at Rwanda some five kilometers across the lake. If we walked to the north end of the porch, we could see Mount Nyiragongo, a volcano glowing red over Goma. The house was pleasant, with three bedrooms, and Saleem gave us a more than fair rate on rent. I called the cellular phone company, switched my account over, and soon had Stan on the line to update him. I then made my first call into the Joint Staff intelligence watch in the Pentagon. We were in business.

Courtesy of Saleem, we had a little white four-door Toyota, and we were out and about the next morning. I realized quickly we were going to need at least one vehicle and probably more. Kate and I dropped the chargé and political officer at the local governor's house. She took me to the airport and we agreed on a rendezvous before she headed off to the U.N. High Commission for Refugees (UNHCR). At around 0930, I walked up to a very fit-looking French Naval infantryman on post at the gate of the French airport compound. Minutes later I met Lieutenant Colonel DeHeul, the French air operations officer. We began speaking in French, and then he switched to English. We kept up the language ping-pong to make sure there were no misunderstandings. I opened with my immediate purpose, arranging support for the USAID director's visit July 18 and said I fully expected a U.S. humanitarian relief operation once Atwood saw the conditions in Goma. I told him the U.S. State Department had asked me to convey a request for helicopter support to Atwood for the visit. I then asked him how the French operation was going.

DeHeul, aside from the accent and French uniform, was a typical air lifter. He was running twenty "heavy" flights a day into Goma using contract Russian and Ukrainian IL76s and AN124s as well as humanitarian agency chartered flights. He had several C160 Transalls for airlift support for the French forces deployed south near Bukavu. His biggest headache was running a simultaneous humanitarian and military airlift operation off a single runway. Mission handling equipment and tarmac space were limited, especially when the wide body aircraft like IL76s and AN124s were on the ground. Even with the French radar in place, night operations were slow due to poor runway and tarmac lighting. As for the Zairian airport officials and technicians, cooperation had been generally good. He added, however, that overall security of the airport needed to be improved, especially with the proximity of the Rwandan refugees. We exchanged phone numbers, and he then took me to see the air base commander. The commander was busy; in high-speed French, DeHeul told him I needed at least one Puma for the Atwood visit. The commander waved his arms and proclaimed this would be "No problem!" I quickly added that Mr. Atwood needed to meet the French commander, Major General LaFourcade. More high-speed French and hand waving ensued before DeHeul echoed his boss. "No problem. I will call you with the details." I took my leave. An hour later I made the noon rendezvous with Kate and the chargé.

We had some lunch—inside the hotel versus on the veranda under the eyes of several hundred thousand refugees—and planned out the rest of the day. The chargé had a tentative arrival schedule for Atwood, who was expected at 0900 the next day. I believed we would get the helicopter support and an audience with the French general commanding Operation Turquoise. There was no helipad pad at the main French compound on the south side of Goma, so we would have to convoy over after the aerial tour. Kate had NGOs for the convoy, and I would arrange French infantry escorts since I had seen some Rwandan military mixed in among the refugees.

Even as we had lunch, we could hear small arms, heavy weapons, and some artillery fire across the lake from Gisenyi. The hotel was only a kilometer from the border, but with its more than adequate menu and unlimited choice of drinks, it could have been on another planet. Refugees were dying of thirst less than one hundred meters from our table. The others in our group had heard the Rwandan military was collapsing. The question was not whether they would hold out but for how long. As firing across the border picked up, so did the intermittent firing by Zairian troops inside the town. True to FAZ tradition, the Zairian troops were stealing everything they could from the refugees. Women were being gang raped at the border and elsewhere by FAZ troops. I had seen two probable victims on my way back from the airport. Both women were stark naked. Both bled from the crotch. And both were in wild-eyed shock. Kate and I teamed up to survey the NGO sites for Atwood's visit. The chargé with the political officer in tow would work the local Zairian officials and the UNHCR. As we split up, I reminded all to be careful. I did not realize at the time that Goma would get worse in a hurry.

Cowards, Losers, and Killers

Kate had been busy that morning, and she knew what NGOs to visit and where to find them. I collected my notes. When we reached the first stop, I stayed outside and made the first call of the day to the Pentagon. Just getting that information back to the Pentagon took nearly thirty minutes of me talking and the watch taking notes, a system soon replaced with a tape recorder. I fielded a few questions and then broke it off with a promise to be back to them in a couple of hours.

That afternoon Kate and I visited four or five NGOs and heard the same story. The refugee flow had been roughly 250,000 per day since July 14. Current plans focused on getting the bulk of those 750,000 refugees out of Goma to camps being established to the north. Those camps would benefit from overland routes out of Uganda, reducing the air bottleneck at Goma. The first camp, Kibumba, was to be a way station, halfway to the main camp at Katale some sixty-five kilometers north of Goma. I thought a way station thirty kilometers distant was a long walk for dying refugees. The plan did call for temporary feeding centers along the way to draw the refugees north, moving some ten to fifteen kilometers per day.

Other needs were standard. Hospitals were overflowing and were likely to be overwhelmed by cholera and other waterborne diseases. The key was water purification and transport. That became my mantra back to the Pentagon: water, water, and more water. We were sitting on one of Africa's largest lakes. We just needed to make the water potable and distribute it.

The NGOs also mentioned the airport. Aircraft loading and off-loading was already slow, and I knew full well the pace of landings was about to triple. The NGOs expressed great concern over airport security as the airflow built up. Anyone familiar with Zaire knew what the military was like. The May deployment to Goma of the 31st Para—leaders of two major military riots in the capital city—had not improved local security. The Goma garrison was already charging the refugees for access to Lake Kivu. An airport tarmac loaded with supplies would be too much for the FAZ or the locals to resist. Getting the camps set up would require civil action teams and engineers. Digging latrines for 750,000 refugees is no small task, especially if you are standing on massive lava plains. There were other needs too numerous to count; some included kerosene-fired refrigerators, generators, and light sets. Our task was to create a tent city for nearly a million refugees and get them there safely before death beat us. It was a race we could not win, and we knew it.

Nevertheless it was interesting to see the reactions of the various NGOs to me as an American soldier bearing the news that the Yanks were coming. Some were openly hostile. Some were almost naively ecstatic. Generally speaking, the more labor-intensive or equipment-intensive NGOs were, the more realistic they were in their expectations. The closer they came to direct human-contact work—doctors, nurses, orphanage workers—the more polarized they became. Some thought we could save the world. Others reacted like we were the same as the Zairian military, at best mere thugs. For example, I would work directly with a Scottish NGO specializing in bulk cargo handling. Aside from language difficulties, we got along fine. They had worked with soldiers elsewhere. When introduced to a Medicins Sans Frontiers (MSF) coordinator, the first words spoken were, "If you have a gun, you must leave. We don't like soldiers here." I let such hostility roll off my back. Besides, we were about to get twenty thousand more soldiers in town.

That afternoon Kate and I were headed from the south side of Goma back to the north. A Dutch MSF Toyota 4-Runner came hurtling down the road toward us, only to slide to a stop sideways in a cloud of dust. The "If you have a gun, you must leave. We don't like soldiers" coordinator stuck her head out of the cab and screamed, "They are shooting everywhere! There are too many of them! They must go back!" She continued the same refrain as she slammed the truck back in gear and took off, generating a dust plume like a crop duster. I mistakenly assumed the MSF coordinator had just met the FAZ. We had just turned onto the eastern loop around the town when we ran head on into the former Rwandan Army. Suddenly we were there amongst some twenty to thirty thousand soldiers who had just lost a war. Many were crammed into Rwandan Transport buses, a common sight and mobile road hazard over the next few months in Goma. Others were in military vehicles, laden with cargo—I saw plenty of ammo cases.

Surrounded by twenty thousand killers, I figured I might as well do my job. I studied the troops and the vehicles to judge their status. It was clear they had been in a fight. I saw plenty of bandages, and no one was in parade dress. Scattered along the route, Zairian soldiers fired their weapons in the air to encourage the Rwandans to keep moving, a technique that made little impression on the Rwandan soldiers. Most walked in formation, and while I did not see many small arms, grenades bulged in battledress pockets. I spotted several twin 37-mm AAA guns mounted in trucks, feed trays filled with ammo, and crews relaxed but ready. All had expended casings scattered around the truck beds. Intermixed between the trucks, buses, and troop formations, three or four Panhard armored cars trundled past us with the track commander standing in the command hatch. I got on the cellular phone back to the Pentagon Intelligence Watch.

"The remnants of the Rwandan military have collapsed and retreated across the border into Goma," was my set up. I got the expected, "How do you know?"

"Because I am sitting in the middle of them" got the watch officer's attention. I described the scene around me for the next ten minutes or so. The gunfire continued as I talked. Even as Kate pushed the driver to go faster, we got slower and slower like a salmon swimming up an increasingly swift stream. We drew more than a few hostile stares from the Rwandan soldiers, and the hair on my neck signaled its concerns. I felt, and then heard, heavy mortar rounds slam into the ground near us. As those rounds impacted, other rounds landed on the southern tip of the airport, suspending operations and sending refugees stampeding past the press compound. Nearly a hundred refugees were trampled to death, and pictures of the panic soon graced the world's morning papers. The French claimed the Rwandan rebels had deliberately targeted the airport to keep any foreign aid from getting to the refugees.

The press jumped on the issue, firmly in line with the French account. Pure serendipity was at play here. The press had found Zaire a very hostile environment. The Zairian military regarded any journalist as a walking pawnshop, albeit in reverse. Zairian soldiers would seize their cameras, and then the luckless journalist would have to buy their expensive equipment back. One such transaction lead to another until the victim was out of money, robbed of his equipment, and perhaps beaten. The only way to stop such a feeding frenzy was to stand up to the Zairian military the first time, quite risky for someone without any diplomatic status or a gun. Several journalists had tried to do just that by threatening to use world opinion against their attackers, as if a Zairian soldier gave a damn about world opinion in 1994 Goma. In one case, a BBC stringer attempted to reach the head of the collapsed Rwandan army. He and his driver made it through one or two check points before their luck ran out. At the next, the Zairian soldier in charge demanded payment. When the journalist refused, the soldier shot the driver and then, turning his pistol on the reporter, said, "Goma!" The journalist eventually made his way back to town and safety. World opinion might be quite powerful outside Africa but it counted for little in Goma.

Even bribes were no guarantee of safety of person or property. To the contrary, the first bribe paid was like blood in the water to the Zairian military. Once tasted, one was certain to be bitten again.

Consequently when the press began arriving in Goma, the only "safe" operating zone for them was the airport under the protection of the French. I was amused; the press, after complaining about media pools in the Gulf War, willingly pooled itself in a small wire enclosure along the main refugee route. One scene, repeated more than a few times, did not amuse me; I saw journalists use the bodies outside the wire as props. The technique was simple: new broadcast, move the bodies to give the viewers a different look. No need to go outside and see what was happening. This was frontline journalism at its best.

The Rwandan Patriotic Army's (RPA) shelling of the airport was a case in point. At the time, I knew the rounds had hit all over our side of the town. I did not know why, but I also knew the French version was probably wrong. A year later I confirmed my suspicions. I was having drinks with a friend in the RPA, Colonel William. Not the least shy, William had told me he was the best of the RPA's tactical commanders. He probably was because others well known to me had spoken highly of the young colonel, age twenty-five at the time of our discussions. William proved his point by telling me how he had pushed the old army out of Rwanda in 1994.

William's tactical technique amounted to being "the biggest, baddest SOB in the valley." He always attacked, even if the odds were three to one against him—which they were in July, 1994, at Gisenyi. William's brigade of some three thousand men had driven the twenty to thirty thousand troops of the old regime out of Rwanda through Goma. That was the hallmark of the RPA: unlike any African army I had seen, they would close hard on their enemies and destroy them. They were, on the other hand, relatively gentle victors. So as William and I had drinks, I asked him about his mortar attack on the airport.

Upon hearing my question about the mortars, William looked oddly at me. I reminded him, "William, I was there in Goma when the rounds hit all over the place. The French said you were trying to close the airport against support for the refugees. Was that true?"

At that he started laughing and pointed across the lake at Mount Goma, a three-hundred-foot lakeside ridge that overlooked the town and the airport from the southeast.

"See that hill?" he asked. "We were trying to hit that damn hill. I was afraid our enemies might put heavy weapons along its crest to fire back at us here."

He had a point. We were sitting on his porch along the Gisenyi ridgeline less than three kilometers from Mount Goma. I remembered the 37-mm AAA the old Rwandan Army had mounted in trucks. "They liked to shoot at us with their anti-aircraft cannon," he added. "We had problems with aiming our mortars' . . . how do you say?"

"Fire direction control?" I offered.

"Yes fire direction control," he affirmed. "We just pointed them in the right direction with compasses and guessed at the rest. I gave up trying to hit the ridge with mortars after about ten rounds. Besides we had heavy weapons that could hit it if needed."

That conversation was a year in my future, amusing to recount a decade later but irrelevant in 1994. William might be missing Mount Goma, but neither the former Rwandan Army nor I knew that in July, 1994. All I knew was indirect fire had started dropping on us. The best place for Kate and me was away from the most likely target, the Rwandan military all around us. The targets wanted out of there as well. Finally we gave up and backtracked. That offered us some maneuvering room, and our driver could turn round. We went with the flow following one of the 37-mm trucks with its loaded guns pointed at our windshield. We retraced in minutes what had taken us nearly an hour to cover. Kate made her meeting, just five minutes late. Meanwhile I ran into the chargé, just back from the border-crossing site.

The Funnel: Leave Your Weapons and Money at the Gate

The chargé had been in meetings at the lake hotel when word came in that the main elements of the old Rwandan Army were coming across the border en masse. Understanding the geography of the crossing increases the drama. Gisenyi and Goma have long been sister cities. Goma had the commercial infrastructure and the crooks to make it a booming smuggling center. Gisenyi had started as a lakeside resort. If you could do it, you made your money in Goma but made your home in Gisenyi. The main road into Zaire from Gisenyi traced the northern edge of Lake Kivu. Stately lakeside homes fronted the road's north side with the lake's rocky beach on the south. It was a natural funnel that ran two kilometers from the luxury Hotel Meridien on the Gisenyi side. There was a border post on the Rwandan side with the usual offices, customs, passport, and military. In July, 1994, none of the normal offices were manned. Next came a fifty-meter stretch of no-man's-land between the Rwandan and Zairian border posts. Like the Rwandan side, a weight-balanced barrier gate marked the entry into Zaire.

In normal times—at least as normal as times ever get—crossing into Zaire is like walking on to the set of a bad movie. Every stereotype about Third World border crossings ever put on the screen is there. The expected buildings squat along the side of the road. Not the relatively pristine white offices found on the Rwandan side, those on the Zaire side are painted like the country's green flag. A yellow circle centered on the lime-shaded walls outlines a dark hand holding a flaming torch, supposedly guiding the Zairians toward progress, a bad joke considering Le Guide Mobutu has taken up permanent sanctuary away from his own capitol city. The green flag buildings are faded and worn, just like Mobutu's reputation. Nevertheless you know right away you have entered the land of the flaming torch.

The other stereotypical features of such crossings are the openly hostile border guards and the associated customs and immigration officials. *The Dogs of War* with Christopher Walken captured this setting at a fictitious African airport. That film could have been cast from the Zairian soldiers and officials at any border post or airport.

The typical Zairian soldier—DSP or 31st Para—looked about the same. Starting with the head and working down, all were medium in height, wiry or stocky depending on ethnic group. The DSP were all Equatorian and therefore somewhat stockier than the Paras who came from a more mixed ethnic group. They had chiseled features, thanks more to a limited diet than any exercise program. All wore berets, usually red or green with an occasional black, marked almost uniformly with a Zairian rip-off of the French Foreign Legion cap badge. Sunglasses, preferably mirror shades, were *de rigueur*. Uniforms were generally French-cut camouflaged battledress accented with glaringly bright rank and badges. Every Zairian soldier wore French jump wings; the Israeli-trained DSP wore Israeli wings as well. Few had ever seen a parachute, much less actually jumped from an aircraft. Some wore unit patches tied off their left epaulet to drape over the left deltoid. That of the 31st Para showed an open parachute, always encouraging for an airborne unit with no aircraft. The DSP at the border had a Dragon emblem, making them select in the larger body of Mobutu's favorites.

They all tended to accessorize their uniforms. A favorite was a rappel seat looped around the waist and tied off with a snap link. A rappel seat is usually just an eight- to ten-foot length of climbing rope used when the bearer is going to rappel out of a helicopter or down a wall or mountain. I carried one in Ranger school but never wore it as a belt. The FAZ liked their rappel seats in bright colors, and every soldier had one. They wore their rappel seats for a reason, one nothing to do with mountain climbing. They never went to the field, and they certainly did not helicopter rappel. The Zairian Air Force had but one operational helicopter, a Puma so worn its tail wagged in flight like a dog begging to sit down and rest. But the rappel seats made handy whips. One could use the knot end for less serious challenges. The snap link could be deadly. I had seen Zairian soldiers throughout Goma beating the refugees to move them through the town.

The other element of Zairian military attire was the personal weapon and its magazines. I rarely saw a soldier equipped with load-bearing equipment for magazines, canteens, or first aid pouch. Usually they stuffed their grenades in their pockets along with whatever else they felt the need to carry.

The grenades sometimes caused problems. A favorite extortion technique was to wave a grenade around. If that did not get the desired effect, the soldier would pull the pin on the grenade. Sometimes they actually threw the damn things, but usually the victim would surrender whatever the soldier was demanding. He would then put the pin back in the grenade and after stuffing it back into his pocket continue with the daily shopping. Grenade pins are steel, and most grenade fuzes are made of aluminum. The steel pins, pulled out and put back in several times, were soon lost in the aluminum holes. Sometimes they slipped out as the soldier walked along. If he was lucky, he might hear the pop or smell the smoke as the fuze ignited in time to get the grenade out of his pocket. If not, his shopping day got cut short.

Ammo was another style issue. The Zairians issued a lot of ammo, especially in a place like Goma. They had been burning up rounds like firecrackers since we arrived. If they did not have magazine pouches, how did they carry their spare ammo? They taped their magazines together in what was a Zairian version of Japanese origami. They carried a variety of weapons. I saw FALs, M16s, G3s, and Uzi's all in the same squad. Every soldier had at least three magazines taped, two down and one up. With thirty-round magazines, that is several pounds of ammo slung beneath the weapon, making it virtually impossible to shoulder fire with any accuracy. While three magazines were standard, I often saw more. Four or five was not uncommon. The most creative was a DSP thug who had managed to tape eight Uzi magazines together like a Nazi Swastika. I would have loved to see him quick-change magazines or even just try to aim the weapon. That too was irrelevant. The average FAZ soldier closed his eyes when firing. Besides, when you are shooting in the air, who needs to aim?

So these were the soldiers who greeted the defeated Rwandan Army as it crossed at Goma. Understand, the Zairians were not just a little scared. They were terrified. They had been beating up, robbing, and raping the refugees for three days. The Rwandan military might not have been up to defeating the Rwandan rebels, but they were more than capable of crushing the Zairians. The local Zairian commander ordered them to surrender their weapons. For whatever reason—they were tired or more likely they knew they had plenty tucked away in their vehicles—the Rwandans tossed their small arms, grenades, and assorted other weapons into great piles along the one-thousand-meter stretch of road past the border check point. As the weapons piles grew, the Zairians grew braver and more shots went into the air. The parade of Rwandan military mounted on buses, trucks, or just on foot straggled on into Goma where Kate and I ran into them. Their entry signaled a new phase in the Rwandan Civil War.

The Atwood Visit

The next day Brian Atwood, the USAID director, and Nan Borton, the OFDA chief, were due to visit. The chargé, Kate, and I spent the evening of July 17 firming up the itinerary. Atwood would arrive mid-morning of the eighteenth. His first event would be a guided helo tour of the Goma area with me as the tour guide. The chargé had arranged meetings with U.N. and Zairian officials at the UNHCR building downtown. From there, we would go to the main French military compound. Since it was on the southern route where the Rwandan Army was still struggling towards temporary camps, I asked for a French military escort to lead us through the area.

The evening ended with a sound and light show courtesy of the Rwandan Patriotic Front (RPF) in Gisenyi and the FAZ in Goma. The fighting had not ended completely across the lake. Flares lighted the sky and tracers streamed out along the shoreline. Just as the RPF had dropped mortar rounds in that afternoon, they were using 37-mm AAA in direct fire against the Rwandan military. Unfortunately, the Rwandan military was concentrated south of Goma with our lake house in the line of fire. President Mobutu's lake resort—just two hundred meters away from my door—was also at risk. Every time there was a boom or a bang in the night, the DSP guards on the gate began spraying the night air. The chargé and I were on the porch watching the show across the lake. Our neighbors started up, and the tracers arched almost straight up. I moved into the door, putting something more solid over my head.

"What goes up, comes down," I said, indicating he might want to do the same.

Before he could even move, a Rwandan rebel 37-mm opened up toward us. The basketball-sized tracers streamed our way. The chargé scooted inside the house. I just stood in the door watching. There was no time to get out of the way and nothing in our house could stop the rounds. As the tracers flowed past us over the roof, I started laughing, though not at the chargé. I laughed because I was glad to be alive. I had a stiff shot of scotch and went to bed. The shooting continued all night.

The morning of the eighteenth dawned with new problems. The most serious was word from MSF that cholera had already claimed victims among the refugees, the majority of whom were still clustered inside Goma. The collapse of the Rwandan Army and its flight into Goma had not been duplicated farther south at Bukavu. The French military maintained a *cordon sanitaire* across southwest Rwanda nominally to allow Rwandan refugees to escape the fighting around the capital city, Kigali. When the Rwandan Army had collapsed in the north, its southern elements moved inside the French zone with an eye to crossing to Bukavu. There were still hundreds of thousands of displaced Rwandans inside the French zone. Later the world would learn the genocide had continued inside the French protected area. Meanwhile, everyone worried they too might flee into Zaire, replicating the developing horror in Goma around Bukavu. No one—except maybe the French military—thought the French would be able to stay and maintain that safe zone. The international community centered in the United Nations in New York focused on resurrecting UNAMIR to stabilize the situation. As if that was not enough, the Rwandan military (ex-FAR) in Goma had refused to declare itself a defeated army and disband. An army in exile presented particular problems. The UNHCR and most NGOs were forbidden by charter or self-declaration to feed an intact military. That left the French forces in Goma as the primary caretakers for their former Rwandan clients. The French supplied the water, and the ex-FAR seized the rest.

In the midst of chaos, one focuses on the immediate. Atwood was due, and we all went to the airport. At my first stop, Lieutenant Colonel DeHeul assured me everything was ready. We waited less than an hour before the French tower reported Atwood was inbound. As his party debarked, the chargé took the lead and introduced us all. Meanwhile, the French began spooling up our Puma so I broke in on the chargé and Atwood, saying "Sir, I have a French helo ready to take you on a tour. If you'll just follow me, Mr. Atwood, I have reserved a position for you by the door."

With the assistance of the crew chief, I got the party seated on the aircraft. I had headsets for Atwood, Borton, and me. The chargé would have to watch without hearing. I put Atwood on the right door seat with Borton beside him. The chargé was farther from the door but would still be able to see. DeHeul had already briefed the crew, and the pilot merely glanced back to get a thumbs-up from me. Tied on by a safety strap, I remained standing as we launched, leaning over Atwood's shoulder. The pilot climbed to two thousand feet above ground level, moving away from Goma to reach altitude. He then turned back and laid the Puma over to where the right side was almost underneath the aircraft. The view was great and I gave him another thumbs-up and thanked him on the intercom. We began a series of lazy 8's looping over the human ant bed below us.

We started with the area around the airport, and I talked the visitors through what they were seeing. I pointed out the pros and cons of air operations at Goma, some obvious, some not so obvious. The number of refugees created another problem. That morning the skies were clear, but I told them the French had suspended all landings the previous afternoon at 1600 hours. Smoke from thousands of cooking fires had obscured the field. From the airport, we flew along the main road into Goma, tracing the refugee flow in reverse. We did not overfly the border crossing. The new owners of Rwanda were not likely to welcome a French military helicopter buzzing their positions. I pointed out the crossing, and I showed Atwood the main road down to the lake, crammed with refugees carrying anything that would hold water. We flew over the main traffic circle and then out along the road where the old Rwandan Army now called home. There were forty or fifty green Rwandan buses below us, many partially or totally blocking the road. We could also see military vehicles, and I pointed out that the Rwandans still had antiaircraft gun trucks and armored cars. We looped around to the north and headed to the "way station" at

Kibumba. The refugee stream north toward it crawled up the single road, surrounded by black magma rocks. The Puma buffeted as we hit the thermals rising from them. As we turned back south toward the airport, I pointed out the local volcano smoking to our west. We soon landed. I got the party off the aircraft, and the chargé led Atwood toward the waiting vehicles.

The French military had their escort up front, and once we were loaded, the officer in charge looked to me for the word to move. I waved, and we headed out the airport gate and into the stream of refugees. The appearance of the hard-eyed French, fingers caressing their triggers, parted the refugees like magic. Atwood, the chargé, and Borton rode with me. We made the UNHCR building on the lake road in record time. As we moved along, Atwood asked me various questions about what he had seen. He did not exactly ignore the chargé but the latter was apparently feeling left out. Atwood then asked me the key question: how many troops would be required to stabilize the situation and get the crisis under control? I had thought about the issue.

I put it in two scenarios. "Sir, if the mission is stabilization and feeding, the keys are controlling the airport and doing something about the Rwandan Army. I estimate they were about 85 percent disarmed at the border. Finishing that job is still on the table. Doing it effectively and safely would require a separate brigade structure," I began.

"How many troops is that?" Atwood pressed.

As I said, "roughly five thousand," the chargé started to interrupt, but a look from Atwood stopped him.

I continued, "That would allow security on the airport with a battalion, a battalion to keep an eye on the Rwandan military, and a battalion to set up the refugee camps, plus, of course, the logistics to move water and food. That's scenario one based on a unilateral operation. The second is a combined operation with the French. They are already here so we augment them. The question is going to be how long will they stay and what they intend to do. The Zairians hate them. The French have always looked down on the Zairians, and the same thing is already happening at the airport. Under the second alternative, we should concentrate on water purification, transport, and airport flow."

Atwood thanked me. The chargé looked at me like I was calling for the invasion of Zaire. As we pulled up to the UNHCR building, I knew what was going to be said inside so I held back. For at least the twentieth time in four days, I got on the phone to the Pentagon with another update.

An hour later, the meeting broke up. The chargé led the party out, and we headed to the French compound. Minutes later we walked inside after being cleared by the guards at the gate. The interior was filled with the heavy blue smoke from the French military's smoke of choice, Gauloise. Atwood met the French commander, Major General LaFourcade. He was in his mid-fifties, a slight-framed man, who stood with a military bearing watching us come in. I also introduced myself. He smiled with a Gauloise smoking off his lips and said, "Yes, I know of you. Our Colonel Bon said you were coming." His grin revealed teeth to make a dentist shudder or perhaps jump for joy. Shrugging, he led us to a long table and pointed out our seats.

LaFourcade then waved to his chief of staff to begin a standard briefing. The colonel laid out the French operation to date in halting but effective English. He described the mission as a humanitarian venture prompted by the collapse of UNAMIR and the failure of the international community to act. It was a not so subtle dig at the United States done as only the French could do it. I listened but thought of the platoon of French Panhards I had seen arriving the day before at Goma. Humanitarian now undoubtedly, but the original operations order had provided light armor with another role in mind. The French intervention in 1991 had begun similarly. Unlike the Belgians, their partners in the mission to stabilize Kigali, the French had immediately deployed north to fight the Rwandan rebels. They had further "invited" the Zairians—always a symbol of stability—to come help. The latter spent so much time raping and pillaging the locals that the Rwandan government asked them to leave. Better to fight the rebels alone than with the doubtful "help" of the Zairians, who seemed intent on converting the locals to RPF supporters.

When the colonel finished his pitch, LaFourcade began his. His main concern was a potential second Goma south at Bukavu. He expected the new government in Rwanda to demand the French withdraw and feared a second exodus would take place. The problem would be worse since Bukavu did not have airfields to support a Goma-style operation. The French were using the Cyangugu airfield on the Rwandan side for their C160s. Neither that airport nor another airport just north of Bukavu could handle larger transport. In the larger sense, he wanted the United States to focus on keeping the French in Rwanda until UNAMIR II could stand up. If Bukavu turned into

Goma II, he wanted to build up helicopters in Cyangugu as well as barges on Kivu. He would need U.S. and international cooperation to do that. I jumped in at that stage to hook him.

In my less-than-Parisian French I said, "That cooperation is vital for us here in Goma, Mon General. We need to share information, people, and equipment to control the disaster at Goma." I knew he did not really want the U.S. military here. France, especially colonial warriors like LaFourcade, regarded central Africa as a fiefdom. I hoped getting his open vow to cooperate in front of his key staff and a senior U.S. government official might actually prompt him to do so.

"*Mais bien sur*, Colonel. We are ready."

We talked a bit longer, but the main deed was done. Whatever the United States decided to do, LaFourcade had promised to help, not hinder. I had visions of French-Belgian cooperation gone awry in 1978 in Shaba as well as 1991 Kigali. I do not think the chargé or anyone else from the embassy really got how difficult the French could be. But we had—I hoped—dodged that bullet. In the interim, the French said they were bringing in more wire to secure the airport perimeter. I told LaFourcade I would be back in touch as soon as we had a clearer picture of what we would do.

We went back to the airport without a hitch. The NGO meeting was pro forma. There was nothing new revealed, but the USAID director could not come to Goma and ignore the NGOs. Kate Crawford kept the meeting focused on the key issues: security, water, and related health concerns. I was pleased with the visit when we saw Atwood's plane go wheels up. I was also tired. By 8:00 that evening, I was delirious with fever, unable surface for thirty-six hours.

Building a Pick-up Basketball Team

Over the next two days, cholera seized the camps, and fever grabbed me, prompted by a massive allergic reaction to constant smoke and dust. I called Stan and warned him that if it had not broken by July 21, I would come back to Kinshasa for a preemptive antibiotic shot. All too often similar attacks had left me vulnerable to secondary infections, a risk to avoid in disease-ridden Goma. I went back to bed to watch the ceiling spin.

That evening Stan called me with good news and not-so-good news. The good news was he had arranged with Saleem's air transport company to airlift our Isuzu to me, selected because diesel was easiest to find. Stan told me he had put a toy for me in the vehicle and that I had better be the one who met it at the airport. As for me coming back, headquarters had told Stan to "tell Odom if he isn't dying, to stay in place." Headquarters promised to look at reinforcements and had told Stan they would let us know the next day.

In addition, they said my reports had proven to be of very high interest in the Pentagon and across the river. I was calling as many as ten times a day as information came to me. But because I had called them into the Pentagon, they were not getting to other concerned commands like U.S. European Command or Air Mobility Command. Their solution was for me to call Kinshasa every time I called the Pentagon watch. Then Stan could write the reports up as electronic messages. The Pentagon has twenty-eight thousand workers in it. I naively believed I could get headquarters to have the watch center, a DIA post, write up the reports. I told Stan it was time for him to come out. I believed we would soon have U.S. airlift inbound to Goma.

I was feeling better the next morning, but I stayed at the house. I called headquarters when I knew the office would be open. I began with the double reporting requirement, arguing DIA could type the reports up. I lost. We then turned to the issue of reinforcements. I came down hard on getting Stan to Goma. I cannot a decade later emphasize how important Sgt. 1st Class Stan Reber was to our air operations in Goma. I knew I had to have him. I was prepared to order him east even if DIA said not to. Referencing the need to double report back to Kinshasa, I told my desk officer, Capt. Rick Moore, "If you want those double reports typed up, you better get someone into Kinshasa to do them. And while you are at it, we will also need someone familiar with airlift operations to coordinate from K-town."

Moore was a good egg, and he genuinely tried to take care of us. As a captain surrounded by majors and lieutenant colonels he got overruled a lot. Plus he had to deal with irate light colonels like me when he had to deliver some variant of the nonsense all headquarters offer. He said he would get on backfilling the office. He told me headquarters had already notified the attaché offices in Chad, Congo-Brazzaville, Cameroon, and the Ivory Coast they might get pulled in under me. Moore said he believed the defense attachés from Brazzaville and Chad would be joining me in Goma. I told Moore I had roles for them already as liaison officers to the French. Maj. Jean-Luc Nash from Chad would go to the main French base in Goma, and the defense attaché from Brazza would go to Bukavu. I warned Moore I would need at least one more vehicle flown to Goma and cellular phones for the two new guys.

Moore called me back later that day with additional details. Nash was coming via French military air out of Chad. The Brazzaville defense attaché would cross the Zaire River at Kinshasa and fly from there on a flight set up by Stan. Moore had gotten the second vehicle approved along with the phones. Stan would put himself, our second office vehicle, and the phones on a "Saleem 707" to Goma. Meanwhile headquarters was pulling the naval attaché in South Africa, Comdr. Dorothy Grant, up to Kinshasa to backfill our office. She was coming with her husband and would stay in my house. Headquarters also pulled an operations NCO out of Cameroon to help her.

Though consideration had been given to pulling the defense attachés out of Cameroon, Lt. Col. Jim Cobb was new and needed to get his feet on the ground. Moore said Cobb might soon be needed to go to Rwanda. The Ivory Coast C12 was staging forward to Entebbe, Uganda, where it would be available to support us in Goma as needed.

Another friend of mine, Lt. Col. "Blue" Keller had moved up from his main post in Malawi to his secondary post in Kampala, Uganda. Blue and I knew each other from the Pentagon. He had done several special operations exercises in Zaire, including one with Dave Scott, my friend from the special operations side of the C130 community. As I remember, Blue and the air force crews had ended up dancing on the bar at the American club in Kinshasa, raising some eyebrows in the diplomatic mission. Finally Moore passed the word that Bill McCoy, a civilian from the Office of the Secretary of Defense for Special Operations and Low Intensity Conflict (OSD-SOLIC), would be coming the next day. McCoy worked humanitarian affairs for OSD-SOLIC and was already involved in relief operations in Tanzania.

Once again I called Stan to make sure he had the same information. I also made it clear I needed him in Goma "yesterday"; he was not to allow anyone to delay his travel. As for the folks coming to pinch-hit at the office, I told him, "Get 'em in and get over here." He told me the chargé wanted me to call him, so I did. He was somewhat exasperated by my headquarters' shuffling of people. After reminding me that the operation would only last a couple of weeks, he wanted to know why more people were coming.

I tried explaining, "This is spooling up as a large operation, and it will last several weeks. I need help, and so will you." He apparently had been in contact with the ambassador in Chad, who also questioned the movements. I ending up promising to maintain tight reins on the visitors, saying, "If anyone steps over the line, they will be gone."

I was pleased we were getting help. But I also knew pick-up teams always had some shaking down to go through. Kate was headed back to Kinshasa the morning of July 21, perhaps to come back, perhaps not. As for the others, I knew the Brazza defense attaché but not well. Stan had worked for and with him as a temporary operations coordinator until a new sergeant arrived in Brazzaville. The relationship had not been smooth, and that worried me. But I also intended he go south to the French headquarters at Bukavu, so friction between him and Stan should not be too serious a problem. I had met Nash at the African defense attaché conference hosted by headquarters in Pretoria in 1993. As he was personable and had a Special Forces background, I believed he would fit right in with the French in Goma. His ambassador had apparently said some harsh things about him, but I am sure my chargé had said some harsh things about me. I would focus on the mission and teamwork to get it done. This was not training, and the learning curve would be steep.

The morning of the twenty-first I took Kate to the airport and wished her well as she left. I expected the U.S. airflow to start that day with an airlift coordination team of some thirty people at 1500 hours. I had asked the French to provide temporary living areas for them until we got sorted out. My office vehicle was due at noon along with the "toy" Stan sent me. Saleem's office said I could keep my driver until Stan arrived. Bill McCoy was due in sometime that morning via Entebbe so I stayed at the airport in case he showed. Jean Luc Nash was supposed to be coming in that day via C160 out of N'djamena. The defense attaché from Brazza would not arrive until the next day. He was crossing the river to Kinshasa that afternoon. I hoped to have Stan shortly after his counterpart arrived from Cameroon, perhaps as soon as July 24. That sergeant could handle getting Commander Grant and her husband settled when they arrived.

Bill McCoy arrived that morning around 1000 hours as expected. As fate would have it, we had crossed paths in the Army Operations Center. Bill was a civil affairs and psychological operations reservist who had been called to active duty during Desert Shield and Desert Storm. We had met in the AOC, which gave us a common starting point, and our relationship soon became a friendship. As a humanitarian affairs coordinator for OSD-SOLIC, Bill had been running emergency food and shelter flights into Tanzania since the Rwandan War broke out in April. He had the ear of senior Pentagon officials, and his presence in Goma proved to be a blessing. We soon developed a tag-team approach to dealing with the Pentagon decision-making structure. Bill would call in on the OSD side, and I would plug in through the watch center to the Joint Staff. We pushed the common theme of water, water, and more water.

Noon was almost like Christmas as one of Saleem's two cargo 707s rolled to a halt on the tarmac. Within a few minutes, one of the oldest Isuzus in Africa was on the ground. Inside the truck, Stan had chained a small portable safe under the rear seat. I opened it up and, expecting one of my Berettas, found a Browning Hi Power 9-mm, marked "FAZ." I dialed Stan.

"Stannnnnn, where did this toy come from?"

He started laughing and said, "It says so right there on the slide. I figured if you had to use it, it would be easier to throw away. I checked it out. It works."

Point taken, and I liked the slim profile of the Browning as a hide gun. Armed once again in Zaire, I felt better already. Soon afterward I collected my final "chick" of the day. I saw a C160 circling and headed over to watch. As it parked, the ramp dropped, and Major Nash walked off wearing a Battle Dress Uniform (BDU) and a rucksack. I briefed him and took him to the French headquarters to meet his counterparts.

Events around Goma grew steadily worse. The buildup of bodies was apparent, and the smell was sickening. The former Rwandan military had shifted west but were still in evidence in town. Efforts to get the main refugee concentration north to Kibumba and on to Katale had progressed somewhat. There were three hundred thousand now at the northernmost camp and some two hundred thousand at Kibumba. Between three and five hundred thousand remained in Goma. Bukavu was up to four hundred thousand, but most of them had moved on south to Kaymanyola. All were dehydrated, and all were drinking whatever water they could find. That meant drinking death.

Megadeath: The Cholera Epidemic

Death, even individual death, is an unpleasant reminder of one's mortality. I had seen death before. All of us had. None of us in the international community in Goma were prepared for the death surrounding us. Even as we arrived in Goma on the sixteenth, we saw refugees dying from exhaustion, dehydration, or wounds. We knew the specter of widespread epidemic was very real. Nearly a million refugees moved through Goma at 250,000 per day. Most had walked more than one hundred miles to reach the border. Based on those figures alone, it would have taken a miracle to stop death from taking its toll.

The dying began with a vengeance on July 18 as the first cholera cases were reported. By the twenty-second, 6,700 were dying each day, a rate that continued for nearly a week. When the worst was over, we used the figure of 70,000 as a baseline estimate. The truth was we could not begin to know how many more had died out in the bush around those camps. We only had a rough estimate of how many were buried in mass graves. Later I found the numbers had been reduced somehow to 30,000 dead, a number both Kate Crawford and I find ridiculously low. To the contrary, I believe the overall refugee death in that summer of 1994 probably approached 100,000.

But I must also say that once you reach a certain plateau of mega-death, numbers become irrelevant. What becomes important is keeping your sanity. One method is, of course, focusing on a cause, something all of us did. Another is religion, and many prayed hard in Goma. There was also humor, appropriately black, to turn even the most ghastly scenes into something we could handle, at least temporarily. In that regard, it became common to refer to the dead as "enchiladas" because they were usually wrapped in straw sleeping mats. Inevitably other names were coined. Overall we cloaked our hearts and our minds with the equivalent of Kevlar body armor; we stayed numb, as emotionally detached as we could. The problem with that technique lies in its premise: you cannot keep such horrors out even when you pretend to ignore them. Sooner or later, they pay you a call no matter how many doors you close in their face.

There was an underlying reality in dealing with the Goma refugees that made these defense mechanisms even more imperative. One assumes refugees are the wretched of the earth, persecuted unjustly until they flee oppression of one kind of another. Not true here. Aside from the very young children—meaning under age eight—thousands of the refugees in Zaire were killers. They were fleeing the slaughterhouse called Rwanda. We were saving them.

With the explosion of the cholera epidemic, the sheer number of corpses created problems of scale. Bodies were literally everywhere, and no one wanted to pick them up. The French military stepped in, and the UNHCR hired locals to assist them. The French military engineers used dozers and trenchers to dig mass graves. Bedford-style medium trucks established regular routes like garbage trucks for picking up the corpses. Once they had a full load, they transported them to the gravesites. One of those was directly across from the airport along the edge of a banana plantation. Inevitably we commented on the prospects for a bumper crop of bananas the next season. The French reported they could only keep a soldier on the detail for a couple of days at a time. Otherwise the soldiers showed signs of depression and possibly worse mental complications.

Sometimes horror springs from horror. Taking a nap in Goma could be dangerous. On more than one occasion, a sick or simply exhausted refugee went into a sleep too deep to be wakened. Family or friends, thinking they were dead, rolled them up and set them alongside the road for pickup. Transported unaware to their final resting place, the first warning these unfortunates got was landing on a pile of bodies in a common grave. Some woke up and screamed. Others waved arms and kicked their legs hoping their movements would be noticed before the next layer of bodies was added. The lucky were rescued. Undoubtedly luck did not favor all.

There was one thing we could never adjust to: the innocent of Goma, the small children and babies who died in the hundreds around us. We never talked about them other than in a sterile fashion, such as discussing infant mortality or perhaps orphanages. We all saw them. The small bundles along the road made for large nightmares then and now.

Operation Support Hope: Welcome Mat

But our focus remained on stopping the dying, and soon Operation Support Hope began to unfold. On July 22, Bill McCoy and I headed to the airport to meet an inbound Learjet bringing in an advanced party from U.S. Special Operations Command Europe (SOCEUR). Bill and I worked well together, a welcome surprise to both of us. We had enough insanity to deal with already without generating our own. We presented a unified and coherent picture back to Washington, critical if we had any hope of getting an equally coherent response. I talked directly with the Joint Staff, and Bill represented OSD-SOLIC. We also believed we had a fairly clear picture of what "Washington" was thinking. We were wrong.

So as the Lear halted, we stood by waiting to meet the team leader. Even as the engines spooled down, the door dropped and out came this huge, black, Special Forces major.

He dropped to one knee, and as he began assembling a satellite communications antenna, he ordered, "This is a classified operation. You will have to move off!"

I guess he thought we were reporters. We were both in civilian clothes and baseball caps. I smiled and held up my ID. "I think I'll stay, Major. I am Lieutenant Colonel Odom, the defense attaché. Where is your boss?"

A voice called out from the door of the plane, "I'm Al Davis, the SOCEUR team leader. We have orders to commence airdrop operations within twenty-four hours of our arrival."

Bill and I looked at each other and then at Davis. We had been pushing water as the principle need. Was someone planning to airdrop water? Davis then asked where and with whom he could get started. Bill and I reintroduced ourselves, and we took him over to our corner of the French compound to begin discussions.

Al Davis blended in well with our efforts. He was a reservist full colonel doing his annual duty with SOCEUR as a marine corps special operator. An American lawyer practicing in the United Kingdom, Al was good with people, a natural diplomat-soldier. He would listen, and he could communicate. He soon had his team out linking up with the international community. Bill and I sat down with him to get an idea of what was happening with the proposed operation. Davis said his mission was to assess the overall situation and recommend solutions back to SOCEUR. Based on what he had been told, he believed that whatever forces were deployed the mission would be along the lines of Provide Comfort, the support operation to the Kurds in northern Iraq. That had been largely a Special Operations show under the direction of then Major General Shalikashvili, now General Shalikashvili, chairman of the JCS.

I gave Davis a full rundown on what was happening in Goma, along with the support structure within the NGOs. I explained what the problems were and that our push had been to get water purification and water transport units deployed. I went into the associated support issues, namely the airport, its security, and its airflow capacity. We also discussed needs for additional medical, civil affairs, engineers, and psychological operations (PSYOPs). I pointed out the Rwandan genocide and the Rwandan exodus were two of the most successful psychological operations in recent history. Directed largely through the Rwandan FM radio station, Les Milles Collines, these two PSYOPs had decimated a country. Les Milles Collines had last broadcast on the seventeenth. I told Davis we needed a counteroperation. I had beaten this same drum with the UNHCR head, thus far to no avail. I finished with an overall security assessment of the area. The immediate danger in Goma was the Zairian military. Not a terrorist threat per se but a largely lawless, undisciplined mob that could be expected to steal everything it possibly could—and some things it could not possibly. They were already gathering at the airport, drawn like flies to the increasing air flights. The Zairian troops would be potential flash points wherever they went. The longer-term threat was the Rwandan military out south of Goma and their associated militias in the northern camps. I reminded Davis that the refugees had just slaughtered a million countrymen back in Rwanda.

I asked Davis for more information about the proposed airdrop. He told us the drop would be emergency or disaster relief high-protein biscuits. He said the mission "came from the top," news to Bill and me. "The White House wants to see U.S. airdrops on television." Davis had a Combat Control Team–qualified air planner due in the next day with the bulk of his assessment team. The issues were pretty straightforward. We needed a drop zone, clear air space, and Zairian approval for the drop. Then we needed cargo handling equipment and security for the drop zone. Davis told us we could expect three to four MC130s, special operations birds with better capabilities for pinpoint drops. Choices for drop zones were limited to existing airstrips.

By now the press compound knew a U.S. military team had arrived and were looking for us. Davis and McCoy went to the press area and held a short news conference. Davis the lawyer took the lead. He kept it short. The United States was looking at various military options to address the refugee crisis, and his team was there to assess the situation. McCoy echoed Davis's comments, adding his office had been involved in similar though less drastic situations in Tanzania. Davis promised the United States would announce its plans as soon as possible. He finished by stating the rest of his team would arrive the next day via a C141.

Our next stop was the French. I introduced Colonel Davis to the French air base commander, their Task Force commander, and the headquarters commandant at the airport. We also took the Brazza defense attaché along; he had arrived that afternoon with another of my vehicles. I hoped to get him headed south as soon as possible. Davis and I explained our airdrop directive to Major General LaFourcade, and he directed his air commander to support us, albeit with two very bushy raised eyebrows. Remember that LaFourcade's original mission probably had nothing to do with humanitarian relief and everything to do with restoring the former Rwandan government, a longtime French client.

LaFourcade had not really liked it earlier when I told him U.S. forces would deploy to eastern Zaire. I had hooked him on his pro forma promise to render *la bonne cooperation* to a Western partner. I already had Jean Luc Nash in his headquarters, so we soon had a Puma recce bird laid on for the next day. I asked the French to coordinate the mission with the local Zairian military and civil authorities. The French agreed and also promised a platoon of infantry to secure the drop zone. I did not want to be on point for negotiations with the Zairians, because I was still not an accredited attaché. The Zairians did not know I was in Goma. Before leaving I got a thumbs-up from Nash that the French had agreed to fly the Brazza defense attaché and the vehicle to Cyangugu on one of their C160s. Meanwhile, Davis's major worked with the headquarters commandant to get a tent and a living and planning space for the team.

Back at the airport, we saw an aircraft with U.N. markings on it sitting on the tarmac. We had not even made it back into our little corner of the French compound when Canadian Maj. Gen. Romeo Dallaire, the UNAMIR Force commander, tracked us down. Dallaire had just undergone one of the most frustrating trials by fire ever endured by any U.N. commander. Aware for months that genocide was imminent and prepared to preempt, Dallaire had been forbidden to do anything. When the war and the genocide started, Dallaire and his force could have still stopped the slaughter. But again, he was proscribed from doing so, and most of his force left in accordance with their individual national instructions. He was holding on in Rwanda, trying to lay the groundwork for UNAMIR II. Upon hearing American military planners had arrived in Goma, he had immediately flown in to see us. He wanted to coordinate our efforts.[1]

Under the circumstances, we had to be very circumspect. Neither Davis nor I knew what exactly USEUCOM was going to do. We believed as I said before it would be along the lines of Provide Comfort. We did not know U.S. forces might actually deploy into Rwanda. So we made broad statements to Dallaire filled with generalities and empty of specifics. We promised to pass on his concerns and wishes, but I am sure he departed frustrated with more U.S. waffling. Bill and I took turns on the phone to call in our conversations with Dallaire and the French as well as news of Davis's arrival.

While I was making the headquarters-mandated call to Stan to repeat everything, he updated me on what was going on back in Kinshasa. The good news was he expected to be in Goma on the twenty-fifth. That was welcome news indeed, because I wanted Stan to work the airport coordination issue. The bad news was the chargé was again questioning deployments into Zaire. When Stan had taken him the country clearance request for Davis's flight, the chargé had demanded a by-name roster. He said unless he got complete rosters of each flight, he would deny them country clearance. The Zairians had already granted blanket air clearances for the operation. By now the White House had announced Operation Support Hope was underway. I told Stan if the chargé wanted to deny the aircraft country clearance then so be it. The chargé could explain it to Washington. Stan conveyed the message, and that ended the demands for names.

Our next big event came July 23 when a gray-green C141 made a look-see pass over the airfield before heading out over the lake to turn on final. I had asked the French controllers to hold her at the end of the runway after she landed. I wanted to brief the passengers before they got out. The press knew the United States was going to respond. The appearance of a C141 was likely to set off a stampede. It did, and as the aircraft set down on the field, I could see journalists running to the main tarmac. Bill and I took the Isuzu and chased after the 141. We held back as the crew turned her around and then cut power. I scampered up the ladder and held up my ID card. "I am Lt. Col. Tom Odom, the U.S. defense attaché here in Zaire. I need to see the person in charge immediately, and then we will get organized," I announced. I saw movement near the foot of the ladder beside me. Some panting reporters began coming up. I did not hesitate.

"Get the hell off this aircraft, and stay off!" Surprisingly enough they did.

I turned back to the now-smiling group on the aircraft and asked, "We got a public affairs team on board?" A couple of hands shot up. "I have work for you outside." They all began laughing now. We had the assessment team off with their equipment in under an hour. The C141 left soon afterward. Davis met them at the compound and briefed them on the situation. They had a small operations tent and a small sleeping tent. That was it. We worked to shuttle them out to their various counterparts in the NGO and the French military compound. Under the helm of his XO, the assessment team spread out and began to work. The airport was a major focus for the air planners. Bill and I had pushed for a full Airlift Control Element (ALCE) to come in. In different phone calls, we had both said repeatedly to Washington, "We have to stop the dying." Doing that meant bringing in most of what was needed by air.

Goma was both the hub and the bottleneck. The air logisticians on the assessment team fixed on that problem. Part of it was equipment. An ALCE comes with mission handling equipment such as fork-loaders and start carts as well as communications. Both were needed in quantity. Another part of it was security. The French had pushed the need for twenty-four-hour operations. Doing that required lights and barbed wire to keep the refugees and the locals, especially the Zairian military, from swarming the field. The other part of the airport puzzle was its multinational contingents and their relations with one another. The French were operating the field, nominally in cooperation with the Zairian air ministry. It was an uneasy relationship. The UNHCR had an air boss to coordinate the U.N. relief missions. Then there were several commercial firms like Saleem's Express Air that contracted ground support as well as air transport. Getting all these parties to work together effectively would take several days. Other elements of the assessment team had individual missions. There were a number of engineer, transport, and water experts to tie into the community effort to resolve the water crisis. Medical experts were there to look at the health situation. They had two missions: see how to help the refugees and also examine the health risks to U.S. personnel. It speaks well of the team's professionalism that Davis had an operational concept ready to go by July 25.

In the interim, our first priority remained the airdrop. Later I learned it was a "specified task" for U.S. European Command. There was no room to wiggle out of this one; the order to execute it had indeed come from Washington. That afternoon Davis, Capt. Dave Burgess, an Air Mobility Command representative, and I did a map recce (reconnaissance) to select several potential drop zones. We ran those by the French, and they coordinated the issue with their Zairian liaison officer. Davis, Burgess, a Zairian Air Force officer, and I flew the drop zone recce.

Out of the three or four potential drop zones, only one was marginally satisfactory. A few kilometers south of the northernmost camp, the drop zone was a one-kilometer-long grass strip, less than three hundred meters wide. It paralleled and was within two hundred meters of the main road, still filled with trudging refugees. To further complicate matters, there was a small hangar with a small single-engine aircraft that belonged to the airstrip owner and manager. The Zairian Air Force officer approved its use over the screams of the Belgian owner who promised to sue us if his property were damaged. I did not care. I owed Davis a drop zone, and this was the only choice. I told the U.S. Air Force captain the MC130s had better be spot on. He said he would coordinate the delivery as a low-altitude five-hundred-foot drop with the aircraft in trail mission. That held the best promise of hitting the target.

Later I learned just how top-driven the planning for this mission was. My air force buddy from CGSC, Lt. Col. Dave Scott, commanded the 7th Special Operations Squadron (SOS); his unit got the mission while "Chode," as he is called, was away in the United States on temporary duty. Based in the United Kingdom, the 7th SOS had less than twenty-four hours to stage its MC-130s into Entebbe, Uganda, for the airdrop. They actually received the mission planning data en route to Africa. Guidance for the mission dripped of politics. The commander of the lead MC-130, now Lt. Col. Frank Fields, was told "higher wants to put on an air show for CNN." As for a drop zone survey, the crews got a faxed copy of a survey showing the drop zone as circular, centered more or less on the northern tip of the airstrip we had picked out. Even so Fields suggested an aircraft in trail approach to maximize accuracy. He was overruled. We would see the results on the drop zone.[2]

That was in our future. Meanwhile our next stop was arranging for transport for the biscuits once they were on the ground. We wanted to recover the pallets as quickly as possible lest we set off a food riot on the drop zone—there were thousands of refugees moving along that road. I decided to tackle this issue at the top. I took Davis and McCoy with me to see the head of the UNHCR in Goma, Fillipo Grandé. As the largest refugee-oriented international organization, the UNHCR was the de facto director of all the international relief efforts in Goma. Fillipo was the chief of Goma operations, and we had talked already on several occasions. I expected this airdrop to be a hard sell.

The issue was simple and understandable. We were going to airdrop some sixteen tons of high-protein biscuits the relief agencies did not require. They needed water purification and transport. Moreover, we were going to drop these biscuits in a densely populated area where if we did not get it right we were going to kill some refugees. And if we did not get them under control very quickly we stood a real prospect of setting off a world record food fight. So that meant vital cargo-handling equipment that could be used to offload sixty tons of medical supplies due to arrive shortly overland from Uganda would have to be diverted to recovering sixteen tons of unwanted biscuits. This was all because the "White House wants to see airdrops."

I went through all of these counter-arguments with Fillipo. We talked and argued for over an hour. Finally I took off the gloves. I stood, and he thought I had given up. As he rose to bid me goodbye, I shut the door. "Fillipo," I said, "if you want U.S. support for your efforts here, you are going to get behind us on this operation. If we go back and say you don't want our airdrop, that will probably be interpreted as you don't want our help. I don't like the airdrop idea, but there it is. What's it going to be?" He blinked and nodded yes. The airdrop was on. Davis followed up on Grandé's agreement by announcing it to the press when we returned to the airport. Bill and I remained uneasy about the whole idea. Still, as I had told Fillipo, you do what you have to do to get the job done.

The Airdrop: Biscuits, Bombs, and Baby Clothes

We got the word the airdrop would go the next day at around 1300 hours. That morning the Public Affairs Officer from the U.S. Joint Task Force (JTF)—currently operating out of Entebbe—briefed the airdrop to the press encamped at the Goma airport. I groaned when I heard the colonel say that the MC-130s could put their cargo in a "pickle barrel." While true under ideal conditions, I had been on more than a few airborne operations. Conditions were rarely ideal, and unbeknownst to us the "hurry hurry" factor was already heavily against this mission. The lead navigator for the mission, Capt. Ben McMullen, was facing a real challenge. To go along with the already poor planning information, the best maps he could get his hands on were the 1:250000 Joint Operational Graphics or "JOGs," as they are known in the business. JOGs are okay for flying high over rough terrain or doing the "big hand, little map" trick when detail is not critical. When you are going to do an airdrop surrounded by volcanoes topping out at fourteen thousand feet, detail gets critical, critically fast. McMullen actually hand drew the landing strip on the JOG for the crew briefings. As if that minor map problem was not enough to jump start migraines, the MC-130 crews drew older army cargo chutes for the mission. That meant that McMullen did not have good ballistic data on the chutes. McMullen did have about 2500 hours of experience in airdrops, which he could call on to plot out a probable drop profile for the mission. Still, there was a lot of guesswork for a mission the media apparatus was already touting as one that would put the supplies in the proverbial pickle barrel.[3]

Blissfully unaware of all that, our USAF Combat Control Team captain Bill McCoy and I hitched rides the next morning with the British Office of Development of Assistance logistics team that would actually recover the supplies on the drop zone. They were experienced hands. Many had been in Bosnia and had handled airdrops before. They were Scots, however, and at times those thick accents made communications difficult. A Swiss NGO that had provided a Bell Jet Ranger helicopter to the UNHCR helped coordinate the operation. We set off for the drop zone at ten in the morning, some sixty kilometers through dense refugee traffic. The day had started sunny and clear. A great day for a drive through the country except it was the height of the cholera epidemic, and bodies were everywhere. We arrived around 1230 hours and hastily surveyed the drop zone. There were a few journalists around, but I maintained my distance. The NGO pilots landed their helicopter at 1315 hours, and the UNHCR air boss said the operation was on hold. The word was that higher-ups were worried about the proximity of the drop zone to the refugees. Twenty minutes later the UNHCR air boss took off again for Goma after telling me he would find out what was happening. Bill, the captain, and I sat down to wait. Meanwhile low clouds moved in and a steady drizzle announced the summer rainy season was upon us.

By 1540 hours no word on what was happening with the operation had reached us. The newsies were making noises about going back—I encouraged that line of thinking with somber predictions of more rain and low clouds. The Scottish ground boss and I did worry that if the drop did not take place soon, we would not have time to clear the drop zone before night fell. He did not want his people driving the refugee-clogged roads after dark. That our promised French security force had not shown also concerned me; the flood of refugees north along the road to Katale continued less than two hundred meters from our drop zone. The only barrier between them and the drop zone was a thin strip of bush. At 1550 hours I heard the Bell Ranger returning. The UNHCR air boss met me under the blades and said the MC-130s had gone wheels up at Entebbe fifteen minutes prior. He walked with me down to the foot of the drop zone, and the Bell Ranger lifted off. They set their bird down on a hill just across the road to watch the show.

Weather on the drop zone had cleared a bit so we had at best a two-thousand-foot ceiling with around one mile visibility. Winds were light out of the north. The captain and I were looking at the northern limits of our visibility for aircraft coming low. We expected to see them before we heard them, a notion soon disabused by the drone of Allison turbines. We searched above us and picked them up as they descended through the clouds about one mile northeast of the drop zone. They were in a "V" formation on a heading of 205 degrees. We watched as they crossed the northern tip of the drop zone. They looked high.

On board the aircraft, Frank Fields was getting more help than he wanted. With the pressure from above to "put on an air show," a full colonel had tagged along to ride on the second aircraft. As the aircraft neared the drop zone, the deteriorating weather heightened the risks. Lightning flashed as the aircraft descended through the soup. Remember, Kibumba and Katale camps were aligned between a series of opposing volcanoes reaching fourteen thousand feet above sea level. Frank continued the mission with his three-ship flight in a V for a Cargo Delivery System drop, CDS being more dramatic though less accurate. Ben McMullen worked with the pilots to kill the formation's drift, calling time hacks off a stopwatch. At thirty seconds or one mile out, they still could not see the airfield. None of the planned landmarks stood out, and the crews tensed until at twenty seconds, they picked up the narrow strip and the orange marker at its northern tip. To their surprise the strip was off to their left at a sixty-degree angle; they had expected to find it dead ahead based on the information they had received. No way to make a down-the-throat approach and ten seconds to decide what to do. The options were limited to calling a no drop, scrambling the formation and attempting to maneuver at the last possible moment, or going with the original heading since the drop zone was circular according to what they had been told. Safety was an issue. At 130 knots with its flaps down, the C130 is not a sports car made for tight turns. As sluggish as a single ship may be under those flight parameters, turning a three-ship formation at the same speeds on a sixty-degree course change in bad weather in mountains is an even worse idea. Meanwhile the full colonel watchdog on the second aircraft started barking at the crews. He brushed aside all concerns and threatened to fire the crews if they did not drop. That might have been a bit overstated, but when you are a captain you have to listen to colonels looking over your shoulder. They held course and prepared to drop. The "CNN air show" was on.

Down on the ground, my captain turned to me and said, "Colonel, I can't raise 'em on the assigned freq. They should be making a turn to the south before doubling back, dropping down, and lining up." He had just finished when we saw the drop warning lights along the belly of the lead MC-130 light up.

"Oooooooh, shit!" I muttered as pallets and parachutes began flowing out the tails of the three aircraft.

As we watched, our French infantry platoon came roaring up. The sergeant in charge saluted and asked for his orders. I watched parachutes and told him to stand by, pointing at the canopies over our heads.

"*Merde!*" he said, matching my earlier sentiments.

I counted five pallets in the air. One of the MC-130s was apparently short a pallet or had failed to drop its full load. The 463L pallets, each with a couple of tons, were coming down fast, a fact we had counted on when we planned the drop for five hundred feet on a north-south axis. Unfortunately the CNN-driven air show was higher, and the V formation automatically widened the dispersal area for the descending chutes. Above us, Frank Fields was flying his planned mission profile, one dramatically different from our expectations. Frank and his crew believed their circular drop zone had been cleared.[4] As the last pallet left the lead aircraft, the crew spotted the U.N. helo on the ground, but it was too late to call an abort. Rather than serve as the actual drop zone, the landing strip was more like a blade in a peep sight. The bull's eye centered on its northern tip, where the captain and I stood. In planning their run in, the crews had used six hundred feet above ground level as their planned drop altitude. In mountainous terrain like the area we were in, six hundred feet AGL in one place could equal fifteen hundred feet in another. The problem of what was, to us, an off-heading, downwind approach added to the difficulty. Not only would they not hit the "pickle barrel," they would probably miss the airstrip. Knowing the light aircraft over in the hangar was safe, I attempted to put a good spin on things and remarked to Bill McCoy, "Well, at least we don't have to buy someone a new aircraft."

The five pallets fell like humanitarian bombs in a zigzag line to the southwest. The first landed directly on the road, setting off a miniature riot. My French sergeant, his Gallic blood boiling, was apparently offended by this impropriety.

"Mon Colonel, *on dois les attaque!"* I held him back. I could just see it on the evening news: we drop a pallet of food on the refugees and then shoot them off it. As I tracked the second pallet, I saw its trajectory merge with the Bell Jet Ranger, sitting on its overlook hill, blades still turning. I cringed as the pallet slammed hard into the ground less than ten feet from the helo, its startled crew diving out of the way. A white plume in the air—looked like smoke—announced the pallet held flour rather than biscuits. The third pallet struck down the reverse slope of the hill with the fourth and fifth landing in a banana plantation to the east. Plumes of flour smoke-marked their impact.

Bill and I, trailed by our French soldiers, scrambled across the road to see what had happened with the helicopter. Meanwhile, the food fights on the road worked to our advantage: most of the newsies were drawn to that scene. We found an enraged Swiss helicopter crew, their pride damaged but skin and aircraft intact. One read me the riot act for attempting to "murder" them before they got back in and took off.

"There goes our ride, Bill," I said to McCoy. "We may be camping this evening . . . now what?"

I nudged Bill and pointed as several laughing Zairians came running up the hill from the direction of the third pallet. All of them had on multicolored balaclavas and mittens. As we walked toward the pallet, one Scotsman approached us.

"What er ya bluuuudy Americans goin ta dew next? Thoot bluuuuuuuudy pallet is na boot winner baabeeee cleewthes!"

Bill and I looked at each other, and we both started laughing. The Scot was not amused and soon left. Fortunately none of the newsies came over to see what the two Americans found so funny. Such was the score for the only U.S. airdrop mission during the Goma Refugee Festival of 1994. Two direct hits on a banana plantation, one near miss on a humanitarian-operated Bell Jet Ranger, one minor food riot that almost sparked a Gallic massacre, and six or seven Zairian field workers who had warm ears and hands that icy July evening along the equator in eastern Zaire.

One could add three very angry MC-130 crews once the news media started in harping about the "military mistakes" in the mission.

Lt. Col. Chode Scott had hustled to link up with his unit before the mission went down but Air Mobility Command (AMC) was running into the same fuel shortages that had slowed French and contract Russian airlift for Operation Turquoise. So Scott did not catch up with his flyers until he found them in the Rhino Pub at the Kampala Sheraton the evening after the drop. CNN was a dirty word at the bar that night.

The squadron commander looked at his crestfallen crews and reached for his wallet. Scott's $1500 travel advance went toward drowning their frustrations.[5] Like all special operations types, MC-130 crews use the term "quiet professionals" to describe their approach to the job. That translates into "do the job right and don't crow about it." In this case, they had done their best on an impossible mission that should not have been flown, and the news media were doing the crowing. Mistakes were made, but they were all at the highest level of decision makers, not operators who had to try to execute a bad mission.

But on the ground in Goma, Bill and I were feeling lonely. The others had gone back with the French troops, which left Bill and me to watch the Scots recover the dropped supplies. The sun was down before they finished, so the Scots carried us to a CARE encampment north of Katale camp. It was the same CARE outpost that had lost its cargo handling teams that day to support the airdrop. Needless to say there was no red carpet for us, and the Rhino Pub was hundreds of miles away. They handed us one Primus beer and one can of tuna to share between us. And they allowed us deluxe sleeping accommodations in the front of a Land Rover. We went back to Goma the next day, determined to avoid the news media at all costs.

Our travel south was harrowing. The weather had cleared, which allowed almost unlimited visibility for the sixty-five kilometers to Goma. It was also fairly early in the morning, and the refugee flow, halted in the evening, had yet to resume. We passed through Katale without incident. Some refugees were stirring, but the crowds typical of most days in the camps had not formed. Yet as we moved south, Bill and I looked at bodies stacked two to three deep along the road all the way to Kibumba. We were following a minivan with the local Zairian district manager and several Zairian soldiers. Unlike Katale, Kibumba was swarming with refugees looking for water and food. Intended as a way station, the camp had not caught up with the demands placed upon it at this stage. One rose early in Kibumba and scrounged. The road just disappeared in the mass of bodies, but the Zairians did not slow down. The driver leaned on the horn, and we followed in their wake.

Near the center of the camp, we entered a relatively clear area, and we relaxed. Then in slow motion, I saw a young girl, maybe four or five, break from the crowd on one side of the road and dash toward the road. The Zairian driver did not swerve or even slow. The Minibus ran over her, rolling her body in the dust. Our driver swerved and we missed her, but she was certainly dead. No one in the crowd reacted as we passed. Normally in Africa an accident like this would have finished us. Any and all passengers in a vehicle involved in an accident are killed out of hand. One never stops to help an accident victim. We did not stop either. I looked back to see a man drag the child's body to the side of the road, just another corpse in the ditch. Bill and I did not speak. There were bodies all the way back to Goma. We never joked about that trip.

Paras, Dragons, and Guarde Civile

The recurrent problem the international community faced in Goma and its surroundings remained the Zairian military. In a normal country, the military acts as an extension of the government. In some cases, the military is the government. In either of those cases, an order from the government is something to be obeyed. Consequently, if there is an incident or a trend of incidents involving the military of a country, other governments or international bodies like the United Nations can *demarche* the government responsible and perhaps resolve the situation.

What do you do in the case of a country that is not by any definition of the word a nation? Zaire remained a creation of European imperialism and its thirst for colonies. Lines drawn on maps in the 1890s remained unchanged in the 1990s. They also remained equally useless as definitions of national identity. The result in 1994 was the Zairian military and its thirty-year tradition of robbery, mayhem, and cowardice. But the basic question remained: how do you fix a broken military that is the extension of a shattered country? The answer was the same it has been ever since the Congo entered the ranks of independent nations: treat the "kleptocracy" as a government, hope for the best, but expect the worst. We got largely what we expected.

From the very beginning of the crisis, the Zairian military acted true to form. The chargé saw it at the border. I witnessed it from the midst of the retreating Rwandan Army. The 31st Para was the worst, raping women, robbing refugees, and repelling the international community with their actions, sort of the "3 R's" of FAZ behavior. During the height of the dying, 31st Paras sold access to the water of Lake Kivu. Others used bodies as temporary barricades to stop and bribe or rob NGO workers. The airport was the pot of gold at the end of the airlift rainbow for these bandits in uniform. The NGO community and the international agencies subjected to repeated indignities at the hands of the Zairian soldiers threatened withdrawal. Ironically, the most effective response to Zairian military deprivations came from the refugees themselves. No strangers to the use of the machete as a debating tool, the refugees killed more than a few Zairian soldiers who pushed them too far.

Nevertheless the official demarches piled up in Kinshasa and Gbado-lité like a snowdrift, and they finally drew a response. Not out of concern over the security of the refugees or the international community but rather out of concern that the flood of international monies into the area, already making the kleptocracy ecstatic, might stop. Kengo, the new prime minister, came out to Goma to review the situation. His visit coincided with the visit of the U.S. secretary of defense, and the Zairian minister promised to improve security. Shortly afterward nearly four hundred more DSP Dragons and some additional Guarde Civile troops deployed to Goma. Kengo also dispatched 1.2 million of the New Zaire notes to pay all of the soldiers in the area. The aircraft that flew the troops and money to the eastern border returned to Kinshasa loaded with weapons taken from the Rwandan Army.

As expected, the new troops soon got down to business, Zairian style. The DSP Dragons were especially brutal in dealing with the refugees. And the latter responded in kind. Refugees killed a couple of the Dragons outside the camp at Kibumba. In response, the Dragons staged a memorial funeral convoy through the heart of Goma. Using military and "borrowed" NGO trucks, the Dragons ran a convoy loaded with Uzi-firing troops down the main street and around the principle traffic circle. This madcap procession nearly ran over me as I was headed out to the lake house. They apparently tried to intimidate the French and earned a few warning shots that reduced their martial ardor. Eluki, the Zairian Army chief of staff, also visited the troops in Goma a few days after Kengo. He too promised that the government would improve the security situation. His promises produced the same results.

Finally, in late August, Kinshasa decided something had to be done to improve the situation out in Goma. The Defense Ministry ordered the illustrious 31st Para to stand down and prepare for redeployment west. Remarkably, the troops complied, and a Boeing 707 loaded with 31st Paras was soon winging westward.[6] The Paras assumed they would be returning to their traditional home base adjacent to Ndjili International Airport just outside Kinshasa. They had, after all, led two parades from Ndjili to pillage the capital city in 1991 and 1993. The Defense Ministry had other plans. As the troops over flew Kinshasa, they were told they would be continuing to another remote post in western Zaire. The Paras were not having any of it; upon hearing their proposed destination, the Paras hijacked the aircraft and forced it to land at Ndjili. They assumed "security" duties at the national airport for the next two days until the DSP forced them back across the road into their old billets. But there was no further mention of exiling them.

Human Rights and Machetes

About two weeks into the Goma operation, we had a flood of visitors. The JTF was just beginning to flow, and for the most part the U.S. troops were camped in the French compound. One day we had the secretary of defense and his party of senior civilians and generals. I remember the chargé asked me to take a senior State Department official and his entourage up to the camps. The chargé said I was to meet the party at the airport at 1300.

Stan Reber and I made our way to the airport at 1245 hours. Stan found the group right away and let them know their "ride" was ready for the 1300 departure. Two from the party soon walked up. Stan with his small man's tapeworm was busily wolfing down an MRE, and they saw him. One asked if we had more MREs, and Stan passed them each a meal. Both took seats in the back of the Trooper and began to tear open the ration packs. I do not remember their names. Both were in some capacity involved in setting up the proposed International Tribunal. They were nice enough, but by this time Stan and I both had a low tolerance for disaster tourists. It was well past 1300 hours and we were broiling in the sun. The two in the back were trying to figure out how to eat their MREs. One was squeezing his beef and rice out of the pack directly into his mouth. He must have sensed Stan watching and paused.

"Is this the way you do it, Stan?"

Reber did not even blink as he replied, "Sure, that will work."

"Why don't you use a spoon?" the other suggested as he showed his MRE spoon still wrapped in the clear plastic. He was eating with it that way, sucking the plastic bag clean each time he stuck it in his mouth.

So there we were, sitting in this '84 Isuzu Trooper, baking in the sun, and listening to visitors slurp their way through two MREs. By now it was almost 1345 hours, and we could see our VIP and a companion still chatting up the press. Finally the senior official headed our way and got into the truck. Meanwhile his assistant continued to talk with the press as the clock reached two o'clock. I finally told him he needed to get his assistant so we could get going. He waved at her, and she headed our way.

One of the most striking black women I have ever seen, she was tall, well over six feet, and finely featured, the perfect model for a Tutsi princess. Just exactly the person you want to visit a camp of diseased, heat crazed, killer Hutu militiamen and their supporters. When she got in at around 1430, we headed north toward the main refugee camps. The first "camp," Kibumba, was about thirty kilometers north of Goma.

We had gone about twenty kilometers when she turned to her boss and convinced him they needed to go back. She wanted more time with the press. When he asked me to about face the truck in a forty-kilometer false start, I agreed but pointed out time was running out. Once back at the airport, she hurried off to find the press. By now it was almost 1530. Stan and I had been on this escort detail for nearly three hours. Meanwhile the assistant lassoed her reporter and resumed her pitch. Fifteen minutes later, she was still going strong.

I was already agitated at the delay when one of the other two guys called from the back, "Can one of you open this door?"

There was an interior latch, but its operation was beyond the technical expertise of the two men we had in the back. The senior official, like me, was sitting with his door open to let in more of the limited breeze. I guess he sensed I was not exactly pleased with the request as I walked back to the rear of the trooper.

Opening the rear door, I said softly, "There you go, guys."

Then in a not-quite roar, I added, "By the way, I am not your taxi driver!"

That got things moving: our visitor called to his assistant to come on. Surprisingly she came, almost immediately. An hour after our first abortive trip, we set out for Kibumba once again. Stan's demon gear shifting showed he was just as angry as I was; he wound the Trooper's four-cylinder diesel up as tight as he could get it. We sped up the road, between parallel files of refugees still marching north.

As we approached Kibumba, I put on my tour guide hat and explained what they were seeing. Kibumba was never intended to be a camp. It was supposed to be a way station to get the refugees to a more habitable area sixty-five kilometers north of Goma. Unfortunately, the way station now had a population of over five hundred thousand refugees; many of them would spend the next two years in that place. Chaos was too kind of a word to describe Kibumba. It was a magma plain beneath the local volcano, and in July it was bloody hot. There were no natural sources of water in the immediate area. Although the worst of the cholera epidemic was over, people were still dying, and bodies were everywhere. Shelter was limited, and the crowds ebbed and flowed like some gargantuan school of fish along the ridges of the magma reef. Their sheer numbers overwhelmed the international workers and their vehicles. We slowed as we approached, gingerly following the meandering road through the insanity.

Even as we pierced the perimeter, and the crowd closed around us, the senior official asked to stop and talk to the refugees. His mission here was to begin the process for setting up an International Tribunal to try those guilty in the Rwandan genocide. The probable defendants were all around us.

I picked my jaw up and replied, "We are not stopping inside this camp. It is too unstable, and the risk is too great."

The woman who looked like a Tutsi princess shot back, "I don't agree with your assessment, Colonel." She demanded a reason.

I was not having any of it. I answered, "Miss, I don't care if you agree with me. I am in charge, and I have the guns. We are not stopping."

She had opened her mouth to say more when something to our front caught my eye. I felt Stan slam the brakes on as we turned a slight corner. We could hear the crowd yelling when the curtain of humanity parted in front of us.

In front of us the crowd parted to reveal a disemboweled young man in front of our vehicle. His throat was already cut, and he was flopping like a fish. Those in the crowd around him cheered as blood spurted in their faces and they spat on him. They chanted "Tutsi, Tutsi, Tutsi!" and they laughed. Two MSF doctors pushed through the crowd to him with a stretcher, and his attacker blended back into the crowd. All of this took place in a minute that lasted an hour. I turned in my seat and looked at my visitors.

"Do you still want to get out and talk?"

We were soon on our way back to Goma.

Tentative Moves

When the former Rwandan Army collapsed and crossed into Zaire, I recognized a fundamental shift had occurred in the region. The new government in Rwanda unilaterally declared a cease-fire soon afterward and accepted the deployment of UNAMIR II. That was a deft move by the Rwandan rebel leaders. It showed them to be accommodating to international concerns—manifested entirely too late in rebel eyes—and at the same time undercut any French desire to keep troops in the area. Still the rebels were not complacently satisfied. On the contrary, as a movement born in exterior refugee camps, the Rwandan Patriotic Front had just won a thirty-year struggle to achieve success. In doing so, it had created what could well become its own albatross: an exterior refugee population of almost two million. Capping that danger was the all-too-real presence of the intact former Rwandan military just across the border, reinforced by an even greater number of Interahamwe militia, the main perpetrators of the genocide.

In July and August, 1994, the former Rwandan military (ex-FAR) was more a brooding threat than an active menace to the international community in Goma. As I have said elsewhere, the Zairian military was the immediate threat, one of pure thuggery. That is what I repeatedly advised Washington and all senior leaders who arrived in Goma. Nevertheless, the ex-FAR was a threat to any hopes for peace in the region, a message I would repeat with tantric regularity over the next twenty months.

At the beginning of the Goma operation, my focus was "stop the dying," a message that became the first priority for the U.S. Operation Support Hope. Yet only a blind man or a fool would either not see or attempt to wish away a problem that the presence of twenty thousand hostile ex-FAR soldiers represented to the region. Early on I raised the issue with Atwood when I discussed using a separate brigade to separate and disarm the ex-FAR and the Interahamwe. Remember, the genocide and the resultant exodus had been organized political movements carried out with the guns of the ex-FAR and the machetes of the Interahamwe and its subordinates. The results spoke for themselves: eight hundred thousand dead inside Rwanda and nearly two million refugees outside Rwanda. Force and its widespread application by the ex-FAR and the Interahamwe had been the catalyst in achieving those results.

For the next twenty months, I focused on the threat those elements represented to the region. I was continually amazed at how many chose to wish the problem away. My first experience came with the arrival of the U.S. commander for the Goma operation. Brig. Gen. Jack Nix, the commander of SETAF, arrived on July 25th as the commander of Joint Task Force-Alpha (JTF-A), the task force assembled to take on the brunt of the Goma disaster. Nix was the airborne soldier's airborne general. He was one of the few serving officers in 1994 who wore two stars on his airborne wings for combat jumps, the first for Grenada, and the second for Panama. He looked, walked, and talked like the airborne soldier he was. He had achieved decisive results in Grenada and Panama. He expected to do the same in Goma.

Bill McCoy and I made sure we were in the briefing tent when Al Davis laid down his suggested operational concept to General Nix. We knew what Davis had in mind, and we assumed Nix did too. Such assumptions often prove wrong and this was one of those times. Davis was minutes into his brief when Nix stopped him.

The general then laid out a three-phased concept for solving the Rwandan refugee crisis. Not surprisingly, he announced we were going to concentrate on stopping the dying, something that tracked with my hours of conversations with the Pentagon. I stood listening and thought; "Well, that's okay so far" when I heard the next pronouncement. The general said the operation would then seek to get the refugees to go home by establishing water and feeding stations along designated routes back inside Rwanda. The concept was to coax the refugees home. He made it clear the U.S. forces were not staying, again something I expected, but he transferred that statement of intent to the refugees. Somehow they were not going to stay either.

Bill and I looked at each other. "Fat chance" was the mental message we flashed each other as Nix continued.

General Nix announced the third phase would be to assist the Rwandan government and the international agencies in reestablishing normalcy inside Rwanda. After that the U.S forces would withdraw. Nix went on to detail how the overall JTF would be divided between operations at Entebbe, Kigali, and Goma. He did say potential operations in the south remained on the JTF planning board in case things fell apart down there.

Nix did not arrive at this operational concept by himself. He was merely transmitting the JTF commander's orders. Support Hope's commander, Lt. Gen. Dan Schroeder, had received equally specific guidance from U.S. European Command and Washington—like airdrops, for instance. In reality, Schroeder's mission and concept evolved as he went, driven by public pronouncements from Washington. His public affairs staff in essence merged with his operations staff in doing their mission analysis. After the fiasco in Somalia, African ventures were suspect, especially in U.S. military circles. The United States had attempted to ignore the genocide in Rwanda. Washington could not ignore Goma. So while the U.S. military was coming, it was coming on what it hoped was a clear, unambiguous mission not given to incremental expansion. Essentially, "Get in, do what you can, and get the hell out," was writ large across the intent of Nix's mission brief. Unfortunately, that's not what the brief said or implied.

In sticking to the achievable, the concept for Operation Support Hope should have started and ended with "stop the dying." Other sub-missions could have been added or "fragged" off the basic mission as necessary. Perhaps some saw that as the road to mission creep. Instead, the plan briefed by Nix came across as concise and with a clear end state. There were two problems. First, the end state was unachievable: there was no way the United States, the international community, or any combination of forces was going to coax the nearly two million Rwandan refugees to pick up and go home. They had just slaughtered eight hundred thousand of their neighbors. They believed an equally bloodthirsty army was waiting for them across the border. They had just marched one hundred miles or more to escape that army, suffering at least seventy thousand dead. The leaders and the executioners of the genocide were all still in the camps. One could draw a line on the map to encircle the bulk of the ex-FAR south of Goma, but there was no barrier on the ground. There was talk then and later suggesting the ex-FAR and the Interahamwe held the majority of the refugees "hostage" against their fates. The truth as I saw it was the refugees were more hosts than hostages for the ex-FAR and the Interahamwe. The refugees would never go back as long as they had the ex-FAR and Interahamwe to protect them.[7]

After the aborted hunt for Aideed in Somalia, U.S. military forces were not going to get involved in disarming the ex-FAR and the Interahamwe. That fact, however, was not apparent in the second phase of the operation concept. Coaxing the refugees back might appear to be a deft solution to the need to "get in, get out." But to the international community in Goma—read NGOs—it appeared to be a long-term commitment. In attempting to limit the operation, the concept promised more than it could deliver. Therein lay its second flaw, one that led to continued friction, most of which could have been avoided, between the military and their civilian counterparts.

Nevertheless, Nix briefed and we listened. For Al Davis and most of his team, it amounted to "Thank you very much but we have a better idea." Nix left some of his party in Goma and returned to Entebbe. He would come back with his full staff on July 30th. Until then Davis was the acting force commander in Goma. In reality, he was merely a caretaker until Nix came back with the rest of JTF-A.

Meanwhile, Bill and I worked the problems in our own way. Bill also understood that the security issues associated with the ex-FAR and Interahamwe would have to be addressed. We knew the UNHCR, with its strict mandate, had refused to feed the ex-FAR as an intact army. Unless the ex-FAR dissolved itself or took matters into its own hands, as proved to be the case, the problem would get worse. For now the French were watering them, but what would happen when the French military left? The other half of the security equation was the Zairian military. The only units marginally capable of enforcing security were in Kinshasa. Mobutu and his henchmen were unlikely to pull them out of Kinshasa to improve security in Goma. Security in Kinshasa after two military mutinies was so bad Mobutu no longer visited his own capital city. He was unlikely to further risk security there by transferring his "best" troops to distant Goma.

So if the international community was not going to do something about the ex-FAR and Interahamwe, and the Zairian military was incapable, whom else did it leave to do the job? I floated the idea of a contractor, itself almost a tradition in Zairian security, and suggested Yigal's guys in black, SOZAIS. The reason was simple: they were reasonably well led, they got paid enough not to steal, and they could shoot whomever they needed to and get away with it. They probably could not disarm the ex-FAR and Interahamwe, but they could offer the international workers better security. I had seen them swarm a Zairian military patrol on the street outside my house in Kinshasa. Stan was coming, and he knew Yigal. I called him and told him to ring up Yigal. He did, and Yigal arrived on the same flight as Stan.

I met Yigal at the airport and took him out to the lake house where he stayed with us for nearly a week. We had never met, but we started talking and hit it off fairly well. My Middle East experience was excellent preparation. Yigal had graduated from the Israeli parachute brigade into special operations. He was an insider to the upper levels of the Zairian military. So there was no need to brief Yigal on the reality of Zaire—he was part of the scene. I ran down the security situation with him and he asked questions. Satisfied, he said he was interested. He too did not believe SOZAIS could disarm the ex-FAR. He could intimidate the Zairian military in the area and the Interahamwe in the camps. That would be his approach to the United Nations or perhaps certain NGOs.

I had already pitched Fillipo Grandé on the idea and had floated it back to the embassy. The embassy leadership said SOZAIS was a company of thugs, an assessment I was in complete agreement with although I saw it as a selling point. My counterparts in the embassy did not and suggested the contractor who provided our residential security. I had caught my guard sleeping too many times to take that idea seriously. I stuck with the SOZAIS idea and suggested it in official traffic. Meanwhile, Yigal networked for the next several days. We had dinner most evenings at the hotel near our place, one of two decent restaurants. U.N. workers were frequent diners there. U.N.-flagged vehicles filled the parking lot each evening. Like most Israelis, Yigal disliked the United Nations and anyone associated with it. All those blue flags in the parking lot were just too much for him. He complained bitterly about the waste of money all the top-of-the-line four-wheel-drive luxury vehicles represented. You could see his body language change into an offensive mode when he passed U.N. personnel. The last night he was with us, he announced after a couple of large beers he was not going back to Kinshasa without a U.N. flag.

As we walked out into the lot, Yigal dropped off in the shadows, called by his mission to capture a U.N. flag. Stan, Bill, and I went to our truck and waited. Yigal materialized out of the dark to tell us he had a "target." "Be ready!" he ordered and took off. Bill followed and

Stan and I watched amused. Yigal had picked a large lorry with an even larger UNHCR flag. Stan started joking and I started laughing as we watched the Israeli commando stalk the vehicle in short rushes from shadow to shadow. Years of training showed in his approach, blown by Bill, strolling along behind him, too tight from the Miitzig beer to care about stealth.

Yigal made it to the truck undetected and wasted no time once on the objective. As he jumped up on the bumper to grab the flag, a startled Scot popped up in the driver's window, exclaiming, "Wot the 'ell!" The cool commando ripped off the flag and raced back to us with a still-relaxed Bill in tow. The U.N. Scot sounded his truck horn and flashed his lights to warn others of the Israeli night attack. Soon heads peered out from the hotel entrance, assessing the situation. No one seemed willing to come farther. I doubled over laughing but managed to get in the vehicle. Stan too was roaring and could barely start the Isuzu. He raced out of the lot without his lights. It did not matter. Yigal's quick attack had left the "enemy" stunned. Had our pursuer wished, they could have tracked our laughter to our house a quarter of a mile away. Unfortunately, Yigal got his flag but he did not get the contract, at least for the time being.[8] Something about SOZAIS "all being thugs" must have disturbed sensibilities.

So as the U.S. operation got underway, I could already see conflicting pressures on it. Somalia remained fresh on our minds and limited our options. Nevertheless the ex-FAR and the Interahamwe represented a "dirty job" that would have to be done by someone—just not the United States. The desire was to get in and then get out. "Stop the dying" made sense. I used the phrase repeatedly in calls to the Pentagon. "Coaxing refugees home" did not make sense unless you planned for the long haul, something Nix made crystal clear was not in the works. That meant this was a long-term problem years beyond the chargé's two-week scenario or even the months as discussed in the early planning by Al Davis and company. Stated brutally, it meant more folks were going to die before it was finally resolved.

CHAPTER 5

Operation Support Hope

Brigadier General Nix's brief signaled the true beginning of Operation Support Hope. Stan arrived just in time to get the main body of JTF-A on the ground. To this day I am grateful I had a sergeant like Stan Reber working for me. No one knew Zaire and Zairians better. Stan just seemed to sense what they might try. Stan did not like Zairians, and he was rapidly burning out on the country. Ten years in the same place is just too long, but the knowledge he had at his fingertips worked miracles. One of his gifts was that he could still get along with Zairians and build a sense of camaraderie. He understood how they felt toward the West in general and the French in particular. That understanding served us well. French-Zairian relations around the airfield were tense. The imminent arrival of U.S. forces meant Stan had his work cut out for him.

The French assumption of air traffic control had certainly made the Goma airport a safer place. The French, after all, had the only functioning radar that would allow night operations. Yet the manner in which they simply took control angered the Zairian officials nominally in charge of the field. It also reduced their access to the bribes that kept them afloat. They were rarely paid, and when they were it was in Zairian currency, hardly worth the ink it took to print it. The tension had become so bad the Zairians had threatened to go on strike—not that the tower officials did any work. But a stoppage would affect aircraft handling, and there was an unstated threat of sabotage of fuel and critically short cargo-handling equipment.

The other bit of international friction was between the United States and the French. When I had first arrived the French provided us a small area within their compound. Davis brought in nearly twenty-five planners on his assessment team, all of whom needed a place to spread their sleeping bags. Their numbers began to creep upward, and so did French impatience. After several days we noticed a trend. Each morning the French headquarters commandant would come over and get a head count. Every time it increased, he complained we were encroaching on his limited operational space. Each time we had one of these visits, one of the Pumas would spool up on the flight line one hundred yards away. The pilot would put it in a low hover and drift over to bury us in a sandstorm of red dirt. Five to ten minutes of this and back the bird would go to the flight line to shut down. The U.S. troops learned quickly to have their breakfast eaten and their gear secured each morning before the commandant came to call.

Cleared Hot to Land: JTF-A Comes to Goma

We knew the JTF was coming, and Nix had given us a good idea of what it was bringing. A water transport and reverse osmosis water purification unit (ROWPU) were deploying from Europe. A battalion of the 325th Airborne Infantry was coming from Italy as security, although we would only get a platoon in Goma. The USAF was deploying a full airfield command element, and there would be additional intelligence, medical, and support as well. I put Stan on getting us a place to set up. He arranged a four-way conference with the UNHCR air boss, the French, the Zairians, and our USAF representative. Stan's first breakthrough was getting all parties to agree to a pool approach in handling aircraft. As the planes arrived, all would work under the coordination of the UNHCR air boss. That eliminated the friction between the French and the Zairians. The latter were so pleased with Stan's mediation they offered a one- to two-acre plot immediately in front of the airport terminal for the Americans' use. The offer snubbed the French; they had wanted the area for some time. The price was a couple of hundred thousand, and the site would have to be bulldozed to clear feces and bodies off it, but space was at a premium. JTF-A now had a home courtesy of a U.S. Army sergeant first class. We could escape our daily dirt bath from the French helicopter.

Units began to flow into the airfield. TF51, the water transport company came in via C5s, which were necessary for the five-ton tractors and five-thousand-gallon tankers. Forklifts and alternate power units, pumps, and tow trucks arrived as part of the USAF element. For the surge of JTF-A, I focused on helping them deal with the reality of Goma. Again Stan shone as the "can-do" sergeant. Although the SOCEUR assessment team and the JTF-A staff had excellent satellite communications equipment, it did not mesh with the local cellular system nor was it as quick. Davis asked for one shortly after his arrival, and I put Stan on it. As I noted previously, normal startup for a phone in Zaire was seven thousand dollars. That paid for the phone and acted as an initial deposit for airtime at six dollars per minute long distance. By this time we had quite a relationship with Saleem's Express Cargo, one of the larger cellular users in Goma. Stan worked through them and got the phones at five thousand dollars each. One went to the JTF public affairs officer, another to Davis transferred to Nix, and a third to the JTF signal officer. The J6 ordered two more to support the visit of Tipper Gore, Vice Pres. Al Gore's wife. We got those as well, but they were never activated. We also provided two other cellulars already paid for by the embassy. Those two went to the airfield control and the water point down at Lake Kivu.

Some of our support was a bit more mundane. I was at the U.S. base camp when the flight surgeon approached me.

"I understand you know this area well. Is there an Ace Hardware–type store downtown?"

I couldn't help but laugh as I said, "You're looking at the hardware store."

He needed spotlights, and we got them. The troops also needed latrines. Through Stan and Saleem's Express Air, we brought in plastic buckets, lime, plywood sheeting, and toilet seats. More plywood from Kinshasa came in for tent floors, and rakes and brooms made the living areas more comfortable.

Four Hundred Cases of Beer on the Wall . . .

Most of our efforts were directed at operational issues, but we did try to better the troops' existence. They had been on the ground for a couple of weeks when I suggested we bring in soft drinks to break up the monotony of Goma. Bottled water and MREs get old very quickly. Nix liked the idea. Stan had gone back on mission to Kinshasa, so I rang him. Nix had agreed to several drinks per soldier so I gave Stan the numbers. The order came to some sixty-five cases of soft drinks. Stan rang off only to call back minutes later with the word the flight would be in the next day. I thought that was remarkably quick even for Stan, but he said he would call the next day once the 707 was on the way. As promised, Stan called me the next day around noon and said the soft drink bird would land around 1500 hours my time.

He warned, "Listen, Saleem said he was 'putting something extra' on the aircraft. I think it might be beer."

"I'll be planeside and see what it is when it gets here Stan," I replied before ringing off.

Three hour later the Express Air 707 cargo landed and taxied on to the main apron. I had alerted the J4, and we stood waiting for the bird. Down came the ladder and out came Saleem's main loadmaster. "Colonel Odom, all is yours!" he pronounced, waving at the aircraft, "All is yours from Saleem!" The task force logistics officer looked at me and I looked at him. We were expecting sixty-five cases of soft drinks and a "little something" from Saleem. Five hundred cases later, including at least four hundred cases of South African lager beer, I was standing just outside Brigadier General Nix's command tent.

"General, I have good news and I have bad news," I offered before delivering the good news first. "We got some extra soft drinks so we should be able to double the ration per soldier."

"What's the bad news, Tom?" he asked, looking out the tent at me.

Even as I replied, "General, we got lots of beer," one of the air force fork loaders trundled by proudly displaying a full pallet of Castle lager.

"There are two more pallets like that one, General," I said, pointing at the grinning air force sergeant. Nix did not share the sergeant's joy: the task force was under a "No Drink, Zero Tolerance Policy," set by European Command. Let me just say the general's reaction was understandably colorful before he ordered me to give the beer away to the French. An "Airborne, Sir!" gave the tactical escape I needed. I took it. Walking away, I speed dialed the phone. I heard Major Nash's voice.

"Jean Luc, I am gonna make you a loved man. Get two trucks and some strong backs. I have some beer for you." Nash arrived with the French in less than thirty minutes. They were soon gleefully loading beer cases. I figured I had at least made Jean Luc's job a little easier.

I was wrong. The next morning the U.S. sentry at the gate sent word there was someone there to see me. As I walked down the hill, I saw Saleem's loadmaster standing there with a local. Saleem's man looked worried, and the Zairian appeared angry. I soon discovered why. Saleem's soon-to-be ex-loadmaster showed me an air bill for the previous day's flight. Apparently, he had misunderstood his boss's intentions. Saleem had told him to set aside a couple of cases of beer for Stan and me, not four hundred cases for the JTF. What made it worse was the Zairian, a local bar owner enjoying a beer sales bonanza with the explosion of expatriates in Goma, had prepaid for the shipment. Now he wanted his beer. All I could tell them was we no longer had the beer, and I would look into getting it back.

Figure four hundred cases of beer at a minimum price of twenty dollars each and you get eight thousand dollars, not something I wanted to pay. I called Stan in Kinshasa and told him what had happened. I explained that Brigadier General Nix had ordered me to get rid of the beer. In keeping with his orders, I had given it all to the French. Getting it back was not going to be easy or perhaps even desirable. I told Stan I would discuss the matter with Nix and get back to him. Meanwhile he said he would call Saleem and let him know what was happening.

As I saw it, Nix had two choices: we could get the beer back from the French and go from there. That was at once the best legal solution and the worst political choice. I had given the beer "*dans le nom du General Nix.*" Asking for it back—regardless of reasons—was not going to endear us to our French comrades. Relations were not exactly smooth. Giving them eight thousand dollars worth of beer and then taking it back was two steps forward, two miles backward. The other choice was to fess up to the JTF commander that we had acquired the beer through no fault of our own. And in keeping with CINCEUR instructions, we had given the beer away as a representational gift to the French. I decided the best solution for the overall operation was to keep the French happy. The operation was costing millions in landing fees, fuel, and flight time to make sure Rwandan killers did not die from lack of clean water. What was eight thousand dollars worth of beer for the French in comparison? That was the pitch I would make to Nix.

Remember the song lyrics, "Send lawyers, guns, and money" from Warren Zevon? Well as I soon found out, someone had sent a lawyer to Goma with the JTF to advise Brigadier General Nix. I went in to see Nix and was in briefing him when a legal beagle lieutenant colonel walked in, announcing he needed to assess the legal aspects of the situation. I ignored him and kept talking to the general. I finished with my recommendation that we leave the beer with the French and eat the costs. Immediately, the lawyer, fresh from the rarified air at U.S. European Command, started in with questions about who had "contracted" for the beer, had the French "signed" for the beer, and on whose authority had I acted in giving the French the beer. I answered the last question, first.

"I gave the beer to the French because the general ordered me to. There was no 'contract' for four hundred cases. There was only a verbal order through a company for soft drinks. A local employee of that company made a mistake. As for the French signing for the beer, you must be kidding!"

I guess he had figured out I was not exactly awed by his presence. He began lecturing me on the task force directive prohibiting alcohol. Nix saw I was getting steamed and dismissed me, telling me he would soon make a decision.

The next day Nix directed me to recover what beer I could from the French. Jean Luc and I took a truck over to the French mess, where several glum-faced Frenchmen loaded some 250 cases on our vehicles. That left us short about three thousand dollars worth of lager, and given the JAG colonel's earlier position it was unlikely the JTF would pay for the shortage. Once again I turned to Stan. He resolved the situation with Saleem, who, since his man had made the mistake, agreed to absorb the loss, a drop in the proverbial bucket to what his company was making in support to the JTF anyway. As for the French, things remained correct but never cordial. Jean Luc took a lot of ribbing about "cheap Americans" over the next few weeks. He was up to it. The French soon asked for U.S. airlift to get home. Nash just pointed out he was the guy making those arrangements.

Un Espion Americain

Although Jean Luc Nash was able to handle the fallout from the French beer bust, our other counterpart from Brazzaville enjoyed less success in dealing with his Gallic counterparts. I sent him to join the French operation in Bukavu. With our office Cherokee, he flew down there on a French C160. His mission was exactly the same as Jean Luc's in Goma: fit in with the French. He was to monitor what they were doing and anticipate U.S. operational needs if the refugee situation there exploded. That was one of the most important questions facing the U.S. operation. The other part of the question was how long the French would stay. The new government in Rwanda was anything but friendly toward them. The Rwandan rebels had fought French troops in 1991. Operation Turquoise had established a protective zone across southwest Rwanda that challenged the new government's sovereignty. Getting blue berets in that area to replace the French without stampeding more refugees out of the country was UNAMIR

II's first priority. That handover was, however, sometime in the not too distant future when the Brazza defense attaché headed south.

His mission was therefore very important. It lasted less than a week. Stan and I had already closed on our lake house at dusk when my cellular rang. It was Jean Luc. He told me the French had accused our liaison officer of spying and demanded his withdrawal. I was more than a little upset at the news. "Okay, I will head out to the airport to see Nix. Meet me there," I said as I hung up. I grabbed Stan, and Bill tagged along as we drove the five miles through Goma to the airfield.

I wondered what had happened. I had emphasized maintaining a low profile to the Brazza defense attaché as the best approach to his mission. For one thing, he was still the U.S. defense attaché to Congo-Brazzaville, an often-troublesome neighbor to Zaire. So when I put him on the French transport, the Zairian authorities believed he was still in Kinshasa for consultations—with me. He was unable to call out from Bukavu as we did in Goma. We set it up with the French so he could pass information through them to Jean Luc in Goma. The French would therefore know everything being said, hence the need for a circumspect approach. We had gotten some good information already.

But we had also gotten some disturbing requests. He had passed word he wanted Stan to get Brazzaville to send out his Israeli load-bearing equipment (LBE), normally worn on field operations to carry ammo, water, and limited supplies. I nixed that request straight away and passed word if he thought he needed his LBE, he was doing some-thing wrong. Next we got a request for him to shift from Bukavu on the Zairian side of Lake Kivu to Cyangugu on the Rwandan side. That was fine with me, and I said, "Do it." But he tagged a request for an American flag he could tape or fly from his Cherokee to the request to move. I nixed that idea too as not in keeping with a low-profile approach.

All of this floated through my thoughts as I headed to see Briga-dier General Nix. I met Jean Luc at the airport, and he could only repeat what I already knew. My meeting with Nix was equally short. He asked who the guy was and wanted to know if he was a spy. But mainly he wanted him gone faster than I had gotten rid of the beer. I explained—he had been told all this already but under the circumstances, I was not about to point that out—that the guy in question was our liaison to the French in the south. I said that was my understanding at present. I assured Nix we would do whatever was necessary to reduce the fallout from the situation.

I went over to the command post to use a secure satellite phone and called Washington. I briefed the desk officer, and he called the division senior intelligence officer (SIO) to the phone. SIOs are the civilian counterparts to the uniformed regional division chiefs in the attaché system. They provide a source of long-term resident experience for the divisions where uniforms come and go every two to four years. I explained the situation to him. I said we would know more soon, but I did not expect any more changes. He asked if there was any way to replace him to keep someone down there. I responded that the French had already made this an issue, and they were unlikely to accept another American. Even if they did, they would stonewall whomever we sent.

"So he comes out?" he asked.

"Yes, sir, he comes out," I answered.

Back I went to Nix. I told him what Washington had said. Somewhat mollified, he looked up and said, "Just get him outta here, Tom. I don't want to see him. I want him gone."

Two days later a C160 landed and dumped the Brazza defense attaché and our office Cherokee on the tarmac. He handed me a one-page report concerning the activities of the U.S. defense attaché in Bukavu as proof of his innocence. My choices were limited to one.

"It doesn't matter. I have to send you out. Just let the dust settle on this because you are finished here," I said. Clearly it was not what he wanted to hear, and it was not something I enjoyed saying. But for whatever reasons, he had to go. I pointed out the Express Air jet.

"Stan has you on that bird. He has everything you brought there waiting." I shook his hand, and he walked away.

I still did not know what had happened, so I read the French report he had given me.[1] It was a remarkable left-handed defense against sending the American out. The author went into great detail about how intrusive and arrogant their American guest had been around French headquarters. He stated that it was his inept social skills that had led several French officers to conclude he was there to spy. He was, according to the report, the epitome of the ugly American. So when he had proclaimed the report proved he had not been spying, he was more or less correct. He did not grasp, however, that he had failed miserably at building any kind of rapport with his hosts.

In his defense, there is another possibility for the Brazza defense attaché's expulsion. Once the French pulled out and U.N. soldiers entered the area, it became clear the French had allowed the former military and the Interahamwe to continue the genocide in the zone. He may have been exposed to evidence of French complicity whether he knew it or not. I know when I first met with the French, one colonel who was the equivalent of the French civil affairs and PSYOPs officer dismissed me in French as "an ignorant American who cannot possibly understand the real situation." He said it in French, assuming I did not understand. I looked at him, smiled, and kept saying, "Wee wee, Kernel," in Texan French, all the while hoping he might amplify his dismissal. He did not, and even if the defense attaché from Brazza had come too close to the truth, that did not change the situation in Goma. He had gotten crosswise with the French. He had to go.

The incident also affected our relations with Nix. He had accepted my presence around the compound and listened to what I had to say. That was especially important when it came to security. The JTF had a small element stationed down at Lake Kivu with the water purification equipment. Our old friends from the 31st Paras resented the U.S. troops. The Americans were giving away the water the 31st Paras had been selling. Occasional shots and constant threats were the norm. Stan and I got involved in easing the tensions. Nix appreciated the assistance. He also learned from it. One evening, a Rwandan bus loaded with 31st troops passed the airport, and the Zairians popped off a few rounds. Nix told me about it the next day and said he had moved his defenses around to give the potential troublemakers a new look, something he did every couple of days. I was glad I had a commander on the ground who listened and learned.

Still, Nix looked on me as an apple in his orange basket. My team was not part of the JTF and not under his command. Stan and I wore civilian clothes and did our own thing. Nix had a ten-man counterintelligence and HUMINT team with the JTF to gather intelligence, especially threat-related intelligence. But to avoid any risk to them, he had restricted their activities. They could go to the water point, and they could ride the water trucks on their runs up to the camps. Otherwise they were restricted to the base camp at the airport. The captain in charge was frustrated and asked me if his team could work with us. I told him they would be welcome, but they would have to wear civilian clothes like Stan and me. Being an enterprising young intelligence officer, he went to Nix and told the general I had asked for help.

Nix refused on the basis that soldiers in civilian clothes were spies. The irony came later when Nix first complained that intelligence support for the operation had been lacking and then told me we had been the only real help to him.

What Crisis?

There was some truth in what Nix had to say. The embassy in Kinshasa showed little interest in the crisis beyond committing the Defense Attaché Office and Kate Crawford to dealing with it. Perhaps the embassy saw it as a distraction to the main goal of delivering Zaire from the hands of Mobutu. Certainly Mobutu saw in it an opportunity to bargain with his former Western backers. The embassy in Kinshasa was, with the departure of the last U.S. ambassador, in a holding pattern, waiting to see when Mobutu would go and what might happen. Even in my ten months in country, I had exhausted the ways to say, "The troops are restless" in describing the Zairian military. The same held true for the other sections in the embassy. The political section—prompted by the piercing wit of Peter Whaley—had started to admit the political "process" in Kinshasa was irrelevant. The econ section had tracked the crash of the New Zaire, but the econ officer had come to see that Western economic models were useless in understanding an economy built on theft. The CIA station seemed adrift in the 60s and 70s when the Agency had been the main player in the country.

Then the refugee crisis exploded. More than a million refugees, including a sizeable defeated army, flooded into eastern Zaire. So did international workers, international monies, and international coverage of Zaire. But despite its magnitude, the rest of the embassy acted like the Goma crisis did not exist. Their focus remained unchanged: getting rid of Mobutu by encouraging democracy in Kinshasa, the focus of all things in the country. The embassy never seemed to understand the reverse was true. When the refugee flood started in July, 1994, Kinshasa became the sideshow. The ultimate fate of Zaire would be decided in the east, not in the capital city.

As a result, Kate Crawford, Stan Reber, and I remained the core of embassy operations in eastern Zaire. We could have used help. Whaley unfortunately was leaving and was unavailable. But the embassy owed the U.S. government a political analysis of what the total disruption of eastern Zaire meant to the country's future. Economically the region was being severed from the rest of the country. The amount of hard currency being pumped into Goma was enormous. Refugees are big business. As for the CIA, they consistently ignored my calls for support. As far as the embassy in Kinshasa was concerned, Goma was just too far away to be relevant.

Scouts Out!

So with the embassy unconcerned, the JTF on the ground with limited intelligence capabilities, and Washington ever thirsty for information, we remained busy keeping everyone happy or at least as happy as we could make them. Just as I had done in southern Lebanon and earlier that year in Kinshasa, I established a routine that had us out looking at the camps whenever possible. We monitored them to see how they were developing and, more importantly, how the Rwandans were settling in. Kibumba and Katale remained the focus of the relief effort, and as those camps improved my interest declined. That was not the case for the military encampments south of Goma. We made a run through the area at least three times a week. Our observations were consistent. The former military remained encamped as an army in being. Uniforms were the norm, and we saw heavy weapons and some light arms. We also saw a lot of hostile eyes when we made the trips.

Interestingly enough, we often had dinner with the officers from these camps. Our favorite hotel restaurant was also the favored watering hole for the former military leaders. It was a sore point with me, because as an attaché there were limits on what I could do to develop information. I had already had requests from headquarters I had turned down due to risk. I could not just pop out to the former military's camp and ask to interview the bosses. The CIA folks back in Kinshasa were the ones to work this area. But I could not get them interested. Consequently, we—the intelligence community—missed an opportunity to find out what these guys had in mind.

Nevertheless, much can be gained from just watching an area. One of the first intelligence requirements came from an unexpected source. Bill and I were at the airport one morning when Brigadier General Nix walked up to us and said he was convinced there were no more than 100,000 to 150,000 refugees in the entire area. Bill and I did a double-take, and Nix repeated his statement. When Bill and I again eyed each other, Nix announced he was putting us on a visual reconnaissance with the French the next day at 0900.

So the next morning Bill and I strapped into the rumble seats on a Gazelle and took off. True to Nix's warning the French pilots did their best to make us sick. That made the flight fun, and Bill and I only grinned. I talked to the pilots, and we headed north to Katale. Bill and I had agreed we would keep our estimates separate, though we did agree a single refugee tarp could be counted as a family. We worked Katale and then Kibumba. I asked the pilot to skirt the border to look for crossers into Rwanda. Then we went south and repeated the process over the ex-military areas. All in all we were in the air for well over an hour. The Gazelle is a lot more fun than a Puma, and I enjoyed that flight.

Once on the ground, we tallied our estimates and compared numbers. Bottom line was we came out with numbers in the realm of 800,000. Armed with a consensus, we went in to see Nix. He listened, and I could tell he did not like it one bit. I went over our methodology and our flight path. I added that we had flown the border and seen no sign of movement back into Rwanda.

"Sir, I was here for the last three days of the mass movement. They walked right down this road," I said, pointing at the airport road just a stone's throw from us. "I had the pilot fly the border. We saw no one either crossing into Rwanda or already there."

To a degree, Nix was correct in his contention: the numbers were probably overstated, but that was a question of method not intent. The difference between a miscount and the number he had somehow arrived at amounted to nearly 700,000. In any case he did send a message into the JTF Main saying he believed his number of 150,000 was right. No one seems to have taken that message too seriously, suggesting it did not really matter. This little vignette was the opening act of the U.S. withdrawal. The next theme would be that reduced water consumption equaled a return of the refugees to Rwanda.

In the meantime, we were still worried about another exodus down south. The French were still in southwest Rwanda, but the new government wanted them out. UNAMIR II was arriving, but full deployment was weeks away. Things were more or less under control in Goma. The JTF was operating smoothly; there were occasional problems with the Zairian military and other locals but nothing that could not be handled. I resolved to take our little show on the road.

Stan and I had already crossed into Rwanda once. It was more of a lark to keep the chargé happy. He asked us to take his wife and him across after the secretary of defense visit. We did the formalities at the

Zairian side of the border but almost nothing on the Rwandan side. All we really did was drive the mile to the Hotel Meridien and turn around. The next week Stan and I headed for Kigali. We had reasons for the trip. First, I wanted a look-see inside Rwanda. I needed to get a feel for how many refugees might have gone back. Second, I figured it was a good idea to take a look at the Rwandan Patriotic Army (RPA). We had taken fire from them in the waning days of their campaign to take Gisenyi. But the area had been quiet for sometime. Finally, there was talk of consolidating the JTF in Kigali, possibly for use in the southwestern part of Rwanda. I wanted a good look at the main road from the border to the capital. On the map, it looked to be a four-hour drive. But maps in Africa are deceiving.

I let Brigadier General Nix and Washington know we were going, and the next morning we set out. The border crossing was not without the usual Zairian demands for bribes. But on the Rwandan side it was a bit different. The officials were all soldiers, and they acted like it. The language was notably English. A captain examined our passports and asked us where we were going. I told him we had a meeting in Kigali, and he sent us on our way. We made it through most of Gisenyi before the other shoe dropped.

We came up on a roadblock manned by four or five RPA troops. Stan stopped and I leaned out the window to talk to whomever came forward. All the troops were armed with AK47s and wore East German fatigues with black berets. There were no sunglasses, no fancy badges, and no rappel seats around these troops' waists. There was no overt threat, but all were alert. A lieutenant appeared and asked in English who we were. I explained we were American soldiers. Immediate grins appeared on their faces.

"You're not French?" the lieutenant asked in confirmation.

"No, I am an American colonel and this is my sergeant," I responded.

At that he saluted and began talking on a handheld radio. "Follow me," he said shortly afterward and headed to a Toyota pickup. We followed him back into town and arrived at what I learned later was the local brigade commander's headquarters.

I groaned inwardly at the delay. In Zaire or elsewhere in Africa, this diversion could turn into an all-day affair. Nevertheless, we were soon inside talking to a major who asked about our business. I went through the same questions and answers with him: Who are you? American soldiers. Where are you going? Kigali. Are you French? No. All of this drew the same grins and smiles. Then I got a real surprise:

the major made a decision without bucking it up the chain as I feared. He told us we could go, and he ordered the lieutenant to escort us out of town toward Kigali. Thirty minutes after being stopped at the roadblock, our RPA escort pulled over, and the lieutenant flashed a salute to wave us on.

There were three salient observations on the next three hours to Kigali. First, we were in a no-man's-land. The next major town along the way was Ruhengeri. All the villages we passed getting there were deserted. Even Ruhengeri was a ghost town. The only beings we saw as we drove southeast toward Kigali were RPA soldiers. We passed through at least ten checkpoints and at each went through the same question and answer routine. The magic words were "American soldiers." They consistently drew grins from the troops, who all were uniformly well disciplined. Not once were we asked for anything. In Zaire, running ten roadblocks would have left us broke.

The second observation was that Rwanda is incredibly beautiful. It was like driving through a Hollywood set that just kept changing. In the northwest, we saw volcanoes and triple canopy jungle and could look back at the deep blue waters of Lake Kivu. As we drew closer to Ruhengeri, we were surrounded by carefully terraced hills lush with tea. From Ruhengeri, we began a series of climbs and descents across high ridgelines and down river valleys. Saying the beauty of the tiny country was stunning might sound trite. But Stan and I were just that: stunned by its deceptive beauty.

The final major observation was that the roads, the towns, and the villages were seemingly untouched by war. The French referred to the machete as the African "neutron bomb," very effective in killing without destroying the surrounding areas. The roads were all tarmac and wide by African standards. Grades were steep, but the builders did use switchbacks to lessen their effects. We saw some small arms and mortar damage in Ruhengeri. But as I mentally compared it to what I had seen in Lebanon, it seemed minor. As we closed into Kigali, we saw more and more signs of war. Some building fronts had collapsed, and there were quite a number of burned-out vehicles. Still, I thought at the time, it looked like a minor war. I was so wrong.

We played Dorothy and "followed the yellow brick road" to the U.S. embassy. Stan had been there years before when the office in Kinshasa covered Rwanda. We stopped at each roadblock along the way and flashed our military ID cards at the troops, many who appeared less than fifteen years old. These "munchkins" all grinned and pointed us in the right direction. Our stop at the embassy was anti-climatic. Ambassador David Rawson and his acting defense attaché, Lt. Col. Tony Marley, were out. Tony was an African FAO who had been working in the Political-Military section of the State Department. He had helped Ambassador Rawson reopen the embassy. Stan and I checked in with the military guys assisting the embassy to let the JTF know we had arrived. We had MREs for lunch outside on the truck hood and after a quick look at the airport, headed back to Goma.

The ride back was the same stunning vista as the trip into Kigali. I can honestly say I fell in love with the country that day. I just did not know how much pain it would cause me. All told, the day was idyllic, a truly welcome break from the stench and dirt of Goma. I guess that is a statement in itself: go to Rwanda for a day vacation from Goma. We made it back that evening just before they closed the border. Stan and I were both tired, but we chattered about the drive like two schoolgirls discussing a cute teacher. Amazing how beautiful a country can be when it does not have any people—at least living people.

Our next sojourn took us north through the camps at Kibumba and Katale. Tony Marley had joined us from Kigali for a couple of days, so Stan and I took him along. We were playing refugee tourist again to see if we could find evidence of any large-scale return to Rwanda. Our route this time ran from Katale to the border crossing with Uganda and then on to Rwanda. We would intersect with the main highway to Kigali just outside Ruhengeri. The camps passed without incident. By this time they were remarkably organized and almost docile. The one thing that had not changed was the open hostility of the refugees. Nevertheless there was a dramatic absence of bodies compared to my trip through the area after the airdrop. But while it might get better, it would never be paradise.

One potential solution glowered and spit over our left shoulders as we drove north. Mount Nyiragongo was the most active volcano in an area infamous for volcanoes. As fate would have it, a casual remark by me in a morning telephonic update had focused scientific attention on the smoking mountain. Just after Stan had come out July 25 or so, I remember my bed marching across the room during an earthquake that lasted several minutes. I had been in California, Turkey, and Lebanon during earthquakes, so the vibrating bed was not a novelty to me. This one happened in the early morning around 0300 hours. The next morning we discovered we were suddenly out of water, a bit strange since our "well" was Lake Kivu less than one hundred yards due east of the house. The house used a lower pump and an upper pump to draw the water to the house. The upper was working, so Stan went down to the lake to check the other. He came back and told us Lake Kivu had apparently dropped, leaving the access pipe a full four feet out of the water.

I mentioned the quake and the drop in the lake level that morning when calling the Pentagon. Apparently that got someone's attention in D.C. because the next day, Rick Moore called me. "You know the report you made about the lake out there dropping? Well the lake did not drop; Goma rose." Apparently, the pressure had pushed up the rock crust Goma sits on from volcanic activity. That was the source of my earthquake.

The problem was this volcano was especially dangerous. It had last erupted in the late 1970s. It is what geologists refer to as a high-speed volcano. Erupting through vents in its side and base, the lava flows at speeds greater than thirty miles per hour. In the 1970s event, lava had caught moving cars. The specter of such an eruption into the very areas where the refugees were encamped was haunting. On the other hand, it seemed entirely appropriate. A combined U.S.-French geology team did come out and examine the volcano. Some of us were disappointed to hear there was little chance of a 1970s-type eruption. For months, we kept hoping they would be proven wrong. God missed a chance to make a statement on genocide.

So we tooled along that morning until we reached the Ugandan border. The crossing went fairly well. The Ugandans were used to the traffic, and the Zairians knew they had little hope of getting bribes from diplomats. From the extreme western tip of Uganda we arced to the southeast and reentered Rwanda. Intersecting with the main road to Gisenyi, our trip back was uneventful but enjoyable. We had just driven a circle around the area made famous in the film *Gorillas in the Mist*. We saw no gorillas, found no guerrillas, and spotted damn few potential "returned" refugees. But the scenery, as before, was stunning. If only Sigourney Weaver had been there . . .

We remained concerned about a southern refugee exodus until the Ethiopians in UNAMIR II took over from the French Operation Turquoise. Stan and I had already been to Kigali; we knew that road was fine as far as the capital city. We did not know how good it was from Kigali to the border at Cyangugu. If it matched the Gisenyi-Kigali highway, it was an autobahn by African standards. I had already talked to Nix about a possible move south. I recommended going through Rwanda rather than trying the western side of Lake Kivu inside Zaire. He seemed to favor that route because it was outside the "war" zone, and he had been told it was less than five hours to Bukavu. My route through Rwanda was at least ten hours.

A glance at the Michelin map said Bukavu was 120 kilometers or so from Goma. And as is often the case, the Michelin map said the roads were good. They probably were good in the 1970s when the map and the roads were last updated. The western shore of Lake Kivu is a series of ridges and valleys that collapse into the lake as part of the Great Rift Valley. The ridges are all fifteen hundred to two thousand feet high and the valleys all have streams that become rivers overnight. Stan was not exactly overjoyed when I told him we were headed south.

"We going back through Kigali?" he asked.

"Nope, we are going down the western side of the lake," I responded. Mild discomfort on Stan's face turned to incredulity.

"I know, Stan, but Nix seems to think he can make that run in five hours with five-thousand-gallon tankers. We are going to drive that road and see for ourselves before the JTF gets buried out there."

The next day we set out early from the lake house at around 0600. Our path took us through the former Rwandan army to the main north-south route along the western side of Lake Kivu, which we reached at 0700. The first twenty kilometers were all on tarmac and went fairly quickly, but that speed ended when the asphalt stopped. Almost immediately the Isuzu began to struggle with the red Zairian clay, her little diesel screaming with the effort to pull us through. By this time it was approaching 0800. We had been on the road along the lake for an hour and had covered twenty kilometers, what would be our best record for the day.

We had only gone another ten kilometers or so when we ran into the nemesis of all travelers in the Zairian bush—a Zairian military checkpoint. It was nothing spectacular, just a log laid across two fifty-five-gallon drums to block the road and a small building set back from the road, with a couple of half-dressed soldiers watching us like buzzards. Nevertheless, Stan and I both shifted into the red zone, alert to possible trouble. It took a couple of minutes for one of the Zairian military troops to break contact with the ground and stand up. As he walked toward us, his partner also stood and leveled an FN (a Belgian rifle, Fabrique Nationale) toward us. The game started as the first walked up to Stan's window.

"Who are you? And where are you going?" he began. He had been drinking; at 0830 under the muzzle of his weapon that was not a comforting thought.

Stan pointed toward the front of the vehicle. "We are diplomats from the U.S. embassy. We are headed to Bukavu to work on the refugee problem there."

The soldier attempted to open the passenger door, but Stan stopped him with, "This is a diplomatic vehicle. See the plates on the front?" The soldier stepped back and examined our CD plates and then returned.

"Come with me," he waved to Stan, who got out and followed.

"I'll be back," Stan said to me.

"I'll wait here for ten minutes and then come in if you are not back," I responded.

As those two walked off, the other Zairian military troop sauntered over and tried to open the rear door. I again used the diplomatic vehicle route, and he seemed to accept it. He too had been into the banana beer. But soon he started with the counterargument that we might be diplomats, but the vehicle was not diplomatic property. We batted this ball back and forth for the next few minutes until Stan returned, followed by his escort.

"Any problems?" I asked.

"Nope. Just a drunk lieutenant who said we could go on," Stan answered.

"But that guy doesn't like it," he added, pointing at the first soldier, who was now deep into discussion with his partner.

Rather than raise the barrier, they turned in unison and headed back toward us. Again they tried to open the doors to the truck, claiming the vehicle was subject to search. We kept the doors closed and refused. Stan reminded them their officer had already released us, but that had little effect. I was not going to consent to the search, because it would only lead to more problems. These troops knew they were crossing a line by stopping diplomats. If we allowed ourselves to be robbed, we became severe liabilities. More than one westerner had disappeared in the bush courtesy of the Zairian military.

"Do we go back?" Stan asked.

"Yeah, we will have to if they insist on a search," I answered.

Even as I said that, the first soldier moved to our rear, preventing any attempt to reverse our course. Stan and I looked at each other.

"No search, Stan," I muttered softly. We started shifting to reach our weapons.

"Idiots! Laissez les passez!" a drunken voice called from the side of the road.

The inebriated lieutenant waved at the barricade, and his soldiers scurried to shift the log barrier. Stan and I were both breathing deeply as we moved off, still riding a jolt of adrenalin. That little drama had cost us nearly an hour by the time we started rolling again, and we hoped it was the last checkpoint.

For the next several hours, Stan and I battled the road with our reluctant charger. The little diesel chugged through hub-deep mud fairly well. She was light enough that the spinning tires pushed along the surface of the mud when heavier vehicles with bigger engines would have just sunk. Outlined by triple-canopy jungle on both sides, the road itself was fairly well marked. In the dry season it might be fairly fast. But this was the wet season, and the road was more like a mud canal between the trees. Nevertheless we pressed on and passed some Bedford lorries buried up to their frames. I could just see one of those five-ton tractors with a five-thousand-gallon trailer trying to get through this stuff.

The little diesel handled the mud flats fairly well, but the ridgelines proved more difficult. As I said before, Lake Kivu marks the passage of the Great Rift Valley through this area of central Africa. The central plateau falls off into the lake with fingerlike ridges spread eastward to the lakes shore. The net effect is an extreme roller coaster of ridges and valleys. What makes the ride extreme is the "engineers" who laid out the system did not use switchbacks to climb or descend the ridges. On a fifteen-hundred-foot climb, the typical road had three five-hundred-foot legs at more than a 15 percent grade. Even in dry weather, such a climb is nerve-wracking. On wet clay-based dirt roads, it got very hairy. Our diesel needed a running start to get up to a momentum to sustain the climbs. We got pretty good at it: the trick was never shifting out of first gear even when she sounded like she was going to blow. Still we had a couple of incidents when we met a descending truck, and we literally had to run backward down the mountain to get out of their way.

About 1500 hours we had some forty kilometers left when we stopped in a small village for a break. That was a mistake. Two Zairian military wives from Bukavu were apparently visiting their families, and they asked for a ride. Their two armed escorts made it difficult to say no. So we loaded the two women, each at least 250 pounds of Zairian delight, and their two escort thugs complete with automatic rifles and grenades and set off for the final leg to Bukavu. There was a positive side to having guests along. We passed through several more Zairian military roadblocks without hassle. Bukavu, and especially the junction of the tarmac road north of Bukavu, was a welcome sight. We closed with the town after spending fourteen hours on a 120-kilometer obstacle course.

Bukavu is one of the classic sad-story towns of Zaire. Built as a colonial resort when the Belgian Congo was a going concern, the little town hugged the Lake Kivu shoreline as it stretched out along a narrow peninsula. During the troubles of the 1960s, Bukavu survived relatively unscathed because of its geography. Easily cut off from land traffic, it was easier to defend, especially with Lake Kivu as a backdoor supply route.

The little town was pretty beaten up by the time I saw it in 1994. Goma was not designed to take a large refugee influx, and Bukavu was even less capable. The refugees could not go around Bukavu or even use multiple side streets to get through it. All essentially had to pass through the center, and then once off the peninsula they could turn north or south. Only several hundred thousand had done so when Stan and I arrived; the town looked like termites had gone through it. Any source of firewood had been chopped down. The avenue of trees along the lakefront was now an avenue of freshly chopped stumps.

As Stan and I arrived, the rains greeted us. We set out to find a place to stay for the evening. Easier said than done, and we soon began to look at the Isuzu as a probable bed. I do not remember the name of the hotel we finally found, but it was really a bar. Stan struck up a conversation with the bartender, a longtime Belgian resident, as we enjoyed two very welcome Simba Lagers. He allowed he had a room not normally rented to white men he would let us have for the night. We were not choosey. He took us back past the restroom—the wall where everyone urinated—and the exterior charcoal kitchen to a small room with a single bed. We fired up some heat tabs and warmed our French combat rations. Stan got the bed. I took the floor. By 2200 hours we were sound asleep, lulled by a drumming rain on the metal roof.

The next day we ate MREs for breakfast and started toward the border crossing, the Rusizi bridge between the sister towns of Cyangugu and Bukavu. Refugees were evident in town but not in the numbers we had seen up north. At the border, we did the usual with the Zairians. That went fairly smoothly, and we eased onto the narrow bridge. At the far side, French soldiers directed us into a holding lot so we could process through the Rwandan authorities. That in itself was rather bizarre. These officials were Rwandan but who they represented was not clear. I could only assume they were holdovers from the previous regime brought back by the French to assist in running the area. Their long-term job security was doubtful.

Once outside the border post we ran into a concentration of several thousand refugees, stacked up along the border but unable to cross. The Zairians had closed the border to refugees. It was raining as we drove slowly through the crowd. Although wet and obviously displaced from their normal lives, these Rwandans looked remarkably better than their Goma counterparts. The reason was obvious enough: the French had provided them a security zone and an escape hatch into Zaire and Burundi. The Tutsis inside that zone were not so lucky.

Stan and I could not linger in Cyangugu. We had a long day ahead of us, at least a ten-hour drive to get back to Goma via Kigali. Our first leg was the longest and by far the prettiest. Once outside Cyangugu, we were back in the tea plantations and their terraced hills. The intense green of the plants and their lush growth made the area look like something out of J.R.R. Tolkien's *The Lord of the Rings.* It was just too green to be real. We soon left that area and entered what felt like an enchanted forest.

For the next forty miles or so, Stan and I went back in time. The Nyungwe National Forest spread out on both sides of the road as we climbed into the highest area in Rwanda. Dense forest and underlying growth both beckoned and warned that this area was not man's domain. The mountains and the weather added to the feeling. At times our little truck would labor up the side of a mountain, hemmed in by low clouds and dense forest. Then we would break out into bright sunshine as we reached the peak. Though it cost us time, we stopped and marveled at the sight.

Buoyed by the beauty we had just seen, Stan and I ran into the reality of Rwanda on the far side of the forest. We turned a corner and ran into a temporary checkpoint manned by French troops. The unit was what only the French could call a CRAP and get away with it. Like our Long-Range Surveillance Detachments, CRAPs are primarily a reconnaissance element. They also have, however, a direct action role more along the line of our Ranger units. This one's position marked the edge of the French protected zone. We chatted with them about the area, and they were curious about our role. The patrol leader recommended we not go any farther. Stan stuck with the "meetings in Kigali" line we had used before. They accepted it at face value. After all, we were the ones headed into what was for them hostile territory.

Out of the forest, we were back in the heavily cultivated areas of Rwanda. Every inch of ground was either terraced for tea production or laid out for subsistence farming. Small houses and huts were scattered through the hills with a smattering of larger communes and villages spread between them on the main *collines* or hills. But this intense evidence of human occupation was like an empty sound set. There were no actors and no signs of life. No cattle or goats moved on the hillsides or in the valleys. No smoke wafted from the huts. We stopped for a break along the main road for about fifteen minutes. There were no sounds or any other indications of humanity. It was remarkable. I had never been anywhere in the Third World where I could be alone for more than five minutes before a local showed up. Here Stan and I were in the middle of one of the most densely populated countries in the world—and no one was home.

Almost with a sense of relief, we soon ran into our first RPA checkpoint of the day. This time the body language was dramatically tenser as we approached the checkpoint. We did not wait for the question.

"We are American soldiers. *Nous sommes Americains.* We are not French. *Pas de Francais,*" we chorused and waved out green military IDs. It worked like a champ. As soon as the RPA soldiers heard the word "American," they relaxed. We chatted with them as we had the French. Stan lit a cigarette and smoked without offering to share. No one asked for a smoke. As we departed, Stan handed half a pack to the senior man.

"I just wanted to see if they would try and get something from us. Can you imagine smoking in front of a bunch Zairian troops like that?" Stan commented.

We saw a lot more of the RPA as we approached Kigali from the south. The no-man's-land feeling continued all the way into the city. There were more civilians in the city and even an occasional vehicle, but it too seemed deserted. We cleared Kigali and headed north to Gisenyi around 1500 hours. Three hours later we squeezed through the border into Goma just as the Zairians were closing for the day.

It was nearing dark when we arrived at the JTF compound to check in. I went to see Brigadier General Nix. I spent about twenty minutes relating the trip and emphasized that any attempt to use the road west of Lake Kivu would be disastrous. A week later, the French proved my point. Their withdrawal was slipping behind schedule, and they decided to push a column of vehicles up that road to Goma. They had no large vehicles. Most of their wheeled transports were Mini-Mog-type 6x6s. When they finally closed into Goma after nearly eighteen hours, every windshield was broken, winch cables were too distorted to rewind, and mud spread all the way across the tops of the trucks. They had made it, but they had paid hard for the trip.

I told Nix what we had seen along the route and the conditions in Bukavu. I showed him where the French zone ended in southwestern Rwanda and talked about the absence of life. He took it all in and thanked me. Then he told me the CIA had apparently decided we needed help. The agency had sent a two-man team to provide assistance on force protection. Nix was less than thrilled and made it clear the spooks were now my problem.

I left and went to see the task force intelligence officer. He told me the same thing, but when I asked where the CIA guys were, he said, "They're in the quarantine tent."

"What quarantine?" I asked.

"Oh, the loggies bought some local beef and all the troops who ate it got sick," he answered, adding, "The last tent on the line, you can't miss it."

I headed for the sick tent thinking. Back when we were discussing the ill-fated beer mission, I had suggested the task force bring in fresh meat and food from Europe for the troops. That is what we did in Kinshasa. One thing we never did was buy local beef or any other meat in Zaire. We had been taking somewhat of a risk eating at the hotel, but they got their meats from Uganda.[2]

True to the description, there was a medical ward established in a large tent. The flight surgeon and medics attached to the JTF had ten to twenty troops all in cots, many with IVs hanging beside them. The story was that all who had the local beef had gotten sick. All who ate T-ration lasagna instead had remained healthy. Nevertheless, the medicos had decided to quarantine the ill just in case some mystery bug was involved. It also avoided concluding they had eaten tainted meat cleared by the same medicos. At the far end of the tent, I spotted an obviously nonmilitary civilian setting up some commo gear.

I went up to him and introduced myself. As it turned out, he and his communicator had been specially dispatched to advise the JTF commander on force protection. That is to say, he was there to tell a general how to make sure his troops did not get killed. I told the guy I had been doing that since the arrival of the JTF lead elements. But this individual had not been sent until nearly thirty days into the operation. Nix understandably had not been impressed with the Agency's sense of urgency. Neither had I, for that matter. Here we were, as it turned out, almost at the end of the JTF's stay, and Langley had decided we needed force protection advice. Meanwhile the station chief in Kinshasa had ignored the entire crisis. Still, this guy took his fate with a sense of humor. His residence in the quarantine tent spoke volumes about his status with Nix. He left to return to the States less than forty-eight hours after his arrival.

Winding Down

Our return from circling Lake Kivu marked the transition of the JTF into its withdrawal stage. Brigadier General Nix and his soldiers had done well in the first part of their stated mission, really the only achievable objective at the time. Still the drawdown of the JTF was not well received in the NGOs and international agencies working in Goma. Working to offset the perception that the job was not finished, Nix and his staff pushed the issue of water consumption as an indicator that the refugees were going home. That had been partially true when the cholera epidemic and a subsequent dysentery outbreak occurred. The number of refugees heading back to Rwanda did increase, although in relation to the numbers still in Zaire, the returnee population was minor. Yet even that small increase in returning Rwandans soon declined and for all practical purposes ceased. I listened as Nix and his civil affairs officer gave a briefing on the operation. The thesis of the briefing was that decreased water consumption equaled a decreasing refugee population. Not true, but it was a sellable point if you were inclined to buy. The rainy season and changes in refugee behavior accounted for much of the decline. Coupled with the fact the Rwandans did not consume as much water as suggested under international health standards, the decline did not add up to the conclusions the JTF wanted. Still it offered an out, one happily taken by a JTF looking to leave gracefully.

The JTF had accomplished its main mission in Goma: "stop the dying."[3] I often heard from various NGO and disaster workers that the United States did not produce as much water as the teams from the United Kingdom and elsewhere. That was true but did not go far enough. The reverse osmosis units we brought in were intended for steady production of potable water for units much smaller than the refugee population around Goma. Our water units had taken their lead from the ODA (British equivalent to USAID) and disinfected lake water rather than go through purification. It was faster. The result was that the U.S. water production effort added enough to the other water production teams to beat the cholera epidemic.

We also added dramatically to the water transport. Those ten five-ton tractors and their five-thousand-gallon trailers moved a lot of water. Taken from war reserve stocks in Germany, they were outdated but fully functional. There was criticism the United States was being cheap in handing them over; they were outdated and would soon breakdown. Therefore, the United States should have brought in state-of-the-art trucks to leave behind. I will offer two points on that idea. First, I saw those same five-ton trucks running the roads in Rwanda eighteen months later. Second, the United States did bring in some commercially bought brand-new tractors to Rwanda. They were broken down inside three months, and they stayed broken.

The JTF briefers and its critics missed the real Goma story. Operation Support Hope achieved what it did through airlift. It is true that in Goma the United States did not produce as much water as the other donors. But for the most part, the United States flew in their equipment along with the bulk of the emergency supplies needed to stop the dying. We funneled a massive airlift through one of the most cramped airfields in Africa. We did it in concert with the French, the United Nations using largely dilapidated Russian aircraft, and a large commercial fleet. There was not a single airframe lost in that effort—though one Russian An124 almost ground looped. What had happened with the Russian copy of the C5 was a pure case of bad maintenance. Inbound to Goma, the Russians lost an outboard engine about fifty miles out. They came on, because there was no alternative. As the jumbo settled toward the runway, the inboard engine on the same side flamed out. The Antonov slammed into the runway and blew most of the tires along the same side. She fishtailed down the runway, but they got her to stop without ground looping.

The crew went straight to the bar, and when the French had the bird repaired, the semi-drunk Russians flew her out. Later in Kigali, I became close friends with a British couple who had survived that flight.

Managing such a polyglot air operation required some sort of agreement. The framework for the working agreement that made it all happen was worked out by one skinny, bald-headed U.S. Army sergeant first class who had ten years in the country. Stan Reber did more than any other to untie the transport knot at Goma. He is not mentioned in the JTF After Action Report.

As for the rest of the JTF in Entebbe and Kigali, they would continue their efforts. Yet they had also already achieved a very real success. The deployment of UNAMIR II was a separate but parallel operation. The focal point for the U.N. peacekeepers in August, 1994, was southwest Rwanda and the former French protected zone. Ethiopia had agreed to send a veteran group of Ethiopian soldiers, all former fighters against Menguistu, to Rwanda. They were to replace the French, who had been ordered out by the new Rwandan government. That handoff took place in the last week of August without the feared second refugee exodus. Ultimately the scruffy Ethiopians proved themselves to be the best of the UNAMIR troops. All of this happened due to U.S. assistance in getting the Kigali airport operating and the U.S. airlift. Operation Support Hope did a lot of other things during its existence. It would do more before the final teams pulled out in late September. But the Operation had already achieved its main tasks: it had stopped the dying in Goma, and it had deployed UNAMIR II.[4]

So as I listened to the briefing, I was not offended, outraged, or even disappointed in the premise of the message. I thought it curious we were not keying on what we had done to stop the dying. The rest of it—return refugees to Rwanda and do something about the security situation—was not on the JTF's mission list. It was on mine, however.

En route to the United States for consultations, Ambassador David Rawson had elected to stop in Goma to get a firsthand look at the refugee situation. I had heard much about David. Ambassador to Rwanda when the war broke out, David had managed to get all his staff and their families out of the explosive situation without loss. That alone made him something special. Prior to assuming the ambassadorial posting, he had been instrumental in setting up the failed Arusha Accords. At the beginning of his career, he had been the embassy consular officer who carried Diane Fossey's mail up to Karisimbe. In his youth, David had been the son of missionaries working among the Hutu in Burundi. No U.S. official had more of a personal stake in achieving a negotiated peace at Arusha. When the accords failed and the genocide began, no U.S. official suffered more than David Rawson.

It was the measure of the man that he had gone back in to reopen the embassy. Now he was headed back to the States to update Washington on the situation. Tony Marley, as his acting defense attaché, had suggested to David that I come over when finished in Zaire. I had agreed on what was supposed to be a ninety-day temporary duty. At the time I still expected my next official posting would be to Haiti. So as I met David for the first time I never expected we would serve together over the next sixteen months. We drove north into the camps, and I could see he was disturbed. Refugee camps are hardly news in Africa. David had seen them before. But as he looked out at Kibumba he said, "This is not going to go away. This is long term. The war is not over."

That simple assessment marked the beginning of our partnership. I told him I would join him in Rwanda by mid-September. We shook hands, and he boarded the plane and left.

If there is one thing U.S. troops do faster than anything else, it is redeploy. Called "smelling the barn," U.S. soldiers lose all pretense of GI grumbling when told they are going home, especially when they are going home from a place like Goma. Once it was apparent that was happening, Stan and I shifted to the same mode. We had already put Nash on a flight to Chad. The Jeep was back in Kinshasa, and we were down to just Stan and me along with Kate. She was staying as the DART representative. DIA had approved State and Rawson's request for me to go to Rwanda as a temporary military representative. They had stepped up the arrival of my replacement, the defense attaché in Liberia. We had been in correspondence for several months.

After forty days I was ready for a change, even if it meant Kinshasa. The JTF was all but gone. The focus of U.S. operations was on Kigali. The quicker I got back, the quicker I would be in Rwanda. We had loaded the Isuzu with supplies and, with Saleem's approval, parked her in the garage at the lake house until Stan and I returned to drive her to Kigali. Stan and I made a 5 P.M. flight to Kinshasa. Finally we could say, "Goodbye, Goma!"

Transitions and Goodbyes

Our deluxe flight to Kinshasa was on one of Saleem's 707s. We had seats, but two Zairian military officers had shown up with female companions, so we surrendered our seats. We did not care. We went into the 707's cargo hold and stretched out on a pallet of beans. Soon asleep, we woke briefly at the interim stop at Kisangani. Neither of us got up. We lay there like two cats, each with an open eye watching our kit bags until we resumed flight. When we sensed we were descending into Kinshasa, we roused ourselves and got ready to debark.

Not a passenger flight, the 707 halted on the apron far from the main terminal. It was night, and there were no lights around us. We saw our Cherokee approach and headed toward it. A self-declared customs inspector stepped in our way and stated we had to go through customs and immigration. Stan and I looked at each other and then at this guy. He now had several assistants, all eager to get in on the action. They were all baggage handlers looking to score. We pulled our diplomatic passports, and Stan, in Lingala, told them to get lost. They knew they had been made and stepped aside. Life in Kinshasa had not changed.

The next two weeks were a period of transitions and good-byes. Some things bear telling as they relate to the rest of my story. First I got to finally meet the rest of my Goma team. The air force sergeant who met us at the airport had done great work handling the Kinshasa end of our airlift. He soon returned to Cameroon. I also got to meet Commander Grant and her husband. She and I had talked on the cellular many times. Grant had done an equally fine job getting the details right in messages back to Washington. She told me the stay at my house had been a sort of honeymoon for her and her husband. They too were soon headed back to their post in South Africa.

I also had the opportunity to meet a new team member. Lt. Col. Jim Cobb flew in from Youandé. He had just arrived in Cameroon when the Goma refugee crisis had exploded. His predecessor had been Lt. Col. Charles Vukovic. Chuck Vukovic and I had as FAO trainees in 1984 made a six-thousand-mile road trip through most of southern Africa. Since USDAO Youandé had responsibility for Rwanda, Chuck had been in Kigali when the war resumed. He had since gone on to a new assignment, and Jim Cobb was his replacement. Cobb and I agreed he should go on to Rwanda until I could get there. We were both under the assumption I would only be there ninety days. Then as the regional defense attaché responsible for the country, Jim would continue to cover Rwanda with periodic visits from Cameroon.

Part of the period was taken up by folding back into the embassy. The second day after I got back was the day for the embassy staff meeting. These were held in the large conference room rather than in the plastic bubble reserved for the inner policy makers. The chargé looked at me and said, "Tell us about Goma, Tom."

I led with, "The Rwandan Civil War is not over. It has merely shifted to the refugee camps outside the country." The chargé made faces for the rest of my talk. I clearly did not convince him. Then as we were leaving, the station chief turned to me and whispered that he knew there were no Dragons in Goma. Stan and I had seen the Dragons in Goma. Based on those two comments, I realized the U.S. embassy in Kinshasa remained unchanged.

Meanwhile the replacements for Stan and me arrived. The new defense attaché moved into my house, and Stan's took over the sergeant's quarters. Stan and I shifted to an empty apartment. My final comment on Zaire deals with one of the hardest things I had to do: say goodbye to Stan. Family health problems forced him to withdraw from the mission to Rwanda. I was not happy to be leaving him behind. He had another couple of months to go on his tour. I sensed my replacement would never allow him to operate as I had done. The new defense attaché felt operations coordinators were best used behind a desk. That was not Stan's style. An officer never had a better sergeant than Stan Reber nor a more trusted friend and comrade. I boarded another Saleem special to Goma wondering what I would do without him.

CHAPTER 6

Land of the Dead

I was lonely on the flight back to Goma, closing a chapter in my life and leaving a close friend. I was also starting a new chapter, at once frightening and exciting. One thing was certain: I was through with the embassy in Kinshasa, a tremendous relief. I managed to keep my seat on this flight. No beanbag special this time. Saleem's flight crews were first rate and I chatted with the co-pilot during part of the flight. Mainly though, I just pondered what I faced.

Goma looked different from the last time I had landed there. The refugees were in tent cities now. The empty JTF base camp remained the most visible reminder of Nix's operation. We disembarked from the plane, and the Express Air service truck took us downtown. I was in a hurry to get on my way, but I did stop in to thank Saleem. We parted, and his driver took me to the lake house for the last time.

The Isuzu cranked immediately. She was loaded with my bags and a full fuel tank. I headed to the border at around 3 P.M. I wanted to get through the routine hassle as quickly as possible. Kigali was a good three-hour drive, and I wanted to be inside the city before sunset. For once the Zairians were fairly fast. I completed the usual formalities and crossed into Rwanda with a mental sigh of relief. The Rwandans were efficient as always, and I was soon on my way.

The diesel labored up the hills as I climbed away from Lake Kivu. It really seemed strange to be alone. Stan and I had spent so much time together in that little truck that it did not seem right without him. I did not like being out on the road solo. It rubbed against years of training and experience. People who travel solo in the bush are just asking for trouble. I worried a bit, but not too much. The truck screamed along just fine, though she lugged down going up the steeper hills. Rwanda had plenty of those to challenge her.

The Rwandan Patriotic Army (RPA)—the military wing of the former rebel movement now controlling the country—remained out in force along the road. Just as Stan and I had experienced together, the new army was cut from a different cloth. The troops wore their uniforms with pride, and they looked like soldiers. I was so accustomed to seeing Zairian military thugs in mirror shades. I never saw an RPA soldier in a pair of sunglasses. That may seem to be a strange yardstick for a military, but looking back I can see it was fair. Any military that has to rely on props like sunglasses to look tough probably is not. The RPA was tough and had no need to prove it. The very fact I was able to transit ten roadblocks by myself and without a problem was positive proof that these soldiers were part of an army.

I rolled into Kigali with the sun setting behind us, and I went straight to the embassy. As expected, Lt. Col. Jim Cobb was there and we chatted. He gave me a brief tour of the embassy; that's all it took. The embassy in Rwanda was much smaller than Kinshasa. Two stories tall, there had never been a marine detachment in this post. Kigali had been something of a well-kept secret in the Foreign Service. Pacific on the outside, the underlying troubles had never disturbed the international community the way they had in Zaire or Burundi. The consular section, administration, communications, and the medical clinic occupied the first floor. The front office was upstairs. The ambassador, the deputy chief of mission (DCM), and the political officer all had small offices rotating off the small reception area manned by the ambassador's secretary. Down the back stairs, you entered the motor pool compound; the back wall was the mechanics shop area and also the U.S. Information Service (USIS) library. All except the ambassador parked outside. The U.S. Agency for International Development (USAID) mission was just up the street as was the American Embassy Club. Virtually all the main restaurants, hotels, diplomatic missions, and ministries sat on this single hill. The same held true for most of the American residences; only the ambassador's residence was outside this central core. Life in Kigali was simple and deceptively peaceful.

Invasion, War, and Genocide

The Rwandan Patriotic Front (RPF) 1990 invasion put an end to that seemingly tranquil existence. Problems suppressed inside the country had come back from the exterior of the country after festering for

thirty years in refugee camps. Rwanda was a land shared by two symbiotic ethnic groups. Hutus and Tutsis had lived together in the region
under Tutsi royalty. The Tutsis were traditionally herders. The Hutus
were farmers. The Tutsis were tall and fine featured. The Hutus were
short and squat featured. The division was not absolute. A change in
marriage or economic status could also change "ethnic" status, making the division something of a caste system similar to that in India.
A wealthy Hutu who bought cattle could become Tutsi. A Tutsi who
failed as a herder could be reclassified as a Hutu. Both groups shared
a common language, Kinyarwandan. All told, the country's ethnic
system was as much economic as it was physiological.

Colonialism changed that longstanding relationship. First the
Germans and then the Belgians used the traditional division of power
to their advantage. They elevated the Tutsis into a class of overseers.
What had been a symbiotic relationship between the two groups
became a rigid social division for more than sixty years. Yet when
Belgium stepped back from Africa in 1960, they reversed this system.
The Hutu became the dominant group virtually overnight. For the
next thirty years the government of Rwanda cultivated the fear of a
Tutsi return to power like a political cash crop. The overwhelming
majority of Hutus were always ready consumers. In a series of massacres beginning in 1960, the Hutu drove many of the Tutsi out of the
country. Many went to Tanzania and Uganda. Others went to Zaire or
Burundi, though the latter suffered its own special version of ethnic
hell. Those Tutsi who remained in Rwanda were required to carry
ethnic identity cards, the basis for life and death in Rwanda. Yet the
West, including the United States, France, and Belgium, dealt with
pre-1991 Rwanda as if it were a success story. It seemed peaceful. It
had an economy, albeit one constantly on the financial precipice. It
was at least nominally a democracy even if the same man had been
president for nearly two decades. Compared to its neighbors, Rwanda
appeared progressive. The reality of course was the country was poor.
It was the second-heaviest-populated country in the world. Only Bangladesh could claim a higher ratio of people to acre. Another million
Rwandan Tutsis lived outside its borders. The political system was by
the Hutus and for the Hutus. And everything they did was intended
to keep it that way.

Outside the country, two generations of Rwandans looked to
undo that machine. The RPF organized itself among the camps and
most importantly among the host nations' militaries. The heart of

Former Rwandan government–issued identification card. Note that ethnic categories are specified at top right.

the movement was in Uganda. That special relationship is a story in itself, one as yet unfinished. The central core of the RPF leadership began their basic training in the bush against Obote's regime in Kampala. They graduated their advanced course by making Museveni the president of Uganda in 1986. In 1990, while the world focused on the war in the Gulf, the RPF judged its moment had come. Several hundred Tutsi soldiers in the Ugandan military quietly slipped away to muster on the northeastern border of Rwanda. The initial five hundred crossed into Akagera National Park to begin the Rwandan Civil War.

Their opponents were the soldiers of the Rwandan Army, or ex-FAR as I called them in Goma. In the beginning, they were a small military suitable for a small African country. Roughly five thousand troops moderately well equipped and fairly well led, the ex-FAR had never been in combat. Their inexperience soon showed on the battlefield. Their leaders were tactically sluggish and entirely predictable. The RPF not only had tested leadership, they had a natural support and intelligence network inside Rwanda's remaining Tutsi population and Hutu moderates. Paul Kagame was the architect of their campaign.

As a major he had been Museveni's intelligence chief and was at the U.S. Army Command and General Staff College when the RPF launched their invasion.

When Maj. Gen. Fred Rwigema, the first commander of the Rwanda Patriotic Army was killed, Kagame returned to replace him. Under Kagame, the RPA fought a light infantry war of ambush, maneuver, and deception. Kagame's objective was to force the Hutu government to accept the RPF as a political force through military means. That meant disrupting the status quo, and the RPA did that quite effectively. President Habyarimana did not look on them as a threat. He considered them an opportunity to strengthen his own power base by overstating their capabilities and their internal support among Rwandan Tutsis. In a classic Machiavellian move, he faked an RPF attack on Kigali, which prompted the French and the Belgians to intervene to protect the capital city. The French shifted roles, openly joining in combat against the RPF and forced a temporary stalemate after the RPF seized Ruhengeri for a day to free its supporters in the prison. Habyarimana then arrested thousands of Tutsis and allowed the ex-FAR to kill hundreds more. Even more darkly, he began the organization and training of the Interahamwe militia as a perverted "Boy Scouts" equivalent of his political machine, the MRND. The French also boosted their training mission and helped expand the ex-FAR to some forty thousand men. At one stage they had Mobutu send some of the Zairian Army to help out. The Zairian military being what it was, the Zairian troops were soon raping and stealing the locals blind. The Rwandan government asked them to leave. Meanwhile, the RPA expanded as well, though not nearly as fast as the ex-FAR. Its core remained the twenty thousand tested troops. Then the RPF finally achieved its goal; an RPA attack took Byumba and forced the Rwandan government to the political table at Arusha, where the accords were signed in August, 1993. As 1994 opened, efforts to implement Arusha sputtered uneasily along. The first U.N. Assistance Mission in Rwanda (UNAMIR) deployed that January, and by April it appeared a new Rwanda was coming.

The new Rwanda did indeed emerge, sparked by the killing of the country's president (probably by Hutu radicals) and transformed by genocide. As UNAMIR circled its wagons under instructions from New York, crippled by the withdrawal of the Belgian and Bangladeshi national contingents, Kagame resumed the campaign against the ex-FAR and its associated militias. The Clinton administration used the

U.S. Mission to the United Nations and the U.S. State Department's African Bureau to try and pressure Kagame into ceasing his military action. When the Bureau could not promise that UNAMIR would stop the slaughter of eight hundred thousand Tutsis and Hutu moderates, Kagame's mission became the salvation of the Tutsis inside ex-FAR lines. The RPF became the new sheriff in Kigali town. Kagame and the RPA had won a total victory. But that victory had come at a horrible cost. And it had come as a complete surprise to the victors. The RPF had set out to win a share of the political power in Kigali. Now they had all the power, and they had to figure out what to do with it.

U.S. Embassy Kigali: Genocide in a Goldfish Bowl

The U.S. embassy was a microversion of the war and the genocide. The news of the president's death at the airport was both stunning and galvanizing. Ambassador Rawson and his team had just achieved a diplomatic victory at Arusha only to have it fall out of the sky over Kigali. The embassy had an emergency plan based on overland evacuation to Burundi. The first stage of the plan was to secure the mission and get everyone safely assembled. The ambassador's residence across the valley was the assembly point for the U.S. community. As fate would have it, the deputy chief of mission's (DCM) residence was adjacent to that of the Rwandan prime minister, a moderate female Hutu. The DCM was at home with a visitor from Washington, a tall American black woman. The two heard the Rwandan Presidential Guard—a central core of the hardliners—arrive next door and begin pounding on the gate. The prime minister initially escaped her attackers by placing a ladder across the DCM's wall and crossing her garden to a neighbor's house. The Presidential Guard followed and caught her. Both she and her Belgian Para bodyguards were slaughtered, the Belgian Paras butchered after they had surrendered their arms in accordance with their orders. In chasing the prime minister down, the Presidential Guard broke into the DCM's compound to see who was there. Finding the American black woman, the soldiers attempted to drag her away. The DCM saved her life, convincing the killers she was American. To mark their visit, the Presidential Guard put several rounds through a refrigerator but left the two women unhurt. They soon joined the Americans gathering across the valley at the ambassador's residence. After forty-eight hours of increasing tensions, Ambassador Rawson led a convoy of vehicles south to Burundi and safety. He did not lose a single American in what rapidly became a horrific situation. And he did so without any direct help from the U.S. government, a singular achievement largely overlooked in the aftermath of the genocide.

American embassies always have a large local staff, and Kigali was no exception. Its local staff reflected the conflicting tensions within the larger population even though it was by definition better educated and better paid. By the time the ambassador and Lt. Col. Tony Marley reopened the embassy in July, fully 60 percent of the staff were dead or missing. One case really stood out, that of the ambassador's driver, Jean Charles. A Tutsi, Jean Charles had married a Hutu woman and produced three boys. Tutsis trace their lineage through the father, so the boys were also classed as Tutsi. The woman was a member of the Hutu extremist organization, CDR. When the killing began Jean Charles' wife made a beeline to the local headquarters. She returned with the soldiers so they could kill her husband and her two older sons. Jean Charles and the boys escaped and survived. The wife ended up in the Goma camps with the youngest son, an infant. Jean Charles has since remarried.

What was happening was the result of months of planning and preparation on the part of Hutu hardliners close to the president. Led by Colonel Bagasora, the Presidential Guard eliminated Tutsi and moderate Hutu leaders who might oppose them. Then they coerced the military to follow suit. They did the same with the Rwandan social structure organized around the communes in the hills. The process started relatively slowly only to build into a sustained killing effort, stopped only by the RPA. UNAMIR Force Commander Maj. Gen. Romeo Dallaire pleaded for troops and assistance to stop the gathering storm. The RPA at one stage proposed a combined operation using the United Nations international forces there to extract their missions, and the units of the ex-FAR not involved in the genocide. That proposal was not acted upon. The killing of the prime minister's ten Belgian bodyguards prompted Brussels to pull out its Paracommandos, along with its diplomatic mission. The French, Spanish, and Italians also staged in and extracted their mission personnel. Bangladesh withdrew its battalion from UNAMIR, and soon Dallaire had little more than a skeleton to work with. Orders from New York soon forced him to order his troops back behind the U.N. barricades. By April 15 a window of opportunity to halt the genocide in its tracks had firmly closed.

So what began as a well-planned but relatively small massacre of moderate Hutus and Tutsis inside the capital city was exported to the countryside. The hardliners pushing what had been labeled Hutu Power swept aside all who hesitated to comply. Many of those who questioned the slaughter were also killed. Inside the city, a six-hundred-man RPA unit fought off seven thousand ex-FAR troops in a full-scale battle pitting them against artillery and armor. Outside, the RPA sent a brigade cross-country in a night forced-march to extract the RPA unit. Carrying only small arms and ammo, the troops marched nearly forty miles to close on the city. International reaction to the slaughter remained relatively mute and decidedly ineffective. The United States moved at glacial speed, first in recognizing genocide was indeed taking place and then on equipping a new version of UNAMIR. By the time the "new" UNAMIR began to close on the country, the genocide and the war were largely over. The French had staked out southwestern Rwanda as a safe zone. Safe being a relative term, the safety of the people inside that zone all too often depended on their being Hutu. When the ambassador returned to open the embassy in Kigali in late July, I had already been in Goma for ten days.

So as I walked around the embassy with Jim Cobb, the scars of the war were evident. At some stage in the fighting, the embassy had taken a heavy mortar hit. The conference room on the second floor had no roof; this is where the ambassador and Tony Marley had climbed in to reopen the doors. The back wall was partially down, scarred by fragments that destroyed the communications antennas on the roof. The offices were semi-pilfered as was the medical unit. The USIS library and conference room were serving as bunkhouses for part of the embassy staff and a handful of personnel from JTF Operation Support Hope. Overall it was a mess.

Nevertheless it was a going concern. Jim and I went upstairs, and I met the young woman acting as the temporary DCM. She had a tour in Burundi and was back in the States in training when the embassy reopened. She volunteered to come out for thirty to sixty days. The ambassador's secretary was also a temporary volunteer out of Washington. The communicator was also temporary as was the administrative officer. The general service officer (GSO) who served as a logistician and administrator for the embassy was the only American there on permanent orders other than the ambassador.

We next went in to see the ambassador. David looked more relaxed than when I had seen him in Goma. He was happy to see me, and we chatted. I had arrived on the tail end of a visit by Assistant Secretary of State George Moose and his deputy. They would be leaving in another couple of days, and David invited me to dinner. Meanwhile, he indicated, I would be living in the old political officer's house with a couple of guys from the JTF. Jim and I took our leave and drove over to the "Lane house," my home for the next fifteen months.

The Lane house was less than half a mile from the embassy. Like almost all homes in Kigali, the place sat on a hillside below the level of the road along the crest. Brick and stone construction, it was a nice little three bedroom with a wonderful wraparound porch on the backside. The civil affairs team from the JTF was still there but was leaving the next day. Jim went on to the old DCM residence now occupied by the ambassador, and I had dinner with the civil affairs types. Our meal was built around T-rations donated by the JTF, standard fare for the coming weeks.

Ambassador David Rawson (at right) and Assistant Secretary of State George Moose (at center) host an embassy press conference during Operation Support Hope. Courtesy U.S. Embassy Kigali. Approved by Ambassador David Rawson.

Initial Meetings: Welcomes and Suspicions

The next day Jim started taking me around to see the city and establish contacts. We began with UNAMIR. Like all U.N. peacekeeping missions, UNAMIR was split down the middle between the U.N. diplomats under the secretary general's Special Representative (SRSG) Shaharyar Khan. The SRSG had a small staff of political advisors much along the lines of a U.S. ambassador and his staff. Ambassador Rawson worked this side of UNAMIR. My targets were on the military side; the force commander, Canadian Maj. Gen. Guy Tousignant, topped my list. Based on my limited experience with Canadian generals—I had met only one other, Major General Dallaire in Goma—it seemed like Canada had a mold for their senior officers. Both Dallaire and Tousignant were Hollywood handsome and Pentagon smart when it came to peacekeeping, products of Canada's longstanding military commitment to U.N. peacekeeping.

Tousignant was personable and professional. He made it clear he not only expected to see me, but he wanted to see me. He ran down where his force was deployed and what he intended to do next. The deployment was not yet complete, and certain sections of the country were not under the UNAMIR baby blanket. He was pleased with the effectiveness of the Ethiopians in the southwest. He credited them with stabilizing that area when the French withdrew after Operation Turquoise ended. He remained concerned, however, as the southeastern area of the country lacked UNAMIR coverage. I told him it was my intention to work closely with UNAMIR. My experience wearing a U.N. beret in Lebanon added to my credibility. Based on that initial meeting, I felt I would have no difficulties getting access to him whenever necessary. I also met the deputy force commander, Ghanaian Brigadier General Anyidoho. He was friendly, but I could sense he was not as forthcoming as the force commander. As long as I had Tousignant's ear, that would not be a problem. In any case, I had enormous collateral to work with; U.S. airlift was still bringing in equipment for the U.N. force. Finally, as we started to leave the headquarters, we stopped in and met the operations officer, Canadian Colonel Arp. Like Tousignant, he was a peacekeeping professional. He openly welcomed the visit; at this point, U.N. forces still operated with restrictions against full-time intelligence staffs. He had a young British captain as his intelligence officer. Information sections filled the need with limited success. The colonel wanted all the help

Here is my UNAMIR identification card.

I might provide. Finished with the headquarters we visited the main Canadian detachment, a communications unit, quartered under the concrete bleachers of Amahoro Stadium along with an Australian medical unit. CANSIG was a standard signal unit but the Canadians had slipped in a small professional intelligence section. The captain who headed the detail provided intelligence directly to the force commander and the operations-intelligence setion. He and I became partners in the coming weeks.

Part of the intelligence problem Tousignant faced went beyond the United Nations's systemic aversion to incorporating active intelligence sections in peacekeeping. As we had done in Observer Group Lebanon for the U.N. Interim Force in Lebanon, UNAMIR had its own observer organization. They were supposed to be the scouts for the force commander and his armed contingents. Yet they were semi-independent in their operations out in the country. All too often the information they gathered was filtered through their own intermediate headquarters and was either not passed on or was watered down. Consequently, Tousignant encouraged the contingents, especially the CANSIG's intelligence staff, to do their own snooping. I would become part of that effort and in turn benefited from it.

That afternoon I met my other partners at the embassy. Maj. Frank Rusagara stopped by to see Jim, and we were introduced. Major Frank, as he was called in the RPA, was the RPA liaison to the diplomatic community and also served as an executive assistant to Maj. Gen. Paul Kagame. Unlike the Zairian military or even the ex-FAR, the RPA was light on rank. Kagame was the only general in its ranks. There was a handful of colonels in key positions at the staff level. The chiefs of staff of the army and the gendarmerie were colonels. The rest of the colonels in the forty-thousand-man RPA commanded brigades in the field.[1] Lieutenant colonels held deputy positions or in some cases national-level positions with special status. One was the G2 (senior intelligence officer) of the RPA. Majors commanded battalions or held special positions like Frank Rusagara, which tagged him as an important figure within the RPA structure.

Frank was one of the Ugandan refugees. He spoke British English and was quite polished. He had what I came to consider an RPA trait: he would listen to what you had to say and then offer a carefully considered response. He was of course quite interested when he heard I had spent several weeks in Goma. We asked him to set up appointments for me to see the RPA leadership over the next couple of days. Jim Cobb was due to return to Cameroon, where he had a full plate of duties. Frank left and called us soon afterward. He invited us over to meet the army and gendarmerie chiefs of staff. This was a far cry from my initial experiences with the Zairian Ministry of Defense.

Army headquarters was just down the street from the embassy, and we were there in minutes. Frank met us at the gate and directed us to a parking spot. Our first host was Col. Sam Kaka, chief of staff of the army. A short and slightly pudgy colonel, Kaka was another of the Ugandans. Under Kagame's guidance, Kaka was the day-to-day boss for the army. Jim took the lead as the defense attaché in this first meeting. At this time I was only a ninety-day temporary like most of the embassy staff. He explained our role and Kaka listened. Kaka then offered that he hoped we would be able to establish a strong relationship. Up front, he said he wanted U.S. assistance in training his army. From there we stepped up one flight of stairs and into the office of the gendarmerie chief of staff. Colonel Nyamwasa had also come from Uganda. In contrast to Rusagara and Kaka, he was almost openly hostile. He listened to Jim's pitch and said we would meet again. I felt at the time he was suspicious of us as foreigners, and I doubted he would change.

Frustrated Diplomats: Dinner at the Ambassador's

That evening I went over to the ambassador's house, the former DCM residence. David, I found, had a relaxed entertainment style, much more refreshing than my associates over in Kinshasa. Of course, if George Moose had been visiting Kinshasa, I would not have been included at dinner. As we entered, David introduced me to his visitors. Moose, a tall stately black American, directed the African Bureau in the Department of State. He was gracious, and thanked me for the work in Goma. As director he was David's boss. The other visitor was his deputy for Central Africa, a manager for David but not a "rater." Given that I was newly arrived, I listened through most of the dinner and offered very little.

It was clear from the discussions that our guests were not happy with the course of events in Rwanda. In itself that was hardly surprising; everyone at the dinner table had invested months in the Arusha accords, only to see them fall along with the president's airplane. But it was equally clear that Ambassador Rawson was more pragmatic in accepting the tragedy and then facing the resultant consequences. David openly accepted the RPF as the new government and was determined to work with it. At the same time, he emphasized the effects of the genocide on U.S. relations with the new government. One of the qualities I most admired about my new ambassador was his candor. David knew he was in for a difficult time with the RPF, and he hung in there. I sensed our Washington visitors were not so willing to accept the sea change effect genocide had on the Rwandan scene. Too much of what they had to say reminisced on the peaceful Rwanda of the past. At the same time, the deputy seemed to believe the Rwandans should put the genocide behind them, not something the Rwandans could do. Overall I sensed they had personalized the war and genocide by laying the blame at the feet of Paul Kagame. The argument ran that the tragedy of Rwanda was caused by the RPF's invasion, and as its leader, Kagame was the main culprit. And we were sitting in the very house that the prime minister had attemped to run to before she and her bodyguards were slain by members of her own government's Presidential Guard. The refrigerator in the kitchen still had its bullet holes as a reminder of the killers' visit that evening.

Initial Travel and Initial Contacts

Soon Jim Cobb was gone, headed back to Cameroon. I stayed very busy just getting to know the city. I also worked my way further into the UNAMIR staff. I made a daily run over to pick up the UNAMIR situation report, and I always stopped in to chat with the ops and intel guys. I also made a habit of dropping in on the force commander's personal staff. Tousignant was candid in his chats with me, and I offered similar fare in return.

But I wanted to get out and see the rest of the country. So one morning, the DCM, a visitor from State, and I piled into an embassy Land Cruiser and headed east. UNAMIR had yet to deploy into this area, but it had been relatively stable in recent weeks. We went directly east to just north of Kibungo and then turned north toward Uganda. Our purpose was not just to get out of Kigali; we were looking for returning Ugandan exiles reportedly headed our way. Roughly a million Rwandans had been in exile, most in Uganda, and now many were coming back to their homelands. They were bringing hundreds of thousands of Tutsi cattle with them.

As we left Kigali, we left the central highlands and entered the rolling plains that flow all the way through Tanzania and Kenya. A series of small lakes marked the north side of the road along with intermittent streams and rivers; this was cattle country. But along the northeastern border of Rwanda lies Akagera National Park. This had once been a prime game reserve with tours and limited hunts for those with the cash. A central lodge at Gabiro had offered a game-filled menu for its guests and visitors. The remnants of the lodge were there, occupied by a platoon of Rwandan Patriotic Army troops. We passed through a number of RPA checkpoints as we closed on the border with Uganda. Evidence of Ugandan emigration was all around us: Tutsi cattle clustered along the rolling hills watched by their herders and the occasional antelope. Lorries loaded with household goods—the African version of North American Van lines—with their owners perched on top hurtled south past us to the "promised land."

Less than five miles from the border as we cleared a rise, I saw the riders of one of those lorries splayed across the road in front of our Toyota. I stood on the brakes and the Land Cruiser fishtailed from seventy miles per hour to a dead stop. One of the accident victims sat up in the road less than ten feet from the truck's front bumper. He must have had a very strong heart; mine was racing, and I was adrenaline saturated as I stepped from the truck. There were a couple more bodies on the road, but most of the casualties were in the ditch along with the flipped lorry. It looked as if the right front tire of the truck had blown, allowing the rim to dig in along the shoulder and flip the vehicle. As many as fifteen passengers had been on that truck; the accident had just happened, because the wheels of the overturned lorry were still spinning. The DCM and I moved among them in an informal triage as our visitor dug the first aid kit out.

Remarkably none were dead, at least not yet. Several had head injuries, and I suspected other internal injuries as well. They were all Ugandan exiles, and they spoke decent English. We loaded five of the worst cases into the Land Cruiser and sped south four miles back to the last RPA checkpoint. I topped out at just shy of one hundred miles per hour and kept it up as we closed on the checkpoint. We came to another tire-smoking stop in front of the barricade, and I waved the alerted soldiers over. The sergeant in charge called on his Motorola, and soon an RPA major arrived. The local sector commander, he looked at our passengers and sent a vehicle to gather the rest. We moved off quickly to a small clinic, run by Medicins Sans Frontiers (MSF). The doctors there could only offer immediate first aid. Again, we loaded the victims, and lead by the RPA major, took them to a hospital at Gabiro.

The hospital was in as bad a shape as many of the victims. I felt guilty leaving them, but there was no alternative. UNAMIR could have helped, but its hospital was two hours away. I would later learn half of them died. But that meant luck and our help had saved half, not bad results after a seventy-miles-per-hour truck crash when most of the victims had been riding on top. As fate would have it, one of those saved was the first cousin of the new Rwandan health minister. He and I would do our best to improve the care available in Rwanda's more remote hospitals over the next year.

Never Written but Widely Quoted: The Gersony Report

In late September, we got another surprise. A USAID-financed contractor working for the U.N. High Commission for Refugees (UNHCR) named Robert Gersony informed the UNHCR High Commissioner he had a "report" documenting that the Rwandan Patriotic Front and Army had systematically and deliberately slaughtered as many as fifty thousand civilians inside Rwanda between April and August. Then he made the rounds of the State Department, the foreign missions, and anyone else who would listen to the "facts" in his report. Gersony stated that credible witnesses outside in the camps and inside Rwanda claimed the killings had taken place and were still occurring. Both the United States and the United Nations had just recognized the new government in Rwanda; there was hardly any choice. But the timing raised fears—immediately felt in the African Bureau still recovering from the damage caused by its statements about the genocide—that great embarrassment was to follow. Ambassador Rawson met with Gersony and then briefed me on the meeting. David told me Gersony had a track record of spectacular revelations that sometimes panned out and sometimes did not. Gersony in pitching his report never produced a thing; he offered a list of atrocities that supposedly were documented by the information gathered in the camps and inside Rwanda.[2]

Of course, he briefed the SRSG and the force commander at UN-AMIR. Tousignant had had troops on the ground in most of the areas for more than two months at this stage, months Gersony claimed were part of the killing spree by the RPF. Ten to fifteen thousand killings a month inside a U.N.-monitored area as small as Rwanda is a startling figure. The southeast district remained manned at minimum levels, but the Canadians and the U.N. military observers were out there. They reported no unusual events. At Ambassador Rawson's request, I linked up with the Canadian Signals (CANSIGS) intelligence section. We made a number of trips out to the places where Gersony claimed recent killings had occurred.

One of those trips introduced me to the genocide. We had gone out in two vehicles, one from CANSIGS and one UNMO team picked up in Kibungo. Our objective was a mission school at ZaZa back in among the lakes southeast of the city. Only about twenty kilometers from Kibungo, the roads were excellent, and we soon arrived at a village with a large open-sided church with a circular roof. The village surrounded the church on three sides, and we stopped to shake the dirt off before continuing. Just five hundred meters north of the church was a mission school where the ambassador's cook, a Hutu woman, had learned her trade. From a distance the school was still impressive: a long single-story brick structure, it formed a U almost one hundred yards at its base and fifty yards along each side. This was the classroom and staff building. There was a dormitory nearby for the students.

Once closer we could see the school had been pillaged. The windows were gone, and sections of the building had collapsed due to fires. The various classrooms had also been ransacked; what could be carried off had been. The rest was destroyed and strewn helter-skelter around the facilities. But on looking closer, we started finding rooms used as killing areas. The first was a shower and toilet facility. Originally white-tiled, it had been set alight and partially burned. The heat had done strange things to the white tiles. All pockmarked, bullet and shrapnel strikes were apparent. But the heat had turned the tiles to a smoky brown and glazed the blood sprays on them into a permanent dark record of the killings. We examined them: we could see where heads had exploded from the bullets. Squatting, we looked for more signs on the floor; bone fragments littered the area. The larger portions of the skeletons had most likely been removed after they were burned clean. We knew there was a communal grave nearby estimated to have several hundred corpses interred in it. Fingers and feet bones were smaller and fell apart more easily. That is what we were finding.

Elsewhere in the compound we found much the same. A room would have been used for killing and then set alight to destroy the corpses. One was especially unnerving: it was the chapel for the school. The pulpit still stood, and I found a broken bronze crucifix, which I kept. Elsewhere in the chapel were the same blood spatters. But there were a series of separate fires, each with a blend of charred wood and blackened human bones. As we worked our way through the facility, we found nothing else until we were outside walking back along the exterior. I noticed a well and went over to check it out. There I found the nude corpse of a woman with her throat cut and her breasts partially sliced off. She had been dead for some time, bleached almost white in the shallow well and pickled at the same time. It was an old massacre site, but you had to wonder about the villagers as we passed through them on the way back. How many had been involved? And how many were staring at us like we were aliens? I guess to them we were. I certainly felt like I had entered an unknown world.

So in checking the Gersony report, we found old massacre sites but nothing new. We briefed the force commander on each of these trips; he made the atrocity investigation a priority for all UNAMIR contingents, especially the U.N. military observers. No one uncovered evidence that the RPF as the new government had ordered the systematic slaughter of civilians in the countryside. The operative word in this hoopla was systematic. All of us, including senior leaders inside the RPF, believed killings had occurred during the war and in the aftermath of the genocide. This may seem unfeeling, but when you weigh fifty thousand against eight hundred thousand, the balance remains firmly tilted toward the latter. Even if fifty thousand had been killed, one had to consider what was happening inside the country at that time.[3] Of course, the African Bureau did an immediate knee-jerk and ordered Moose's deputy back to Kigali to take Kagame to task over the Gersony report. By now I was up to speed on events in Rwanda, and I cautioned the deputy against rushing to judgments.

"Consider what has happened in this country. The RPF is not blameless. Certainly killings have occurred. Kagame and the others will tell you that. But I have been out with UNAMIR looking at these sites and we have found nothing. UNAMIR is a five-thousand-man force. Tousignant is not asleep at the wheel and neither are his troops. They have reported nothing to suggest the government is directing these killings—if those killings are in fact occurring. I believe they are, but at lesser numbers than suggested by Gersony. I do not believe they are organized above individual-unit levels and most are probably individual acts of revenge. Before you judge the RPA too harshly, consider this: I would not want to command an American infantry unit, come home to stabilize its own town after the neighbors had killed my soldiers' families. It would be grim. Very grim."

I do not believe my words had much effect on the deputy's session with Paul Kagame. The U.S. government in essence demarched the vice president over a report no one was sure of. It was rather like punishing someone for something they might have done. Wisdom finally prevailed at higher levels. The UNHCR, UNAMIR, and the United States turned their collective backs on the Gersony "report" as a non-issue. Critics abounded at the time, and they still do regarding that decision. It could have been worse, much worse in derailing our efforts in Kigali. Still it added more weight to the emotional baggage at the State Department's African Bureau. "Gersony was right" became the emotional equivalent of "the RPF caused the genocide by starting the war."

By addressing our Washington visitor directly on the matter, I suspected I had already been tagged an "RPA sympathizer" within the halls of Foggy Bottom. Maybe I was; when you wade through genocide sites, it does give you a different perspective from those more concerned with the legal definition of the word. Ambassador Rawson had established a firm rule: no visitors came to Rwanda without paying a visit to a genocide site. His reasoning was clear: you could not understand post-genocide Rwanda without getting a glimpse of the savagery that had taken place. He and the DCM had made sure George Moose and his deputy made the hour trip to Ntarama southwest of Kigali. I remember my first visit there, sometime just after the Gersony uproar, like it was yesterday.

Ntarama Church

Ntarama was just another of the thousand hillside communes in Rwanda, that is before the genocide. It was in an area where the killing was slow to start, so slow the organizers of the genocide bussed in Interahamwe militia to encourage the locals. Like most communes it had a local church serviced by the Rwandan clergy. There were two main churches in Rwanda. The strongest was the Catholic Church. The second was the Episcopalian Church. While there were a few foreign clergymen in both orders, the majority of the clergy were native Rwandans, mainly Hutu. The reason for that ethnic association lay in pre-1960s Rwanda when the church was one of the few avenues of advancement open to Hutu males. After the Hutu "revolution" some Tutsis did take up the cloth, but the Hutus remained dominant. In the post-1960 massacres and even as late as the post-invasion atrocities, the churches had offered sanctuary to those threatened with death.

Yet the Hutu Power movement spawned by the government had made great inroads into the clergy, undermining its foundation as a symbol of mercy. The genocide gathered momentum by threatening all who might choose to stand aside from the killing. The clergy were not exempted from that coercion. Some held out against it and died. Others gave in and cooperated. Some took the lead in organizing the killing among their flocks. The vast majority of those threatened saw the churches as places for sanctuary. As the genocide gathered in intensity, its victims gathered at the churches. The result was Rwanda's churches became *abattoirs.*

Ntarama was just one example. Entire families of Tutsis had fled to the tiny chapel. It was a simple place and a small place to die. Maybe twenty-five feet by fifty feet, it had a small, elevated pulpit and low benches for its worshipers. In normal times, you might expect maybe a hundred worshipers to gather there in comfort. Far more crammed in there to escape their killers in the madness of 1994. Perhaps one of the cruelest jokes played upon them was they often paid their way to get inside. Bribes and offers of sex got them past their oppressors to churches all over Rwanda including the chapel at Ntarama. In more than a few cases, it was the clergy who collected their offerings and granted them sanctuary. Ntarama was one of those cases. But the beaters had driven far too many of their victims to the tiny chapel. Women, children, and the elderly were passed inside, perhaps as many as four hundred. The remaining men gathered outside the church to await events. Numbers are unclear, but they certainly exceeded a thousand.

As I said before, this was an area where many of the locals were reluctant to slaughter their neighbors. So as the pocket of Tutsis clustered in and around the Ntarama church grew larger, those who were willing to kill them called for help. Those locals who refused to murder soon joined the would-be victims inside the pocket. Soldiers and Interahamwe arrived via bus to begin the business of killing. The soldiers attacked the church with rocket-propelled grenades, blowing holes in its walls. They followed up with grenades and automatic weapons, killing most of those in the church very quickly. Interahamwe and their recruits moved in with machetes to finish the rest. In their frenzy, they chopped up the already dead with those still alive. The victims in the church were fortunate to die so quickly.

The men and the handful of women still outside the church were not so lucky. Herded by guns and machetes, the men were tied two to three to a tree all over the hillside. Bound by their hands, they were hamstrung to prevent their escape should they even manage to free themselves. The women were gang-raped repeatedly, and they too were often hamstrung. Over the next several days, the men were slowly hacked apart. Once they died, they were beheaded and their corpses left tied to the trees. The women were similarly killed if the savagery of their repeated rapes did not kill them first. Then they too were beheaded. Once the several days of killing stopped, the killers left the bodies where they were to mark the event.

You could smell the dead from a kilometer away, and the ever-present crows signaled from even farther. It was now more than sixty days since the killings, and the carrion eaters had gotten to those left tied to the trees. The crows in Rwanda were indeed quite fat that year. Partially clothed and partially picked clean skeletons slumped in clusters around the trees. The forest was fairly dense; the trees stood less than ten feet apart. So as you walked toward the church, you walked through a low forest of trees, each with the remains of two or three victims jumbled together at its base. Their blood, leaving the soil sickeningly pungent, darkened your path. The coppery smell left a twang of taste in your mouth. You might get rid of the taste; you would never get rid of its memory. I was reminded of the smell of blood bait used for catching catfish in my youth. I would smell that hill for months after leaving Rwanda.

So after a gauntlet of horrors, one arrived at the small church. The unwise might assume nothing could be worse than that grove of trees. The church soon rendered such assumptions foolish. A low-slung rectangle of a building, the chapel had three windows on either side, all blown out. There were additional holes from rocket-propelled grenades in both ends of the building. A small door stood open to beckon the unwary. It was clear that day, and the bright sunshine closed my pupils against its glare. As I started to look in through the door, it was almost like sticking your head into dark water. If the blood-soaked ground had warned you not to go any farther, the smell from the church threatened your sanity with its intensity. Some heeded that warning. I did not. Almost gagging, I stuck my head into the pool of darkness at the door and waited for my eyes to adjust.

Black turned softly into gray light offered through the windows. And there they were. Some several hundred dead packed so tightly along those narrow benches that their corpses supported one another. Others lay in rows between the benches and along the walls, all pockmarked from bullets and shrapnel. Separated heads lay everywhere. Their size gave clue to their ages. Many—all too many—were the small skulls of children. Unlike the skeletons by the trees, these corpses were partially mummified, desiccated by Rwanda's altitude five thousand feet above sea level and sheltered by the sun. Flies hummed as they feasted. I felt like my ears would explode from their buzzing. My sense of smell seemed to shut down after the initial assault of rotted meat. Still I was sickened physically and emotionally. I pulled my head back from inside the pool of darkness and looked directly into the sun. I wanted its blaze to burn the vision of those church pews from my soul. Hell does not go away that easily. I wish I could say that I prayed for the dead. I did not. I prayed their killers would suffer similar fates.

You could leave Ntarama, but it never left you. Part of it was physical; the very smell soaked into our shoes and saturated our clothes. I stank of Ntarama church. The most lasting effects were mental. I cannot tell you the day, nor can I tell you who was with me. But I remember rolling the figures of the Gersony report over in my head, thinking about the alleged fifty thousand dead as I returned to Kigali. My initial mental response was "so what?" But as I brooded on Ntarama, the fifty thousand dead again came to mind, and my response became, "Not enough."

An Embassy That Worked; An Ambassador Who Led

The pace in Kigali was just as demanding as the early days in Goma. We worked seven days a week, often sixteen hours a day just to keep up with the events in Rwanda and demands from Washington. Our living conditions were austere and would remain that way for months to come. It still rained every day in the embassy conference room, and you had to be careful around electrical equipment. Entertainment was non-existent; the American club remained closed, although State had given us money to get it started again. Some folks still lived in the "barracks" of the USIS library. David had the old DCM house, and I had the Lane house. We lived off a diet of T-rations and whatever could be scrounged in Kigali.

The city was at once a ghost town and a military camp. Nights were eerily dark in a city with no streetlights. RPA patrols circulated in the blackness, and you had to be careful when forced to move at night. The troops were disciplined, but they were well armed and equally willing to shoot. The reopening of a Pakistani restaurant was a major event towards the end of September. As it turned out, the family had two daughters who were graduates of Texas A&M. Swapping Aggie jokes over croissants or curry was a welcome break. It was a small community, and we seemed to live in each other's pockets.

Ambassador Rawson was the one who made it work. Our country team meetings were just that: team meetings. David was the senior reporting officer, but he was tied up with the community political scene. That was quite a show in itself. The Belgians and the Germans soon reopened their missions, ultimately joined by the French. The U.N. community included every field agency plus UNAMIR. NGOs were everywhere, and they multiplied daily. Then there was the new government to work with, a challenge that left us drained at times.

David and I arrived at a workable division of labor. To the new government, he remained a symbol of Arusha and U.S. hesitancy in responding to the genocide. But he could work through the office of the new president, a Hutu. As a military officer, I was welcomed by the RPA, and I focused on them. David and I merged efforts through the office of Vice President and Defense Minister Kagame. Our high road–low road approach worked well, and we did the same with UNAMIR. He focused on the SRSG and U.N. policy while I concentrated on the force commander and the military. If that had been all we had to do, it would have been enough to keep us busy.

But we had other duties as well. The embassy was still a mess. The temporary DCM left around the end of September, and I became acting DCM. We still had temporary communications, administration, and secretarial staffs plus a support officer who was struggling. Our security officer was nominally covered out of Burundi, but that did little for us in Kigali. We had a series of security visits from Nairobi, Uganda, and Burundi to point out problems already apparent to us all. We had to solve them.

Meanwhile we were getting larger as USAID reopened, joined by the regional Disaster Assistance Response Team (DART) from Entebbe, led by Kate Farnsworth. She was an invaluable addition to our eyes and ears. She brought with her a team of experienced disaster workers. On the USAID side, the mission was struggling to resume operations, challenged by staffing and physical damage to the mission itself.

So between playing DCM and serving as the main reporting officer, I stayed busy. But in early October I got a real break. The DIA's main analyst on the Rwanda crisis, Maj. Rick Orth, came out to help for almost six weeks. Rick was an armor officer who had commanded a company of the 1st Infantry Division in the Gulf War. He understood war and its fallout, plus he was a go-getter when it came to Rwanda. Our first evening together he was on automatic, rapidly firing questions at me as we prepared our T-ration dinner. Finally I said, "Rick, let's eat dinner. You are not going to solve Rwanda's problems this evening." It pulled him up a bit short, but weeks later he thanked me for saying it. He said it kept him from burning out. Even so I never had to encourage Rick to get out and about.

Goma Getaways

With Rick on board, I was ready to revisit Goma. My replacement in Kinshasa had not been out there as yet, and we needed to see what was happening. I was nominally still on the roles of the embassy in Kinshasa, so I did not bother asking for clearance. I knew if I asked, the leadership in the Kinshasa embassy would block the trip. Better to beg forgiveness than ask permission goes the old saying. Kate Crawford was still there as the DART representative and although she focused on humanitarian relief, her comments on security issues deserved follow-up. So one morning just after Rick's arrival, we headed west. For Rick it was a first look at what he had been studying back in Washington for more than a year. We crossed the border without real problems, and Rick got his first look at the Zairian military.

We planned additional trips, so this first one was more of an introductory tour. I made a stop at Saleem's and said hello before we headed out toward Sake through the ex-FAR. Much had changed and much had not. The ex-FAR was still there, but their encampment had become more organized. The green buses were no longer parked hither and yon. They were running the roads ferrying passengers, Rwandan and Zairian alike. Of particular interest to us, most of the heavy weapons had disappeared; their whereabouts remained in question for several months. We wheeled through the area and then reversed course for the airport and the northern camps.

It seemed strange to see the airport so empty, but we stopped for a moment. I pointed out where things had been during Operation Support Hope, and Rick as always fired questions. We then went north to Kibumba. I had already seen the shift toward permanence. To Rick it was all new, and his silence told me he was absorbing it. We passed through Kibumba and went on to Katale. I pointed out the drop zone for the ill-fated airdrop as we passed it. Katale like Kibumba was becoming a permanent community built of UNHCR plastic. Once north of Katale, we again reversed and headed back to the border and Kigali. We closed on its outskirts as the sun died. Our day trip had taken the full ten hours of sunlight available to us in mid-October.

From that initial trip in October until December, I would cross into Goma or Bukavu to the south at least once every two weeks, often once a week. The idea was to monitor the situation, and that meant getting out and looking around just as I had done in Lebanon and in Kinshasa. We also stopped in and chatted with the UNAMIR elements in the area.

Two trips to Goma were of special note. On one, David asked me to look up two of his main contacts in Goma, a pair of Tutsi brothers who had been raised by American missionaries and educated in the States. One was tied into the political network that bridged the Goma-Gisenyi divide. We had a beer with him, and he showed us his front-lawn parking lot. As the former government officials had arrived in their upscale cars, they had dumped them inside his compound rather than risk having them stolen by the Zairian military. It was like a bizarre used car lot; he had the cars but could not sell them, legally that is. Over the next few weeks their numbers decreased, perhaps reclaimed by their owners or even less-righteous folks.

His brother was even more a character; he owned a somewhat shabby second-tier hotel in Goma. His nickname was "Tex," and he wore a Stetson to commemorate his formative days in Houston. Now he was tied into the commercial side of life in Goma. He had some interesting things to say about arms smuggling and training in the camps. Both of the brothers were regarded with equal suspicion by both sides of the Rwandan ethnic equation. As Tutsis, the Hutu used them cautiously as intermediaries in contacting the RPF. The RPF saw them as opportunists and crooks and approached them with equal caution. That made them excellent sources of information, if that information was carefully weighed.

Another visit involved an anachronism dating back to WWII. The security of the camps and the local areas remained an issue—as it would until finally resolved in 1996. I had made my stance on the camps crystal clear. The camps were festering boils that would have to be lanced. It would be painful, but the pain would have to be accepted. As for the Zairian military, I had taken an equally clear stance: the Zairian military was part of the problem and could not therefore be part of the solution. I noted with dismay that my replacement in Kinshasa seemed to be rehabilitating the Zairian military on paper; unlike me, she had gotten her accreditation from the Ministry of Defense. She swallowed Zaire's stance on the camps hook, line, and sinker. According to the Zairian government, the ex-FAR had been completely disarmed, there were no militias in the camps, and absolutely no military training was taking place. Any and all security problems were due to the number of refugees and the chaos caused by them. Of course the NGO and international communities disputed such claims; security conditions were growing steadily worse. They wanted the United Nations and its various bodies to do something. Meanwhile Madame Ogata, a Japanese national, remained head of the UNHCR. In that role she pressured her countrymen to assist her in addressing security problems in Goma.

Banzai Africa Korps!

They did. In the first out-of-area deployment since World War II, the Japanese Defense Forces deployed a company to Goma. Their doubtful mission to increase security in the area was made even more dubious by the restrictions placed on them by Tokyo. The company deployed to Goma with but two light machine guns mounted on two lightly armored personnel carriers. The troops were not authorized to carry their individual weapons. The Japanese attaché from Nairobi stopped at the U.S. embassy in Kigali and asked me to go to Goma to brief the Japanese commander. Off to Goma I went.

The Japanese military mission in Goma was without a doubt the most bizarre I had ever witnessed. They had occupied the site used by the JTF and simply camped out. That's really all they could do. The two armored personnel carriers were parked side by side; the machine guns were stored inside. The unarmed troops stayed inside the doubtful security of their barbed wire, the only foreign military presence in Goma. I met the commander and his staff, and we sat down to talk. I briefed them on the situation as it had evolved since July. I paid particular attention to the dangers posed by the Zairian military. Their eyes got increasingly bigger as I talked. Finally the commander stopped me.

"Colonel, you must realize everything you have said is exactly opposite from what the French told us. They said we should make immediate contact with the Zairian military leadership. That we could trust them." I was not surprised; the Japanese attaché in Nairobi had intimated the French had been less than honest in briefing the force before it deployed.

"Colonel, look around you here. You have seen the Zairian army here at the airport. Do they inspire trust?"

He shook his head negatively, and I continued, "No? Well, Colonel, those are the best Zairian troops in this area. The others are worse." It did no good to be kind, and I did not sugarcoat my thoughts.

"Colonel, forgive my honesty, but I must tell you you can do nothing there except risk your men. If the Zairians figure out how poorly you are armed, you will have problems. You should get your men out of here as soon as possible." He did. They left in less than sixty days.

Good NCOs Are Like Gold

Toward the end of October, I got an unexpected phone call at the embassy. "Hey, sir, this is Chief Dunham. I am coming out as your OpsCo next week and I wanted to confirm what I should bring," the voice on the line said. It was a complete surprise but a welcome one. Rick Orth would have to go back soon enough, and I would again be a one-man show. I did not know Dunham from Adam when he called me, but I liked his enthusiasm. Less than a week later, Rick and I met Chief Michael "Mickey" Dunham at the airport. He was a bull of a man, about five feet, eleven inches with a twenty-two-inch neck and equally proud waistline. Redheaded but balding, Mickey looked like an Irish poster child. It did not take me long to figure out I had gotten truly lucky again. I had another self-starting, smart non-commissioned officer.

Mickey started getting us organized on a more normal basis. He was a navy intelligence–special operations type. As fate would have it, he had served in the DAO in Tel Aviv with Don Zedler after Don had left UNTSO. Don had been one of the U.N. military observers in the car that had gotten separated from Col. Rich Higgins. Don had also been my chief instructor in the attaché course. Mickey was not a headquarters sailor. He was ill suited to the flagpole, and he knew it. He liked being a chief, but he wanted no further promotions to pull him back from the line. And I understood that. Since his rotation from Israel back to DIA headquarters, he had already served a volunteer temporary tour in the Middle East. When he heard of the new mission in Rwanda, he volunteered for it. I liked him right away. So did Ambassador Rawson, and that really meant a great deal in internal embassy relations. Mickey was there as an operations coordinator, but like me he also got a full plate of additional duties. With his background in special operations and intelligence, I dubbed him the embassy security guru until someone permanent came on board. David, after talking to him about the mission, asked him to take on getting the club up and running.

Mortar Rounds and the U.S. Air Mobility Command

As the world's premier airlift coordinator, Air Mobility Command sometimes has a tendency to do what it pleases how it pleases, an attitude that sometimes sifts all the way down to some of the crews. In Zaire, I had learned very quickly from Stan to watch AMC missions carefully lest we have problems. AMC published the air clearance guide on what was required country by country for landing rights, fees, customs, and other regulations. Defense Attaché Offices were the primary source for this information, and that was the case in Zaire. Unfortunately many of the crews failed to read the guide, and if they did they often ignored what it said. In Zaire, the airport, as was the case in many Third World countries, was considered a strategic installation by the government. That meant photography was forbidden, and the guide said so in clear English. But in my year there, I had more than one crew pop out cameras like tourists, a move that set off alarms in the airport security people. In one case, I had a C141 come rolling up with the navigator standing up in his hatch on top of the fuselage merrily snapping away. He was almost arrested, and his camera was seized. We let him stew on it and then bribed the security official to return the camera.

You could do that sort of thing in Zaire and get away with it. It did not work in Rwanda. The airport security apparatus was professional, and they watched what foreign aircrews did on the tarmac. That was especially true on U.N.-related airlift, even those involving U.S. Air Force aircraft. We were still hauling in equipment and, in some cases, troops for UNAMIR. We had an edge since the JTF had helped train the Rwandans to run the place, and that made them favorable towards us. I wanted to keep it that way. Mickey got us airport passes so we could drive in through the back gate at will. We knew the security folks, and they knew us. We soon had the landing clearance process streamlined for efficiency.

That fall the United States was still involved in Somalia in a big way. U.S. airlift continued to move supplies including ammunition for the U.N. forces still on the ground there. U.S. airlift was doing the same thing for UNAMIR. When a U.S. mission supporting UNAMIR came in, UNAMIR coordinated the missions and we backstopped them. To be allowed to land, the aircraft commander had to declare in advance exactly what was on the aircraft before the Rwandans would grant a clearance. Given the poor relations between the government and UNAMIR after the genocide, the Rwandans watched these missions like hawks. Just after Rick arrived, a U.S. C141 landed at Kigali with a load of equipment for UNAMIR. The manifest declared no weapons or ammunition were on board. Yet when the tail doors swung open, there were two or three pallets of mortar ammunition destined for Somalia. AMC had decided to save gas and have a UNISOM C130 meet the C141 in Kigali to transfer the ammunition. They had told no one other than UNISOM and the C141 crew.

In response, the Rwandans seized the ammunition and then demanded an explanation. I put Rick on it, and he came through like a champ. He unraveled what had happened at UNAMIR and at AMC. I fielded questions from Washington. In one case, I turned off an irate action officer in the Pentagon who demanded I "go tell Kagame he had no business seizing the ammunition." I told him if Kagame had shipped ammunition for Burundi through Washington National without telling us we would probably do more than just seize the ammo. That made him think and tempers soon cooled. But to make a point, the government held the ammunition for another four weeks before we could get it on its way to Somalia.

Building Relations with the Boys

During this same period we had broadened our contacts with the RPA. Maj. Frank Rusagara introduced me to Lt. Col. Karake Karenzi, the intelligence officer or G2 of the RPA. Karenzi, a medium-build Tutsi, was another of the Ugandans. He was a true survivor: when the war broke out, Karenzi was the RPF liaison officer to UNAMIR. His name was near the top of the kill list for the Presidential Guard. He managed to link up with the RPA battalion in the city and then slipped out to escape. Karenzi and I built our relationship over the coming year. He did not give away much at first, remaining closemouthed and cautious. Six months later we were swapping jokes along with the information we shared. The next year, I would attend his wedding. At the personal direction of Paul Kagame, Karenzi issued us weapons permits. He often coordinated travel for us with the border posts. On one trip back from Goma, the RPA officer at the border had tried to search our vehicle, but I backed him down. I also warned him I would be seeing Karenzi when I got back to Kigali. That really made him blink, and I did mention the incident to Karenzi when I saw him. The next time I passed through the border, the officer in question started in again until I handed him a signed memo from Karenzi warning all improper behavior toward diplomats would be "dealt with ruthlessly." In the Rwandan context, that was not a warning to be taken lightly. From that point on the officer went out of his way to keep me happy.

The G3 or operations officer of the RPA became another key contact, often a partner, over the next fifteen months. Col. Charles Muheri had been born in eastern Rwanda but fled with his mother when his father was killed in the 1960 massacres. He became a lawyer and then a soldier in Museveni's campaign against Obote. Charles was one of the original eighty guerrillas who took to the Ugandan bush with Museveni. I met with him that fall once it became clear we would in fact be able to establish a demining operation with the Rwandan military.[4]

I also met and soon became friends with the Rwandan minister of health, Dr. Col. Joseph Karamera. Dr. Joe was one of the most personable of the RPA inner circle. Tall and polished, Joe had a sense of humor that extended to himself as well as others. His family members were in the truck crash I had stumbled across in Akagera. We used that chance contact to establish our relationship. Once Bill McCoy got clearance to start shipping excess equipment out of Europe, Joe and I took all of it we could get our hands on. Joe served another role as well. He became the "unofficial" official messenger for the RPF. When the inner circle—referred to as the Council of Colonels—had a message for the U.S. government they did not want to make official, Joe would call me and ask me to come over and chat.[5]

Then of course there was Vice President and Defense Minister Maj. Gen. Paul Kagame. Undoubtedly one of the thinnest men I have ever met, Paul Kagame could cross his legs and keep both feet flat on the floor. He is a soft-spoken but thoughtful man. And he has an iron will well tempered by the ruthlessness necessary to fight and win a war of rebellion. We met for the first time in his office; I was there with Ambassador Rawson to discuss a coming visit. Kagame was well dressed in a suit for this meeting. Often when I saw him afterward, he would be in his fatigues—the "dress" uniform of the RPA. When Mickey arrived, he brought in a SigSauer 228 9MM as his personal weapon. The airport security team seized the pistol but told us to contact the Ministry of Defense. When we went over to see about weapons permits, our host was General Kagame. He directed his staff assistant to make sure we got our permits forthwith. Kagame always dealt with me in a straightforward way. I told him early in our relationship I was there to help convey his concerns to my superiors in Washington. I promised to do so even if I did not agree with those concerns. I also promised I was there to tell him what he needed to hear as opposed to what he might want to hear.

With access to the top leaders in the RPA, building other contacts became simple, although it did take time. The RPA was an accomplished but immature military organization. Kagame admitted that to me; he had never dreamed he would be sitting in that particular office. One of the signals you were "in" with someone was their telling you their last name. The RPA was a guerrilla army with years in the bush. The only one routinely referred to by his family name was Paul Kagame. Colonel Charles was Col. Charles Muheri. Colonel Joe was Col. Dr. Joseph Karamera. Colonel Karenzi was Lt. Col. Karake Karenzi. If you had to ask what Colonel Joe's last name was, you clearly had no need to know. That same caution spilled over into our relationships as military men. The last thing the Council of Colonels wanted was a patron-client relationship with a Western military, a la the French and the ex-FAR. So even as they proposed closer ties with the U.S. military, they had a definitive framework in mind for that relationship. What I found most refreshing was that their top priority was always training, not high-dollar equipment.

By the end of the war the RPA and the ex-FAR had both grown to almost fifty-thousand-man forces. Again the core of the RPA centered on its twenty-thousand veterans; the remaining "twenty thousand" was a soft number at best and included camp followers and genocide survivors who flocked to the rebel army. The bulk of the ex-FAR had fled into Zaire where I had greeted them in Goma.

The RPA then divided the country into brigade sectors with the size of the brigades tailored to meet their responsibilities. The military districts served more as an intermediate communications node between the brigades and Kigali, linked largely by handheld Motorola radios. The RPA used repeaters to keep the links intact and Kinyarwandan double talk to keep them secure.

With such efficient communications, RPA commanders could shift their forces fairly rapidly. Most movement was by foot, certainly, out in the mountains, it just about had to be. Elsewhere it was light trucks. The Toyota 4-Runner was the "Jeep" of the RPA. The RPA usually mounted a squad in the back of the vehicles facing out from two parallel benches as the standard troop carrier. Gun trucks with pedestal-mounted machine guns or recoilless rifles added punch to an RPA column. Commanders used Land Cruisers and Nissan Patrols as their command vehicles. Only the unwise failed to clear the road when an RPA column blew through. Normally the RPA moved by platoon or company; a battalion movement was fairly rare and was usually in response to a threat. When that happened, there were no speed limits.

UNAMIR made a convenient motor pool for the RPA, much to the frustration of the force commander and his staff. White Toyota 4-Runners in Rwanda multiplied like oversexed rabbits; UNAMIR used hundreds of them as standard transport for the staff, the UN-MOS, and the various U.N. contingents. U.N. agencies also used the same vehicles, as did many of the NGOs. The RPA was quite adept at stealing the vehicles. Open hijackings were very rare; U.N. workers were sufficiently careless that the RPA was able to do its shopping in a non-threatening manner. Soon the white vehicles would be spray-painted green and black; it was not uncommon to see them with the underlying white showing through.

Of course, this drew howls of protest from UNAMIR and grumbling about the "bad" RPA for stealing "good" U.N. workers' vehicles. We naturally protested the thefts, but one needs to keep in mind the RPA's perspective on UNAMIR. They clearly saw the U.N. force as an interloper with an ill-defined mission that would have served well in halting the genocide but now only interfered with the legitimate government's affairs. Kagame had accepted UNAMIR to make the international community more comfortable with the new government. He did not intend to offer the same comfort to the U.N. force, lest it stay longer than the minimum. Meanwhile U.N. New York could help equip the RPA.

Even as the RPA adjusted to its new reality, the leadership planned to reduce its ranks. At its later stages, the Rwandan War had become a children's war. Both sides recruited teens and even pre-teens into their ranks. The RPA's self-applied nickname was "the Boys." When I talked to Colonel Charles, the G3, he often used the name, saying "The boys near . . . made contact with militia" or whatever. They referred to the kid soldiers as "the Little Boys." Originally recruited as messengers, carriers, or batmen, the Little Boys were drawn into the fighting, and a number were killed. Kagame, seconded by Colonel Joe as health minister, wanted to get the Little Boys out of the army as quickly as possible. But how do you reintegrate nine-year-old boys who have seen combat into society, especially a society torn by genocide? The challenge inherent in that question was one to give social workers nightmares.

Gako: Integrating the Ex-FAR

Elsewhere the RPA was engaged in another remarkable integration effort. The RPF was not as its critics implied a pure Tutsi organization. Habyarimana's campaign against the RPF used that as its central tenet: the RPF was Tutsi and all Tutsi supported the RPF. That led to the series of anti-Tutsi massacres every year from 1990 to 1994. The RPF was born in the camps in Uganda, and its central core of leaders was Tutsi. But it offered a power-sharing program to the Hutu, and a number of them had accepted even before the war resumed. They paid heavily in the genocide; witness the fate of the moderate Hutu prime minister. Yet in establishing a new government, the RPF had attempted to comply with some of the power-sharing agreements reached at Arusha. Hence the new government had a Hutu president, and much of the government was built around the old Hutu bureaucracy.

Truly remarkable was that the RPA was attempting to do the same thing with elements of the ex-FAR. I learned a special reintegration program had been established at Gako Training Center just south of Kigali. The RPA had a couple of hundred ex-FAR officers there who had volunteered to be reeducated and integrated into the RPA. This was not a new concept; it was a key element in the Arusha accords. There was simply no way Rwanda could support a combined military of one hundred thousand men. Obviously most were going to have to go, and the pre-genocide target was a post-Arusha army of thirty thousand, still high for such a small country. Another part of the agreement was that officer ranks would be frozen until after the war. Common sense dictated that one, and common sense soon undermined it. Looking ahead as it lost the war, the ex-FAR began promoting a number of officers to colonel and higher. In contrast, the RPA finished the war the same as it had started it, with a single general in command.

So once the dust had settled after the war, the RPA invited ex-FAR officers who had not been involved in the genocide to undergo indoctrination into the new army. Several hundred took up the offer and returned. They would be retrained as officers of the RPA at Gako. But the RPA was an African military, and African militaries reflect their societies. They are therefore built on consensus to keep ethnic and social pressures in check. The previous Rwandan government had used those pressures, cultivated over thirty years and concentrated by war, to set off the genocide. Kagame and every RPA officer I met said the RPA could never hold Rwanda by force. Consensus was the only way that could happen, a consensus from both sides of the ethnic equation to reestablish a new equilibrium for the future. That meant borrowing from their common past and adding a new sense of tolerance to the social mixture. The Gako integration center was an initial foray in that effort.

Imagine if the Israeli Army had decided that in the interest of moving past the Holocaust, it would attempt to integrate German Army officers into its ranks. For that was what was happening at Gako. This was not the first time some of these officers had met off the battlefield. In January, 1994, the U.S. embassy had offered an International Military Education and Training (IMET) Course on military justice. Held in the USIS conference room, the course had concentrated on the role of the military and how such an institution fits into democratic society. As the U.S. ambassador, David Rawson had been a key host for the course, attended as well by Maj. Gen. Romeo Dallaire. I had found pictures of the RPF attendees including Frank Rusagara and others. Often they were seated beside ex-FAR officers now wanted for war crimes. Other ex-FAR officers were there who did not get involved in the genocide. Quite a number of them were at Gako, where to a large degree the RPA was recreating the naval justice course.

Rick, Mickey, and a new acting DCM, Robert Whitehead, went with me to visit the Gako facility. Bob Whitehead had ties to Rwanda. Married to a Tutsi he had met while assigned in Africa, Bob had volunteered to come in as DCM while David was back in the States on consultations. At Gako, we met the commandant of the camp, another RPA major. He explained what the program entailed. As we expected, it concentrated on building compromises for the country's ills. Candidates applied for attendance, and RPA security vetted their records. If clean, the candidates were accepted; in many cases, their letters of acceptance had to be smuggled into Zaire. Once in the course, they became equal to all other students. Prewar ranks were placed on hold pending satisfactory completion of the course. Ranks granted in violation of the Arusha promotion freeze were rolled back. Everyone wore East German fatigues without rank.

What made the course especially interesting was that half the students were RPA. Every ex-FAR officer had an RPA counterpart. Part of that relationship was spying and part was mentoring. The RPA officer kept an eye and an ear on what his ex-FAR compatriot did and said in the course. But it went further, because the RPA student was also getting graded. At the six- to eight-week completion of the course, the ex-FAR students would be assigned to RPA units as supernumeraries. The RPA students would also go to units where they would get their own ex-FAR supernumerary.

The commandant took us in to where we could meet the students. They were just finishing an assembly, and the major introduced us. I was still in my semi-stealth mode, so I had Rick offer a few words as the U.S. military representative at the embassy. At that time, I was not at all sure I wanted my presence in the mission widely known. Rick hit the right notes, stressing reconciliation and rebuilding for the future. As he finished, the class broke up and headed outside.

I was talking with Bob Whitehead when I heard, "*Je suis le* General Rutasira," over my shoulder. I turned, and there was one of the students. I knew his story. He had been one of the moderates in the ex-FAR, and he claimed to have helped save a number of Tutsis in Kigali. But he was also one of those who accepted a boost to general officer rank after the Arusha accords had frozen promotions. He had also been accused in some sectors of having a role in killing certain Tutsis and Hutu moderates even as he saved others. "*Non pas de tout. Vous n'etes pas un general ici. Vous etes un étudiant. Periode,*" I said, looking him in the face. His RPA handler heard the exchange, and the "general" soon walked away. My doubts about him were later confirmed. He showed up in the embassy several times to complain to the ambassador about his status in the RPA. When the allegations against him grew stronger, he fled the country once again and became a self-declared opposition leader in Nairobi.

That little scene pretty much said it all for the RPA's hopes for integrating the ex-FAR. It also said volumes about the chances for full political integration. At best we were talking years of healing and a gradual transition. That the RPF and the RPA were even willing to try at this early stage—less than three months after genocide—was remarkable. A full brigade of ex-FAR was integrated into the RPA in late 1995. Yet the West led by the U.S. was pushing them to move even faster. I heard more than one senior U.S. diplomat say Kagame and his people were just going to have to get over the genocide.

Kagame Visits Washington

Just before Thanksgiving, I made an unexpected trip back to the States to see my wife. She had undergone mandatory medical treatment after being evacuated from Haiti. I went back as a concerned husband and returned as a marital casualty. As fate would have it, my personal troubles coincided with the U.S. secretary of defense's invitational visit of Vice President Kagame. I had already made my presence known over at the Pentagon and was soon involved with arranging the visit. I had earlier worked up the secretary of defense's talking points before I left Rwanda, thinking at the time I would probably never see Kigali again. Looking back, the visit was a personal Godsend; it kept me busy and kept me sane. I reported into OSD-ISA Africa as temporary help.

The assistant secretary of defense for international security affairs in 1994 was Dr. Joseph Nye. His deputy (DASD) was Mr. Vince Kern, a senior civil servant long focused on Africa. His military staff included four African FAOs whose paths had crossed mine earlier in our careers. Col. Gus Lorenz was the senior military officer in the shop; he had taken French with me in 1983 before heading to Zaire. Two of the others were also French course alumni; Lt. Col. Greg Saunders was still on active duty as an Africanist. He had completed tours in Senegal and Mozambique. Mike Johnson had retired from active duty but stayed on as a civil servant within Vince Kern's office. Mike had hosted me for two weeks in Somalia in 1984. Finally, Maj. Mike Bittrick was a young Africanist who had been in the Army Intelligence and Threat Analysis Center during the build-up for Operation Restore Hope; we had shared information in the Army Operations Center. All four had tracked what had been happening in Zaire and Rwanda. It was like old home week for us. To my delight, Lt. Col. Roy Lauer, who had been with me in Lebanon and Egypt as a U.N. observer, sat in on the discussions as a representative from another section of the Defense Department. Roy had been one of the five UNMOs hijacked in southern Lebanon on their training tour. Finally Bill McCoy also joined us from down the hall at Defense humanitarian affairs to complete our team.

I thoroughly enjoyed working with this crew. All knew Africa and all wanted to do something constructive. OSD-ISA was more than a little frustrated with State over Rwanda. State had surrendered some of its lead after the shoot-down of the president's plane. But the diehard Arusha fans just could not accept the RPF had won the war and were now effectively the only game in town. OSD-ISA had a similar struggle with the U.S. service staffs who saw Rwanda as another Somalia.

As we crafted suggested policy options and talking points for the secretary of defense to use with Vice President Kagame, we had to simultaneously educate our audience. Our focus was on providing the new government the tools to survive; that meant security as well as humanitarian assistance. We knew Kagame was going to ask for a lifting of the U.N. arms embargo belatedly slapped in place after the genocide began. I pitched the ideas we had discussed back in Kigali with the government and inside the embassy. One was demining, an excellent entrée into a wider program. Bill McCoy was a big help, just as he had been in Goma. His office would support the demining program as a humanitarian operation through U.S. European Command. Plus he could broaden the defense effort to include support for rebuilding the medical and educational sectors.

I pushed the envelope by suggesting we should look at pure military programs. The RPA wanted to "lose weight" and become more flexible. That meant downsizing and improving mobility along with command and control. Tactical radios, trucks—I knew helicopters were beyond the pale—and training were the big three for the RPA. The need for assistance was based on an internal threat and the festering external threat from across the border. Inside OSD-ISA, that was easy to sell. From Vince Kern on down, we knew the RPA was a different kettle of fish. The difference started at the top: Paul Kagame did not mince words, and when he said something he meant it. That translated out at the tactical level into a military that would close with its enemies and destroy them. At the same time, the RPA maintained discipline remarkable in the Rwandan context.[6]

Outside OSD-ISA, the sale got tougher. Within certain segments of the Pentagon UNAMIR was offered up as an answer to internal security issues. That was relatively easy to answer. The UNAMIR mandate was designed for intervention in stopping a war already over. The peacekeepers' continued presence in Rwanda rested on the good graces of the new government, willing to cooperate for a while to gain U.N. recognition. Once that happened, UNAMIR's stay in the country would be limited. Another point was the ability of the peacekeepers to affect the situation around them. Certainly the Ethiopians had been a success story. They often did what needed to be done and let the fallout from their actions take care of itself. Their willingness to fire back when attacked or harassed or to intervene in tense situations actually endeared them to the RPA commanders in their sector.

Other peacekeeping units were less effective. One of the logistical stumbling blocks that had slowed UNAMIR's deployment was the provision of armored personnel carriers to the Ghanaian Battalion. Knowledgeable persons suggested the Ghanaians lacked the technical expertise to use and maintain M113s, the former standard armored troop carrier of the U.S. Army. Instead, African experts—read army FAOs—pushed wheeled armored personnel carriers like V150s or Light Armored Vehicles as more appropriate and user-friendly for the African peacekeepers. Wheeled armored personnel carriers would meet 99 percent of any tactical situations the Ghanaians might face, plus they were less destructive to the roads. Unfortunately, the United States did not have stocks of Gage V150s or Light Armored Vehicles sitting around waiting for a coat of white paint. We did have hundreds of M113s and their availability made them the easier choice. Yet once decided, State engaged in a three-month marathon negotiation to lease the armored personnel carriers to the Ghanaians. My buddy Blue Keller made a special trip up to Entebbe to help prepare the tracks for turnover to the United Nations.

In one of Rick Orth's trips outside Kigali, I had him take a look at how the M113s were being used. We had already heard the RPA was considering banning the tracked armored personnel carriers on surfaced roads. The Ghanaians were not used to negative steering with tracks—locking one track and pivoting the vehicle around it—and the roads in their sector were suffering accordingly. Rick went through their sector in a trip down to Cyangugu. Passing through a Ghanaian checkpoint, he saw one track towing another. More properly said, the first armored personnel carrier was dragging the other in an attempt to break free a frozen drive. Rubber track pads crumbled and scattered like blown retreads on an American eighteen-wheeler, and as the steel tracks underneath dug in, sparks flew as the steel links ate the road beneath. Off to the side, another M113 sat, equally derelict but not completely out of action. The Ghanaians had converted it into a chicken coop. The master of his own little empire, the resident rooster perched on top of the track commander's hatch. Such is the material of interesting and sometimes amusing reports back to Washington. I fired off a cable to Washington highlighting the cultural problems inherent in providing Third World militaries equipment that was beyond their capabilities.

I could not resist using the phrase, "the chickens have certainly come home to roost," on the fallacy of giving 113s to the Ghanaians. The report made the rounds inside the Pentagon, and someone made a single-frame cartoon capturing the relevant issues. Perhaps somewhat frivolous, it did drive home the point about UNAMIR. The force had an excellent commander and was capable of certain basic functions. But it had a limited mandate and its components were of unequal quality. We had already examined the possibility of using UNAMIR to resolve the refugee situation. When I had flown out on the U.N. C130 to go back to Washington that November I sat next to Sam Melessi, a friend from Zaire who was in Kigali studying the issue of the camps. His company was attempting to land a contract for policing the camps like I had suggested for Yigal's SOZAIS. I told him to make sure he could shoot people and get away with it. He laughed but said "broadly interpreted powers" would be part of the contract if he landed it. He did not.

Neither did the United Nations. That fall Tousignant had established a special planning group to determine whether or not the force could deploy into Zaire to establish control over the camps. Of course, such a move would require additional troops and the force commander recognized reinforcement was unlikely. U.N. New York would probably assign the mission and expect him to make do. He could not as a U.N. commander pull me in on the planning group. But we did discuss the issues privately, and when a U.N. fact-finding group arrived in eastern Zaire to study the situation, I just "happened" to be there. All of that aside, UNAMIR was marginally capable of executing its mandate inside Rwanda. It would never be able to address effectively the security problem lurking in those camps. As I had told Sam Melessi, any force charged with policing the camps would have to be able to shoot bad guys. The same rule applied to any U.N. force charged with controlling the camps.

As I pushed the need to assist the RPA in restructuring and training, others looked to resurrect a long dead horse, the Zairian military. The main culprit was the U.S. embassy in Kinshasa, especially the new defense attaché. As mentioned earlier, I had noticed that she seemed ensnared by the myth of an effective Zairian military. She was not a newbie in the business; she had done well on earlier assignments. But that did not prepare her for Zaire, and she ignored the most knowledgeable member of the mission when it came to matters Congolese. I made a point of looking up Stan while I was in Washington. He had spent another couple of months in Kinshasa working for the new defense attaché, and I wanted to know how it had gone. Stan confirmed what I had feared as I left for Kigali: as soon as I was gone, she told him his job was behind a desk. She would do all the collecting and all the reporting. She chose to ignore the advice of a senior sergeant who had ten years in country and had just turned in a stellar performance in Goma.

All of that showed in what she was writing about the situation in eastern Zaire. First of all she had accepted the Zairian and former Rwandan government line that the ex-FAR was no longer a threat. She declared there was no training going on in the camps, a line she would maintain for the next year. Every trip she made was under Zairian military escort; she saw and heard exactly what the Zairians wanted her to hear. Most importantly, she completely overlooked the issue of will to fight, something the Zairians had never ever shown.[7]

When the need for security forces around the camps became more pressing, she stated that units of the FAZ could do the job if they were paid. This gave rise to the Contingent Zairoise pour la Securité des Camps (CZSC), a derivative of the DSP and perhaps an extension of SOZAIS, Yigal's security company. The United Nations, with Western backing, in essence paid the leadership of the DSP—General Nzimbi—to provide a special security force around the camps. The troops of the CZSC actually got some of the money, but it was the same old story again. With senior Zairian personages like Nzimbi controlling the purse, most of the funds never made it to the actual troops. And even before the first Western dollar went into the coffers of the CZSC's leaders, the severity of the problems facing them grew with every passing moment. The ex-FAR, the Interahamwe militias, and the hardliner ex-Rwandan government officials had enjoyed a period of several months to get organized, an opportunity they had definitely not missed. So even though the CZSC mercenaries were the best the Zairian military had to offer, the "best of the worst" would never stop the training or the infiltration into Rwanda. Still, fielding the CZSC gave the United Nations and the West a way out to dodge the security issue; it was a Band-Aid on a sucking chest wound.[8]

Kagame in the Pentagon

All of these issues were on the table as Secretary of Defense Perry met with General Kagame. As a member of the U.S. embassy in Kigali, I sat behind the U.S. delegation. There were no surprises. Kagame spoke on the points I had told Washington would come up. He welcomed friendship with the United States and looked to the U.S. military for training. He did not ask for big budget items; his focus was on getting the U.N. embargo lifted. Kagame said he understood the role of UNAMIR but expressed frustration with its earlier impotence during the genocide. He hinted it would be allowed to stay, but its future in Rwanda was limited. Kagame highlighted the threats facing his country from eastern Zaire and said if the United Nations wanted to be proactive that was where it should focus its efforts. He made it clear Rwanda would not accept the refugee camps or the displaced persons camps inside its own borders as permanent fixtures.

The U.S. message was less clear. The secretary focused more on recognizing the efforts the new government had made to stabilize the country. He called for the new government to continue those efforts and said the United States would support them as appropriate. Training and other military assistance might come later. Meanwhile, Defense would continue humanitarian assistance but with a greater focus inside Rwanda. The most important message was that the U.S. government would look to getting the U.N. embargo raised. To support that effort, he suggested further consultations in Rwanda should take place. That meeting was the high point of the Kagame visit. He did lay a wreath at the Tomb of the Unknown Soldier, and there were some other functions. I attended one and met with Karenzi, Rusagara, and Karamera. The next day I left to return to Rwanda.

Back to Kigali

As I came down the steps at the airport, Mickey met me. I grinned at him, and we shook hands. "Well, looks like you're gonna be okay, Boss," he said. "I was worried. Some guys fall apart when their marriages collapse. You are gonna make it." That might seem a bit forward, but Mickey and I were already friends just as Stan and I had been in Zaire. I appreciated his concerns and resolved to live up to his optimistic expectations. Besides, I owed it to him; Rwanda was not a place to allow one's attention to wander.

Mickey told me the ambassador was back, and we had a high-level U.S. delegation due in the next day. National Security Advisor Anthony Lake had liked what he had heard in Washington and was on his way for the follow-up suggested by Kagame. Tipped off that Tony Lake was coming, David had returned to the mission while Kagame and I were in Washington. The entourage would include Lake, his NSC Africa staff, State, and Defense personnel. They were coming via a Special Air Mission out of Andrews AFB. It was to be a quick in and quick out mission; the ambassador arranged for them to meet the Rwandan president, a Hutu, as well as Kagame, the UNAMIR force commander, and SRSG. All of this had to take place in a single day. David had turned to Mickey to make it happen.

The Mick lived for tasks like that. He contacted the Rwandan Ministry of Defense to let them know about the visit and coordinated the landing rights for the special air mission 737. The main airport terminal was still pretty shot up, so the Rwandans offered the VIP reception area normally reserved for heads of state. Lieutenant Colonel Jackson became Mickey's main contact with Kagame and his entourage still in D.C. Jackson was an interesting story. He had been a local hire in the U.S. embassy in Bujumbura for years. All that while, he had been an RPF organizer and operative. No doubt he had worked the embassy to glean intelligence on how the United States stood on the RPF. Once the war began, he joined the RPA in the field and became one of Karenzi's main counterparts on the intelligence side. Since the end of the war, he had shifted towards more straight security duties, hence the assignment to coordinate Lake's visit.

By the time I arrived back in Kigali, Mick had the schedule locked down cold. Lake's visit was to concentrate on consultations with the president. With our high road–low road division of labor, that put the ambassador in the lead. I had met all the others—at least so I thought—so I would be more of a tagalong for the entourage.

The morning of the visit virtually all of the embassy staff was committed to meeting the visitors. There were more of them than of us. They included Tony Lake, the NSA to the president, members of the NSC, State, State-U.N. committee, Defense, and the Joint Staff. The embassy policy group—the ambassador and I—met them planeside. The Rwandan Foreign Ministry officials were there, but the real player was Lieutenant Colonel Jackson, Mickey's main counterpart in setting up the visit. Jackson wore his RPA fatigues with a red beret and French Para wings dating from his days in Burundi. Mickey, I noted, treated Jackson the respect he would show a senior U.S. Naval officer.

To my surprise, the ambassador called me over and asked me to take charge of the security detail. I had left my piece at home in case I was asked to come in with the entourage, so I borrowed Mickey's. Jackson had his boys on point and trail security in small sedans. I climbed in the lead vehicle and off we went. The Boys seemed determined to impress me; they did. Kigali is not a big town and in December, 1994, the traffic was light. The security escort's main technique in clearing the road was by playing chicken. They drove straight at the oncoming traffic until the other driver squawked and pulled over.

Once at the president's house—the lawn still showed signs of the April crash of the previous occupant's aircraft—Mickey and I chatted with Jackson while the ambassador went in with Mr. Lake. We were smoking and joking, both of us in casual civilian clothes, when two of the entourage came out in the garden. Both were in civilian clothes, one a very attractive young black woman, the other a white guy who looked military. He approached us.

"Are you guys State security or CIA?"

Mick and I both laughed, and I said, "No, we are the Defense Attaché Office staff here."

I introduced Mickey and myself as the woman came over. We entered into a discussion on Rwanda and Kagame. The guy was an air force major on the NSC staff. He launched into a diatribe against the RPA as a bunch of "warlords just like Somalia," and I was ready to cut him off when his comrade blasted him before saying, "sometimes there are good guys and bad guys."

Mickey and I looked at each other and grinned. Susan Rice was our kind of diplomat. She was director for international organizations and peacekeeping on the NSC. We knew at the time she was on her way up. Over the coming months she looked to our reporting as the most reliable source of information. In any case, the visit proceeded very well. Lake promised the U.N. embargo would soon end and U.S. assistance would follow in a variety of forms. By the end of the day, we were glad to have had them but even gladder to have them gone. Talking to Susan was a highlight of the visit. We felt someone was indeed listening to what we had to say.

In a way, the Lake visit was a watershed event. It marked the end of a State filter on information flowing out of the country. The president's national security advisor does not go to a region unless there is a need for a fresh set of high-level eyes on the program. Looking back, it is clear there was a vast difference in the views of Defense and State. Kagame's visit to D.C. and his reception at the Pentagon had heightened those tensions. Lake was there to make the final decision, and based on what I heard Susan say, the decision would be one of action—long overdue with regards to Rwanda. It did give us in the embassy the vector we needed, and with David at the helm, we moved off smartly. David's standard question to all future visitors who came wanting concessions or to offer advice to the new government became, "What are you going to offer the Rwandans?" Our actions from that point forward would be aimed at helping the new government rather than standing back and criticizing it while longing for the old government. I soon found myself engaged in a bureaucratic struggle with my own headquarters that might have removed me from Rwanda altogether.

DAO Wars: The Push for USDAO Kigali

If you were to believe after the Washington tour and my high-profile reporting during the Goma crisis that I enjoyed unfettered support from my handlers in Washington you would be naively mistaken. The opposite seemed the case. Or maybe it was just too much of a good thing. Remember that when the refugee crisis broke, my head-quarters wanted me to go to Goma, and they did support me in doing so, so much so they did not want me to stand down when I fell ill. In a similar vein, headquarters supported my going to Rwanda on a limited ninety-day duty. And they would enjoy the high marks my cables on the camps and what was happening inside Rwanda received from the Washington analysts and decision makers. But that honeymoon was soon over.

The initial notes of discord had begun earlier that fall when Ambassador Rawson and I wrote a five-year projection for the region. Entitled "Central African War," the cable laid out our considered judgment that the Rwandan War was not over, and its continuation had regional consequences. Stability in Rwanda affected stability in Burundi, Uganda, and Zaire. We predicted the war would continue for at least another five years and might explode into a regional conflict. The key, we believed, was the quick resolution of the refugee situation in Zaire and a concurrent program to assist the new government in Rwanda. As the ambassador, David stated bluntly that he needed a full-time attaché office in Kigali. He admitted State and government of Rwanda relations were at a low point after the war. As a military government, he believed the new central authority would be more likely to listen to a fellow military officer. He further named me as the attaché he wanted in a position made permanent. That message went to the Departments of Defense and State, the National Security Council (White House), and of course the DIA.

"WHHHHHOOOOAAAAH, horse!" was the word that came back from my headquarters on such an idea. The powers that be—in particular the middle-level managers at the DIA—did not like that suggestion at all. They had other goals in mind, goals rooted in the break-up of the Soviet Union. As the new Russia emerged with a brood of hatchling independent republics in tow, the Cold Warriors could not let go. The belief ran that to cover all those "new" threats, the intelligence community would have to restructure itself. That translated into "borrow from Peter to pay Paul." Peter was in this case intelligence coverage of low-priority areas like Africa. Paul was the newly emergent states of the former USSR. Within the army's FAO program, suggestions were made that Middle East FAOs would be used to cover these largely Muslim states, an idea that had us Middle Eastern types shaking our heads. As for African FAOs, we risked becoming extinct, because the DIA was realigning its attaché offices accordingly. Wherever they could close an Africa shop, they would. That was the reason my first boss at headquarters had in November, 1993, suggested we close Kinshasa when he learned I had not been granted full status as a diplomat. Fortunately, I had gotten to Major General Leide and killed that idea. Otherwise the Zaire shop would have been closed when the Goma crisis erupted.

I was something of a dilemma to the folks inside the Defense Humint Service and the DIA who wanted to cut offices in Africa. It was difficult to make a case on closing African stations when my presence in Zaire had proved so important. I had received written congratulations from the DIA director, U.S. Air Force Lieutenant General Clapper, on my reporting and handling of the crisis. Clapper and I went back to the Gulf War when I had briefed him as the air force intelligence boss on our templating of the Iraqi forces in Kuwait. When I went to Washington that November, he told me, "Tom, I just wanted to tell you I have been getting some very good paper on you. Keep up the good work." He made that comment recorded in a message to me in the field. Army Chief of Staff General Sullivan had done the same inside the army staff after his visit to Goma, referring to me by name as an example of how important FAOs were to their ambassadors. Then Maj. Gen. Pat Hughes as the Joint Staff J2 had done the same after Goma writing:

Please accept my appreciation for your recent superb accomplishments in Goma, Zaire, both prior to and during operation SUPPORT HOPE. The information you provided via your daily telephone calls was simply outstanding, enabling us to provide the best possible intelligence to the Secretary of Defense and the Chairman, Joint Chiefs of Staff. I cannot overemphasize how important it was to begin a briefing with " . . . we just spoke with the DATT and . . ." Moreover as a result of your extraordinary efforts, you significantly contributed to the success of operation SUPPORT HOPE which saved thousands of lives.

Thanks for a great job. Come by and see me when you're in town.

General Hughes added a penned comment on the flag note, stating "Outstanding as usual. Even Jim Pardew thinks you are a great soldier doing a great job."[9]

I had continued to perform in Rwanda—and the performance was needed and noted by Washington. Vince Kern, the deputy assistant secretary of defense for Africa told me there were two standing topics for discussion at every meeting of the National Security Council: Bosnia and Rwanda. My reporting had prompted Susan Rice to remark to Vince Kern, "At least someone knows what is happening out there." The same held true in the front office of the Defense Humint Service. Maj. Gen. Jack Leide—the FAO's FAO—was still the DHS director in November, 1994, when he sent me the following:

R 041700Z NOV 94
FM D.I.A. WASHINGTON DC //CC//
to am embassy kigali
personal for col odom from mg leide
SUBJ: JOB WELL DONE (U)
1. TOM, I WANT TO LET YOU KNOW HOW IMPRESSED WE WERE WITH IIR 6 825 0040 95. IT WAS IN TUNE WITH ANALYTIC NEEDS, PROVIDING EXPERT OBSERVATIONS, ANALYSIS, AND BOTTOM-LINE. THE SUGGESTIONS FOR HOW LOCAL SECURITY MIGHT BE IMPROVED WERE APPROPRIATE FOR BOTH POLICY AND THEATER DECISION MAKERS. A TRULY EXCELLENT IIR THAT TYPIFIES A CONSISTENTLY OUTSTANDING EFFORT.
2. CONGRATULATIONS ON A JOB WELL DONE. KEEP UP THE GREAT WORK, MG JACK LEIDE.

So I was getting through to the senior leadership in Washington on what was happening in Africa. The idea of standing up a DAO was well received inside Defense, the Joint Staff, State, and the army staff. After the chief's comments about me in Africa, I enjoyed great credibility inside the Pentagon. One evening, the major general in charge of DAMO-SS, the element of the operations staff responsible for strategy, called me at home in Kigali. The subject was the need for a Defense Attaché Office in Kigali. I ran it down for him.

"Are you volunteering for the job, Tom?" he asked.

"Yes, Sir. I will take it and stand it up before I go to Haiti," I responded. This was of course before I knew about my soon-to-be-failed marriage.

"Good, I will tell the chief we need a DAO there, and you are my choice as the DATT," he stated and rung off.

The exact opposite was happening inside the middle levels of my own headquarters. While there in November, I did a formal debrief with the analytical community in Washington who really liked the news that I would be returning to Kigali. My bosses—with the exception of Rick Moore—were openly hostile. Moore pulled me aside and warned me not to raise the issue of a new DAO. Official policy—meaning the mid-level of the Defense Humint Service—was against any suggestion of creating a new attaché shop. Moore said any lobbying on my part would be seen as disloyal, disloyal of course to DHS. I told Rick then I had already stated my position and would not raise it as a matter of course. Of course, I could and would restate that position to anyone who asked me.

It seemed utterly incredible my managers thought they could ignore the needs of the policy makers. Still I knew I could not fall on my sword over the issue, because they would use it against me. My loyalty was to the U.S. government in general and the U.S. military specifically. That meant outwardly toeing the line drawn by management until reality caught up with those drawing that line. My supervisor was merely the messenger boy. On the issue of the intentions and capabilities of the ex-FAR in Goma, my headquarters trapped itself.

The CIA and the DIA generate their budgets through collection capabilities. You want information then you must pay the bill to collect it. As I said earlier, the head CIA spook in Kinshasa had ignored the Goma situation too long. The opportunity to divine the intentions and capabilities of the ex-FAR had been when its leadership was hanging out at the lake hotel bar. That opportunity had come and gone, but the collection requirements remained. My supervisor had then volunteered me to fulfill them—from Kigali. When I received my collection taskings, the requirement to identify senior ex-FAR leaders in Goma, assess their intentions, and evaluate their military capabilities drew my attention. I could fulfill all the other taskings and was already doing so. But the DIA preaches risk versus gain as the yardstick for judging the feasibility of any collection mission. To do what he was asking me to required I cross into Zaire—where I was no longer even a non-accredited attaché—go into the camps, and then sit down with killers who would regard me as an RPA spy since by that time I am sure they knew my name.

The death of Rich Higgins at the hands of Lebanese terrorists came to mind. He had attempted to complete a mission that could not be done. He and his family had paid for it. His death had not changed a damn thing. The same was true here. We were not at war. I was reporting what needed to be reported already. If the policy makers were not going to respond to those reports, additional details were not going to make any difference. Mama Odom's little boy Tommy was not coming home in a body bag. Neither was Mama Dunham's little boy Mickey. I cabled back accepting all the missions except that one, saying the risk was too great for the doubtful gain. But in the same conversation, when my supervisor nixed any idea of a permanent DAO in Kigali, he resurfaced this collection task in Goma.

"You know we don't like to go back to the collection tasking meetings and say we can't do what we have already said we could do," he said. If he expected me to give in, he was sorely mistaken.

"I have already told you why I cannot do that mission. I could give a damn about how you look at collection meetings," I responded.

What made it truly bizarre was I had developed a contact that could and would do some scouting around the ex-FAR camps if compensated. My boss—the same guy complaining about collection meetings—refused to approve that operation, saying that was not our approved method of operation. I told him if that was the case, then get the CIA to do the mission. I got the same response.

"We don't like to admit we can't do things. It's bad for budget battles."

It was not long after the Lake party left Rwanda that headquarters moved to limit our operations. The first step was to direct that all our cables had to go through the Defense Attaché Office in Youandé, Cameroon. Rick Moore called me one day and told me that from now on I would not be allowed to transmit reports as USDAO Kigali. The bureau's new position was that there was no USDAO Kigali; I was there as a representative of the U.S. Defense Attaché Office Youandé. Jim Cobb supposedly remained the defense attaché for Kigali as part of his regional coverage. Consequently, we would have to transmit our reports to Youandé for release as that station's reports. This eliminated all mention of USDAO Kigali and supposedly reduced my visibility as an acting attaché. The major effect of all of this was to slow down reports Washington needed and expected. I merely added this delay into my bag of arguments in favor of making USDAO Kigali official. If all this seems silly today, it seemed absurd to me in 1994. But it was important: effective policy depends on accurate intelligence, and we were focused on that mission. For a variety of reasons, both clear and obscure, headquarters and our sister agencies and missions pursued other agendas.

Then Rick dropped the other shoe. He told me that I was henceforth restricted to operations inside Rwanda. No more crossings into Zaire without specific approval of the embassy in Kinshasa and our headquarters. I guess since I would not take on the suicide mission to interview ex-FAR generals and militia leaders I was no longer considered an extension of the Zaire mission. From then on the new defense attaché in Kinshasa would report events in eastern Zaire. I could see the handwriting on the wall. She was already advocating the Zairian Army—a main culprit—as the solution to security problems she denied even existed. She advocated money would motivate them to do the job. VdW—my old friend the organizer of secession and mercenaries—would have laughed at that.

The RPA and UNAMIR: Marking Turf

Losing the Goma missions hardly left us bored inside Rwanda. Kigali remained very much a frontier town emerging from war. UNAMIR attempted to run patrols in the city with some successes and quite a number of failures. The RPA remained in force in the city and began to set up traffic controls. They also continued walking patrols, especially at night that required extra care from those who encountered them on the dark streets. It was an explosive mix. Part of the problem was with the RPA; they had just won a war and were at a loss with what to do with it. Complicating the RPA's internal problems were the discipline issues associated with the "Little Boys" and the

Burundi Tutsis who had joined in the latter stages of the war. More Tutsis were returning to Kigali along with a handful of Hutus from the camps in Zaire. The RPA and the NGOs had occupied various houses in the city. The Tutsi returnees from Uganda and Burundi had squatted in others. Tutsis who had been in hiding and Hutu returnees came home to find their homes occupied by RPA, fellow Tutsis or Hutus, and NGOs. That meant a lot of short tempers and demanded great wisdom in sorting it out. The NGOs could get on the emergency radio and call for help if someone tried to evict them. UNAMIR was the local equivalent of "Dial 911" in these cases. The other part of it was that UNAMIR's charter, true of almost all U.N. peacekeeping organizations, guaranteed it the right to go anywhere at anytime it wanted to, something the RPA did not understand and certainly did not like.

As a result we had repeated standoffs between the RPA and UNAMIR patrols or reaction forces. Two of the UNAMIR units got into more of these than their comrades. They were the British Engineers from the Para Brigade and the initial Australian infantry unit assigned to protect their national medical contingent. The Brits were a special case. They had deployed to support UNAMIR but were not officially under UNAMIR's control. They did excellent work in repairing bridges and light engineer work. But they tried to use the same intimidation tactics used in North Ireland with the RPA in Kigali. That just did not work. For the Aussies it was, at least initially, the same problem. The Aussies came in under an outdated mandate, and it took a while for that to sink in. The difference was that the force commander could take steps to improve their behavior he could not with the British. No one got shot in these confrontations. Typically the RPA held its ground until the offending U.N. unit complied. It was a lesson in humility for the British Paras; they departed very quickly. The Aussies in contrast took pains to train the next unit on how to deal with the local military, the RPA. Meanwhile Kagame and the RPA leadership kept careful rein on their troops without conceding their sovereignty inside Kigali.[10]

Xmas and New Year's in Kigali

Aside from these tensions, Kigali was remarkably pacific. We even left the doors of our house open at night, something I would never have done in Zaire. Our circle of friends broadened, and we even went to an occasional dance. We approached Christmas with the thought that things had to get better.

Reality means you do the best you can with what's at hand and let the rest sort itself out. That's what David was doing as ambassador. He had a shot-up embassy, a war-torn policy called Arusha, and a hodge-podge staff including me to work with. But he made it work because he truly cared about his people. Christmas was special. David hosted it at the old DCM house. The dinner was nice, and we all sang Christmas carols. We finished the evening at an NGO bar.

The next week went quickly. Mickey proposed we host a New Year's party at our place. We whipped out some invitations and started scrounging for food. Nearly fifty folks showed for the party. We were rather loud, and it became louder as the night moved toward the end of 1994. The dance hit of the evening was Foreigner's *Dirty White Boy*. That song just seemed to fit. At midnight, every RPA troop with an AK and more than a few UNAMIR soldiers let loose skyward with their weapons. Tracers arched across the city and coupled with grenade blasts and *Dirty White Boy* it was a hell of a sound and light show. Bullets that go up must come down, so we sat on the floor below window level to wait out the fireworks. Soon we could hear the not-gentle tinkling of expended rounds falling on the metal roof of the house. So ended 1994 in Kigali, Rwanda—a Land of the Dead finally showed signs of coming back to life.

CHAPTER 7

Resurrecting a Country

I t might be a new year, but it was still Rwanda and the troubles were not over. David and I had stated that the goal of policy making in Rwanda had to be reducing the killing. Stopping the killing was impossible. Although the refugee camps across the border remained the most serious threat to stability, there were internal parallels. When the French had established their security zone in the southwest, the fleeing Hutus were soon gathered in displaced persons (DP) camps inside the area under French control. There were DP camps near every large Rwandan town in the southwest. Attended by the U.N. High Commission for Refugees (UNHCR), they soon began to take on the same aspects of permanence that were appearing in the camps in Zaire. Worse still, there were a number of smaller camps closer to the border with Burundi, populated by a mix of Burundians and Rwandans.

Help from Burundi

These camps were a natural staging base and refuge for hard-core militia determined to carry on the fight against the Rwandan Patriotic Front (RPF) in the countryside. They also served as staging bases for Burundians doing the same against the rampaging Tutsi army in Burundi. As one would expect, the Rwandan Patriotic Army (RPA) established ambushes and roving patrols to intercept these groups as they moved across the border. The inevitable happened: an RPA unit intercepted one of these militia groups and pursued it into one of the smaller DP camps on the Rwandan side of the border. Summoning reinforcements from the sector commander, the RPA platoon moved into the camp. The leader soon lost control, and his troops killed a number of civilians before the reinforcing RPA commander arrived and stopped the action. The U.N. Assistance Mission in Rwanda (UNAMIR) was notified, and the blue berets soon arrived as well. The RPA commander actively cooperated with the UNAMIR force and soon UNAMIR helicopters were ferrying wounded to the U.N. hospital in Kigali. The cooperation continued after the melee was over. RPA and U.N. Human Rights Officers investigated the incident in tandem. The RPA platoon leader was relieved and disciplined. The unit was moved out of the sector altogether. All things considered, the incident was just that, an incident hardly noteworthy in the context of Rwanda's killing grounds. What made it remarkable was the cooperation between the RPA and the United Nations. I reported it as a matter of course within the UNAMIR situation report I transmitted almost daily back to Washington.

Enter our ambassador in Burundi, a vehement spokesman against the depredations of the Tutsi-controlled military inside Burundi. Often he was too outspoken and so alienated the government they shut him out. Later that year, the Burundian army or its militia supporters tried to kill him in an ambush in northern Burundi. They failed, and State attempted to tone him down to no avail. David and I were about to get a taste of his vitriolic reporting. The ambassador in Bujumbura got wind of the camp incident inside Rwanda and headed north to interview survivors who had fled back into Burundi. One supposed survivor spun a tale worthy of Oliver Stone.

According to this source, the militias who were attacked in the countryside by the vicious RPA were no more than peaceful farmers moving back in from the fields. The RPA chased them into the camp and then summoned more RPA and UNAMIR troops to finish the job. According to him, U.N. helicopter gunships led the combined RPA-UNAMIR attack. They fired rockets and machine gun fire into the area, and the ground forces then mopped up. The village was supposedly leveled. The U.N. and RPA troops then hid all the bodies by throwing them down wells in the area. The death toll was supposedly in the "hundreds or thousands."

Without any corroboration, our neighboring ambassador put all this into a cable and fired it off to Washington. David called me in and showed me the report. I read it and was torn between laughter and rage. This sort of thing gets ambassadors relieved. I told David I would put out a full report on the matter. I made a special trip out to UNAMIR to verify what they had said before, and I checked with Colonel Karenzi on the matter. I related the full story in a separate report and added a none-too-subtle dig about UNAMIR "gunships." The United Nations had a contract with a Canadian company to provide five unarmed twin turbine Hueys. I had flown on the birds, and I liked the guys who flew them. But their birds were just slick helicopters with no weapons or even weapon hard points. David read the report, and we sent it off with Burundi as an information addressee, believing it might make the ambassador in Burundi pause.

Two days later, David again called me in and handed me a cable to read. It had come back from State as a retransmission. Apparently unsatisfied by my report—as well as UNAMIR's—the ambassador in Burundi had cabled the African Bureau requesting permission to investigate independently the events in southwest Rwanda. So independently he had not even put Kigali down as an information addressee. The African Bureau had of course not approved the request but had forwarded it on to David for his consideration. David was one of the most patient men I had ever worked with, but he was angry now. He had talked with State and been told he could nix the investigation. But if he did so, his fellow ambassador might continue to make noises about a cover up and eventually draw a reaction from the press a la the Gersony "report." We could answer any such media enquiry, but it would be simpler to kill it before it started. And preemption was certainly better for our relations with the new government and UNAMIR. We decided to invite him up and then rub his nose in the facts.

Again I went back out to UNAMIR, this time headed to the force commander's office. I took the original Burundi message about U.N. gunships and slaughter along with my rebuttal cable. Tousignant read the first, and I could see his ears turn red with anger. Then he read mine and visibly relaxed. "So, Tom, you have already solved the problem. What's up?" he asked.

I handed him the request from our ambassador in Burundi to visit Rwanda independently, and for once the smooth Canadian two-star was speechless. He summoned his new chief of staff, Indian Army Brigadier Sivakumar and introduced us. The force commander ran down the problem and then turned to me, saying, "Are you going to let this guy in?"

I explained that David and I felt it better to invite him in and then bury him with the facts. The two peacekeeping generals got the idea right away, and the Indian brigadier took on the job. He was the complete military professional. I mentioned my U.N. days in

Lebanon and said I understood how heavy the blue beret could be for the wearer. We bonded on the spot. Then we sat down and came up with a plan, soon approved by his commander and my ambassador. We sent an invitation to the ambassador in Burundi to meet us at Butare, Rwanda, in two days.

Mickey and I drove down to Butare on the appointed day. Halfway to the site of the incident, Butare is the first major Rwandan town on the road from Burundi. We waited at the Rwandan National Museum until the ambassador's Cherokee joined us, then headed west to Gikongoro. Our destination was the sector U.N. Observer headquarters where the Indian brigadier met us. A UNAMIR Huey waited on the pad beside the building. We then went for a briefing attended not only by UNAMIR but also the RPA sector commander.

The briefing started fairly well, delivered by a Canadian officer who had been in on the investigation of the killings. Our visitor's first question dealt with the subject of U.N. gunships, and I could see Brigadier Sivakumar begin to fidget in his chair. The briefer pointed at the Huey and remarked that UNAMIR did not have armed helos. Then as the briefer continued, the ambassador brought up the claim that U.N. troops had helped throw the bodies into the wells. That was too much for the Indian general: he jumped out of his seat and took over the briefing.

Sivakumar stood spread-legged directly in front of the U.S. ambassador to Burundi, pointed his finger at him, and ran down the events of the incident without pause. Briefing finished, the ambassador, Sivakumar, and I boarded the Huey while Mickey returned to the Butare Museum with his Cherokee.

Once in the air, the pilot headed for the scene of the "RPA-UNAMIR" attack. I talked our visitor through the scene as viewed from the air. We were down to less than two hundred feet. The "destroyed" village was clearly intact. There were no signs of rocket or machine gun attack. The only thing noteworthy was that the village stood empty; the inhabitants had displaced to Kibeho, the largest DP camp in the southwest. He just nodded, and once finished, I directed the pilot to head to UNAMIR headquarters where we would meet my ambassador. Twenty minutes later we were on the ground and headed to the force commander's office in Ambassador Rawson's car. Tousignant turned on the charm and went through the briefing again. Briefing over, we took leave of the two generals and headed downstairs.

Outside, David pulled me back. "Take him back to Butare and put him back in his truck. Make sure he is headed south before you leave him."

We headed to the pad and boarded the Huey for the hop back to Butare. The visitor sat silent all the way there. We landed, and as he headed to his vehicle, he turned.

"Colonel, I appreciate all the effort you put into this visit. I must tell you somehow I am not totally convinced." In keeping with David's instructions, I made sure I saw his rear bumper leave Rwanda.

New Nightlife

Up until that spring our entertainment choices were limited. We had reopened the embassy club earlier, and it was a disappointment. The staff was lazy, the food choices limited, and the prices way too high. If you have a problem, give it to a navy chief and stand back. Mickey had gotten to know the staff at our neighborhood NGO bar and restaurant quite well. He learned they were closing out the operation and made them a deal. They would run and maintain the club on a turnkey contract. The results were great. We soon had the main watering hole for the internationals in Kigali. The buffets offered good food at a reasonable price. One could order steak, burgers, pizza, or fried chicken if the buffet did not appeal. There was always someone to talk to, and many folks came for the Sunday brunch and made a day of it. If something were going down, I would often hear about it first at the bar of the embassy club.

Of all the things we did for the embassy and the international community, the club was probably the most important. What really bugged Mickey and me was criticism from our boss at headquarters. We had sent in an activity report including embassy support, and he complained that we were "doing too much," that State was somehow getting over on the DIA. I called him and asked exactly what the issue was. He said we should only be doing those duties normally associated with a DAO. I first reminded him that we were living in State housing that had not cost the DIA a dime. Then I asked him if there was some problem with the quantity or the quality of our reporting. When he answered no—we were still getting kudos from senior officials in D.C.—I told him that I would continue to support the embassy in any fashion I could. He never did grasp how important such support was to our operational mission.

The End of the Tunnel

Nevertheless, the constant sniping from my own headquarters was getting to me. I had long wanted to be a defense attaché in an action area. That's why I had gone the way I had, and I had accepted the costs. Certainly I would never be selected for command; the board that had considered my year group for battalion command had met. I was not selected. I stood a good chance for full colonel. The War College non-resident course list had come out, and I made it, normally a signal you were on track for full colonel. I felt I had done well in Zaire and in Rwanda thus far. Certainly the upper echelons felt that way, and I sensed I was winning the battle to get a new DAO set up in Rwanda. Rick Moore had asked us for a list of what would be required to formally open the shop we were already running. He would not have asked had the rear been reconsidering the issue. That was rewarding in itself. But I was sick of having the same folks on my back or, worse, on the back of my NCOs. Our immediate boss had been on Stan's case constantly in Zaire and he was doing the same with Mickey in Rwanda. Mickey was past retirement, and he could not have cared less. Still, like me, Mickey was trying to do what was necessary. He actually had gone home to get married and then came back because he knew I needed him.

I had to consider where I was going next as well. My assignment to Haiti was a dead issue. The U.S. embassy in Zaire had been bad, and Rwanda had its own special touch of hell. I had lost count of the massacre sites that I had visited. I had literally walked in blood for more than six months; we learned that diesel fuel poured on our boots cut the smell. My ability to put the horror aside and function came at a cost I could only guess. There were limited choices in front of me. That was the African FAO reality. I had asked for Kenya and been told it was going to a guy who had closed the shop in Sudan. Branch, speaking through my bureau, offered me Chad, another garden spot. I asked about Kenya once more and was offered Angola. My choices kept getting better and better. Looking at what I had done in Zaire and Rwanda, I could not see an equally challenging job on the horizon.

The other consideration was personal. My marriage had gone off the rail, and I needed to close that out with a divorce. So I notified headquarters I would be retiring the next year at twenty years. Better to get on with life after ending my career on a high note. I must say that I had no regrets then in making that decision. I have none now.

There was one immediate effect, one most gratifying. I could concentrate on doing my job and let the chips fall where they wanted. Folks could snipe all they wanted, but I had just taken away the target. From that point on I operated on the principle that the less headquarters knew the better.

Demining: The Initial Steps

All the time I was wearing my spook hat collecting information and my DCM hat trying to smooth embassy operations, I was also wearing the hat of U.S. European Command's military representative to Rwanda. While in Washington, I had worked with friends in the Pentagon and other agencies to get the demining proposal moving. The U.S. Agency for International Development (USAID) had the money and AID Chief of Staff Dick McCall had said they would fund the initial part of the program. U.S. European Command and U.S. Special Operation Command Europe also had monies and had verbally signed on to the idea. To use the AID monies, I was designated the AID project officer with power to disburse funds. Back in Rwanda I conferred closely with the RPA leadership about a demining operation. Their concerns were straightforward: they could provide good soldiers to be trained and little else. That is what I had already pitched in Washington and to European Command. Both had accepted that reality. I also suggested to Col. Charles Muheri, the RPA operations officer or G3, that we use a "train the trainer" approach to establishing the program. That would make the program sustainable in the long term. Muheri, ever the practical man, immediately agreed, and then we talked manpower. He promised the RPA would provide an initial contingent of fifty to seventy screened soldiers for training. They would undergo medical testing for disabilities that might limit their effectiveness. The last thing you want is a deminer with a nervous condition. They would also be screened for intellectual ability. He asked about the language barrier. I told him the more English speakers he could provide the faster the learning curve would climb.

SOCEUR Demining Survey

European Command and its subordinate Special Operations Command Europe (SOCEUR) knew all about the agreements I had worked out with the RPA. They had hard copy cable and I talked to the

European Command Demining Office on a regular basis. In order to dot all the "i's," they had to send down a Demining Survey Team to make things official. The team would consist of the European Command Demining program officer, a marine lieutenant colonel, an army master sergeant deminer, and a couple of representatives from 3d Special Forces Group. This group had the army special operations mission for Africa. Their representative was a young captain who had been in Goma at the latter stages of Operation Support Hope and a young staff sergeant. They would monitor what was agreed upon and give 3d SFG a heads-up on what was coming down the pike. There was also a representative from the Pentagon, Col. Bob Bailey. Bob had been with me in basic French back in 1983. I stayed with him while I was in Zaire on FAO training in 1984.

Mickey and I alerted the RPA and UNAMIR that the European Command team was coming. I had worked with Colonel Charles long enough to know he would have things ready on the RPA side of the house. I went to see the UNAMIR force commander to coordinate things with the peacekeepers. Working through operations, our main U.N. contact was the UNAMIR staff engineer, an Indian captain. He maintained the UNAMIR UXO (unexploded ordnance) and mine database and was the staff officer who said yes or no to proposed demining by UNAMIR engineers. We set up a program for the survey. After an initial morning of consultations in Kigali with the RPA and UNAMIR, the combined group would take a look at mines and UXOs around the capital city. The next day we would fly to Ruhengeri and, under U.N. military observer escort, survey mined areas in the northwest. The following day would be much the same thing due north of Kigali in the Byumba area. Finally the team would spend a day wrapping things up and head back to Stuttgart.

Things went quite smoothly that first day. Ever the gracious diplomat, David held a cocktail party in the team's honor and invited personnel from both UNAMIR and the RPA. The key RPA people came, including a Maj. Joseph Mbaraga, command designate for the demining program. UNAMIR showed as well, including the force commander and key staff. That set the cooperative tone for the next day's meetings and tour of the Kigali area. Since I had already negotiated the basis for the agreement, the meetings went quickly. The RPA would provide the bodies. We would provide the trainers, the money, and the equipment to make things work.

The second day we loaded the UNAMIR helicopters and flew northwest to Ruhengeri and the Tunisian sector. Colonel Charles had an RPA escort laid on to meet us at the pad along with the local U.N. observers. Our first stop was the observers' local headquarters where they would brief us on the mines and UXO concentrations in the area. This sector had been a final redoubt for the RPA after the French intervention. There were areas resembling the conventional defensive lines of earlier wars. What made them especially nasty was both sides had been adept at booby traps as well as mines.

The senior U.N. military observer in the sector was a Russian colonel. The last time I had seen him was on OP duty in Sinai back in 1988. He was one of the kamikaze drivers who had given Colonel Gasche, our French commander, such headaches when the Soviets were first released to go into Sinai. There were a number of Russians under his command along with other nationalities in Rwanda. We had just finished the briefing and were loading up the vehicles when another Russian proved some things never really change. Mickey had gotten into one of the Toyotas when the Russian U.N. observer started the vehicle beside him. The guy gunned it and cut the wheel hard as he backed up. That slung the front end of the U.N. vehicle into the side of Mickey's and destroyed the doors on the passenger side. Mickey just barely missed getting his leg cut off. The Russian did not even stop as we headed out for the Tunisian headquarters.

Once again it was another sector briefing, and there were really no surprises. We listened politely as the Tunisians repeated what the U.N. observers had just told us. But from here we were going up to the old battlegrounds for a first-hand look at that terrain. We walked out and again began getting in our assigned trucks. Mickey had to use the other door on his Toyota. He had just gotten inside when the same Russian U.N. observer started his truck beside him. Again, the Russian put it in reverse, tromped the gas, and cut the wheel to back out. This time he destroyed the other side of Mickey's Toyota and completely demolished the front end of his own vehicle. But this time he did not just drive off. He got out of the vehicle and staggered to the front to look at his handiwork. At 1000 hours he was completely drunk. Colonel Charles watched this performance and just shook his head. Mickey and I got in the RPA truck for the rest of the trip.

North of Ruhengeri, the area is heavily forested and crossed by ridgelines. The RPA had withdrawn into this area to wait out the French and their clients, the ex-FAR. Both sides had set in positional defenses built along the ridges. They had built trench and bunker systems on the military crests and used mines and booby-trapped UXOs to close the gaps. I explained to Charles that in setting up a demining program, this area would be a last priority. It was well known and no longer inhabited. The density of the mines and the UXOs would make it challenging and better left to a time when his deminers had more experience. He agreed. For me it was interesting to see the battleground, especially with the senior operations officer of the RPA.

The following day we flew to Byumba where the Nigerians had their battalion headquarters. Unlike many of the UNAMIR contingents, the Nigerians had a combat engineer platoon attached for ordnance disposal. We landed at the helipad and trekked up a low slope to be greeted by the battalion commander. A lieutenant colonel, he looked like an African sumo wrestler. He was the fattest soldier I had ever met. Clearly he had never humped the hills in his sector. In any case, his engineers gave us a briefing and showed us a collection of supposedly inert UXOs they had gathered in the area. That set off warning signals; you never, ever gather UXOs, especially inside a building you live and work in. You blow them in place because the slightest movement can set them off. I began to have serious doubts about these Nigerian engineers right then. So did Mickey, Charles, and the SOCEUR survey team. We all just sort of slid toward the doors and away from the collection of duds.

The next step was a field survey and we went up to a village abutting a known mine and UXO area. As we walked up, one of the elders came up and started talking to the Nigerian engineer leader. Charles listened in and told me the elder had found a shell near the village well. The Nigerians followed after the old man, and we watched from the road. Minutes later here they all came back with the senior engineer in the lead waving an unexploded mortar round. As they came closer, we backtracked. The Nigerian wanted to show us his prize, one I preferred to view from a safe distance. Finally Charles stepped forward and ordered the Nigerian sergeant to stop. We had seen enough in any case. As we loaded the vehicles, the Nigerians tried to put the dud round in Mickey's vehicle, but he waved them off. If they wanted the damn thing for their collection they could ride with it. Later I debriefed the force commander on the Russian U.N. observer and the Nigerian engineers. I also warned the UNAMIR engineer officer a visit to the Nigerian's dud munitions display might be in order before one of the rounds blew up.

Bad drivers and suicidal engineers aside, the SOCEUR demining survey was a success. The team leader agreed that the concept I had worked out with Colonel Charles was the right way to go about it. We set up a series of milestones. We would establish a national demining office to direct the deminers and to coordinate the mine awareness program. The deminers would need equipment, vehicles, and communications equipment. The 3rd Special Forces Group would provide the demining trainers; the mine awareness trainers would be a mix of psychological operations (PSYOP) and civil affairs soldiers. The next step would be to get 3rd SFG's site survey team in to start making logistic arrangements. The sergeant who had been on the SOCEUR survey would most likely be the point man for that effort.

But before we put the survey team back on the plane to Europe and the States, we made sure they visited a massacre site as part of their Rwandan experience. This time we went to Nyamata Church south of Kigali. Estimates held this church had seen the execution of more than four thousand people. It had been cleaned up, and a mass grave lined one wall of the one-thousand-square-foot chapel. We arrived at the church mid-morning on a sunny day and entered the church. My first thought as my eyes adjusted to the dim light was I had entered some bizarre disco holdout from the 1970s. Pinpoint lights danced across the floors and walls, highlighting the flickers of dust in the air. Yet as my pupils enlarged I could make out the internal details. I was grateful that this site did not have the stacks of bodies Ntarama Church held. The low benches were empty below a raised pulpit and choir stand.

Unlike the rest of the church, the pulpit stood bathed in a tube of sunlight that poured through a four-foot hole in the roof. As my eyes adjusted further, the origin of this "skylight" became clear. As the focal point for the congregation, the pulpit had been the slaughter zone for the massacre. Some four thousand people had died at that one point. The concrete floor around the pulpit was stained a dark red that no amount of bleach would ever reduce. The roof around the hole was matted in red and organic material, largely brains, bone, and hair. The only way that could have been done was to march the victims to the pulpit, put a gun barrel under their chin, and blow their brains through the roof. The disco lighting effects were from various stray rounds that had gone through the roof. Naturally this story horrified the members of the team; they had never been exposed to this level of savagery. I found I was changing in a disturbing way. I was no longer surprised or shocked by the evidence of genocide. I was more frustrated. I wanted to kill those responsible. I wanted them to wait for their turn at the pulpit of justice until the executioner came for them. I wanted to be that executioner. Humanitarian assistance like demining was okay, but I wanted to see some non-humanitarian assistance for the Rwandans.

Parallel to the demining effort, I was making progress on assistance to the Rwandan health and educational sectors. Bill McCoy played a key role in this effort. As equipment became available in Europe, he would notify me and ask if I wanted any of it. I finally told him if he could get it shipped, I would take it. By January, 1995, we had already gotten in two aircraft loads of hospital beds and equipment. I expected we would also be getting school desks and playground equipment. Bill's office also helped transfer water trucks left behind by the JTF; we passed the paper trail through the embassy down to the UNAMIR motor pool. These were top-of-the-line Volvo trucks purchased in Uganda, all at top-dollar prices.

A Garden from the Movies

Working the humanitarian side of the house put me in contact with one of the true heroines of Africa, Ms. Rosamund Carr. An American adventuress, Roz had come to Africa after WWII with her husband when the Belgians still controlled the Congo and Rwanda. They had established a pyrethrum plantation in the hills northwest of Ruhengeri. The business had succeeded where the marriage failed. Roz stayed on with her flowers and her farm. It was she who sheltered Diane Fossey when the latter was run out of Zaire in the 1970s. Roz's house was featured in the film *Gorillas in the Mist*.

Roz was one of the last Westerners to evacuate Rwanda when the war resumed followed by genocide. She hid her Tutsi staff members from local Interahamwe militias until the killers turned on her. Along with a handful of other expatriates, she managed to escape through Goma and return to the United States. As soon as she learned the ambassador was going back, she started making her own plans to return and arrived in Kigali shortly after David. He attempted to get her to leave but she was not having any of it. Her only concession was agreeing to live in Kigali for a few weeks until UNAMIR was fully deployed. She had stayed in the Lane house with the civil affairs guys until the week before I crossed over to Rwanda from Goma.

Up country, Roz found her home had been pillaged and most valuables stolen. Her staff had suffered, and a number had been killed. Yet her stalwart friend Sembegare had made it. Sembegare was actually Roz's right-hand man, not that of Diane Fossey as portrayed in the film. The producer had liked the name and enjoyed his company, so they wrote him into the film as Sigourney Weaver's main guide. Roz's beloved dogs had also survived, as had the basic structure of the house and the lovely exterior gardens. Gradually over the coming months, she managed to reacquire many of her possessions taken in her absence.

But Roz being Roz, she was not content to merely rebuild her own existence. Though well past her eightieth year, she soon opened an orphanage on the farm using the pyrethrum-drying barn as the basic shelter. When I first met her she had fifteen or so children under her care. By the year's end she would have more than thirty. She was madder than a wet hen over a reporter who had reneged on a promise not to mention her age. She feared that might be used against her getting funding for the orphans. Roz specialized in those children whose families were dead. She did not really want the kids who would stay a few weeks or months and then move on to be reunited with family. She grew too close to them to stand losing them again. I got to know her over the next fifteen months, and I felt privileged for it. Roz would do anything for her kids, and she unabashedly begged for assistance from any source she could find. I introduced Dr. Joe the Heath Minister to her and through his office made sure she was well stocked with blankets and other items I had brought in. She also made use of UNAMIR; the Aussies adopted her and rotated platoons up to her farm for weeks at a time. They rebuilt the barn and put in floors and partitions as walls.

Roz, however, had an uneasy relationship with the RPA. She was an outspoken critic of the RPF; like many she blamed them for the war and the genocide. They had disrupted the quiet world she had built for herself, and she found that unforgivable. "Things were so peaceful here before they invaded," she remarked to me once at lunch. Comments like that did not exactly endear her to the RPA. Nevertheless, the local commander kept an eye out for her welfare. Since moving back, she had become a target for the militias. As things grew unstable in the countryside, he stationed troops on her farm to protect her. Mid-year they intercepted and killed several militia members who may have been there to kill her. We talked about what had happened, and we agreed to disagree about the RPF. Her views on the subject come across clearly in her book, *Land of a Thousand Hills.*[1] The bottom line was that Rwanda was forever changed from what she had known. A year after I left Rwanda, militia attacked her farm and burned down the pretty little house as well as the barn-orphanage. Roz picked herself up once again and reopened her orphanage closer to Gisenyi.

Kibeho: Disaster Foreseen

Meanwhile the Lane House had turned into a boarding house for single males. Our most recent addition was Peter Whaley, who had volunteered to come over from Ghana as the political officer. A bit eccentric but outspoken, Peter fit right in with the rest of our Lane house crew, though he was the only one given to wearing silk robes. His presence added political depth to the mission reporting, plus he served as the consular and information officer, duties I avoided at all costs. Peter also volunteered to sit on the club board.

Peter arrived on the verge of a serious crisis involving the government, the RPA, UNAMIR, and the entire international community. UNAMIR had made a valiant effort to encourage the refugees to come back to Rwanda, even setting up home visitations for would-be returnees. Though there had been some successes, no great influx had taken place—to no one's real surprise. Inside Rwanda, Kagame had warned the U.N. and international community in October, 1994, that the displaced persons (DP) camps were not going to be permanent refuges. The U.N. response was Operation Retour that had returned some 300,000 internal refugees to their homes by December. By the spring of 1995, UNAMIR, UNHCR, and UNREO (United Nations Rwanda Emergency Office) had reduced the DP population from its high of 1.2 million to some 250,000 in the camps near Gikongoro. The Rwandan government played a hidden role in those successes: RPA liaisons went in ahead of the United Nations and made it clear it was better to cooperate with the United Nations and go home. Otherwise the RPA would return and clear the camps through decidedly less gentle means. When the U.N.-assisted movement out of those camps ceased, the Rwandan government made good on its promise. Commencing that spring, the RPA began—with the U.N. bodies anxiously looking on—closing the smaller camps in the southwest. In many cases, the Rwandans in the smaller camps merely picked up and headed to a larger one. But by April their choices were dwindling.

In early April, the RPA gave warning that Kibeho was next on the list for closing. Southwest of Butare, Kibeho held 125,000 displaced persons encamped around a small school and hospital complex set on a horseshoe hill. The camp had been a source of continued militia activity and was considered a hotspot by both UNAMIR and the RPA. As force commander, General Tousignant ignored U.N. New York orders to withdraw a Zambian company from the area. He said later that he felt the order was immoral and illegal. In any case the Zambian company stayed in place as an RPA brigade moved in around Kibeho on April 15. They immediately began to tighten the noose around the camp, a move inadvertently helped by the positioning of the Zambians dead center in the area. Meanwhile UNAMIR reinforced the Zambians with another company and an Aussie medical unit. The Aussies brought an emergency surgery team that established itself beside the Medicins Sans Frontiers (MSF) medical facility near the Zambians. The DPs packed in around the U.N. peacekeepers like sardines in a can, and not a few were actually trampled to death.

Keep in mind just who those displaced persons were. They were would-be refugees who had halted behind French lines rather than cross into Zaire at Bukavu. Many were directly involved in the genocide—some of the worst slaughters had occurred in this area during the war. An MSF report covering the event states "tensions between the RPA forces and the camp population increased."[2] That is the understatement of the decade. The RPA brigade around the camp included many soldiers whose families had been killed in the area. The RPA high command and the average RPA soldier knew who was in the camp and what they had done. As the RPA tightened the noose, there were incidents where displaced persons were killed. Those killings only heightened the fears inside the tightening cordon. As indicated by former SRSG Shaharyar Khan in his book, hardliners inside the camp began killing their fellow inmates as soon as the RPA arrived. The motive was simple; they intimidated them into not agreeing to be processed for return to their homes.[3]

We monitored the situation from the embassy and through UNAMIR. The ambassador had a string of visitors who painted a darkening picture of what was happening at Kibeho. They included Alison Des Forges as the Human Rights Watch principal investigator on the genocide, as well as NGO representatives. All told the same story: the RPA was on the verge of committing a large-scale massacre. Yet no one, including us in the embassy, could offer any possible solution other than what was about to unfold. UNAMIR and the other U.N. bodies as well as the international community had not been able to dissolve the remaining camps. In fact the international community was directly responsible for creating the camps and then maintaining them. Kagame had been raised in a refugee camp; he knew what would happen in the camps outside Rwanda. He certainly was not going to accept the continued presence of similar camps inside Rwanda. He had asked, warned, and stopped just short of begging the United Nations to arrive at a unified solution to the displaced person camps. The United Nations had failed. Now the RPA would act.

Firing began around and inside the camp the morning of April 22. There were three separate periods of shootings. Kibeho main camp sits on a sort of horseshoe ridgeline with the MSF and Zambian position as the heel of the shoe to the north. The RPA had completely sealed off the camp, but most of its firepower concentrated along the two "prongs" of the horseshoe. Most of the shooting was done by the RPA, and displaced Rwandans were killed indiscriminately as the RPA commanders lost control. There were killings going on inside the camp, as well, as hardliners drove those less willing first against the UNAMIR perimeter and the exterior perimeter of the camp. Finally a surge of fear-maddened inmates—several thousand in number—broke through the perimeter and stormed down the narrow valley out of the horseshoe. It was therefore a natural killing zone for the RPA troops along the ridges, and they fired into the crowd as it fled. Weather also played a role. Windy, rainy, and cold, the action petered out as darkness set in. Initial reports stated a couple of thousand had been killed. Within hours that had grown to four thousand plus, and by dawn the next morning, reports that eleven thousand had died at Kibeho were circulating.

At midnight on the twenty-second, banging told us someone was at our front door. A retired USAID guy who worked on contract as a Disaster Assistance Response Team (DART) representative was pounding on the door as I opened it. Peter was standing behind me as the guy said, "UNREO and UNAMIR have requested the U.S. military emergency airlift in a mobile surgical hospital to handle thousands of gunshot wounds at Kibeho." I made him repeat it, and when he did, I dialed Ambassador Rawson. He answered almost immediately and suggested we meet at the embassy in thirty minutes. Mickey and I would make a quick run by the UNAMIR ops center. Peter would go with the DART guy and check in with UNREO. I told the contractor to go back and reconfirm that the force commander and the SRSG were behind the request.

Our side trips complete, the three of us from the Lane house and the ambassador huddled in the front office. The DART contractor came in and said UNREO might request U.S. military medical assistance through UNAMIR; the UNAMIR medical units could not handle the load. We compared information. This was the only time I ever saw David Rawson shaken up over anything. Now he was visibly agitated and equally emotional.

"They're killers! They have driven those people to desperation—" he exclaimed before I cut him off.

"No, they didn't, David! Those people were desperate people when they went into that camp. Many of them were hip deep in the genocide. This was inevitable. We just have to sort out the results."

That was also the only time I think David Rawson considered firing me. It also made me respect him even more. Because he was shaken, he was distraught, and he was angry. Yet he allowed me to pull him up short, and he listened when he needed to listen. A lesser man would have unloaded on me. Clearly, everyone else in the room thought he was going to, because David just looked at me for nearly thirty seconds before resuming.

We laid our plans for the morning. Mickey made a quick call to UNAMIR and got us two seats on the first Huey scheduled in the morning. Peter would continue to work the Kigali end of things. David knew he faced a steady stream of phone calls from Washington. We put our initial reports into a consolidated cable to Washington. I called the Pentagon as well, then at 3 A.M. we went back home to grab some sleep.

Five A.M. and we rolled out of the driveway for UNAMIR headquarters. We stopped in at the ops shop and found it in near chaos. I got a chance to talk with the operations officer, Colonel Arp. The numbers game was in full swing; eight thousand dead was now the "accepted" number. Arp kept saying the RPA was actively hiding all the bodies, and he was trying to get as many U.N. troops on site as possible before all the evidence was gone. SRSG Khan echoes this claim in writing about Kibeho, saying the RPA brought in floodlights and trucks to carry off bodies; it is a strange claim given trucks were not supposed to be able to get into the area because of the deep mud.[4]

I was already questioning the eight thousand dead figure. How did it jump to that number from the four thousand reported earlier that same morning? It had been cloudy, rainy, and dark. Who could count bodies accurately under those conditions, especially on what was in reality a battlefield? As for the bodies being hidden, every time a killing took place, someone came up with the idea that the bodies were being put in wells. I knew that it happened in the genocide. I had seen the bodies in the well at the mission school at ZaZa. I also knew that it often did not happen. In the spectacular cable from Burundi, the ambassador in Bujumbura echoed a claim that UNAMIR and the RPA had hidden bodies in wells. How many wells does it take to hide eight thousand corpses—especially at night and in the rain?

It was evident we were not going to get good information here, so Mickey and I went out to the UNAMIR helo pad. Our bird was due to lift at 0600. Dense fog greeted us at the gate to the airport. We sat down to wait. Mickey flaked out in the back of the Land Cruiser, and I crashed in the front. No birds lifted for more than four hours; at around 1000 we started to get glimpses of blue through the fog and low clouds. Finally at around 1100 we lifted off for Kibeho, landing at the pad some thirty minutes later. Mickey and I studied the ground independently. We had agreed that the way to do this was walk the area and talk to the troops without comparing notes. Once we were done, we would then collate our findings to determine what we had learned. As we started, General Tousignant arrived and began his own tour.

As we landed, I fixed the horseshoe layout of the hill in my mind. We were landing at the tip of the easternmost prong with the heel to our north. I could see the cluster of blue berets inside the Zambian position, as well as the tents set up by the Aussies. One thing caught my eye immediately: the "killing ground" between the ridge we were standing on and the one to our west. There were no bodies in evidence. I also saw no mortar or RPG divots or burn marks on the area. Covered with short green grass, the Rwandan soil was dark red, and explosions from mortars or rockets should have torn that green carpet. We walked on and passed a number of RPA positions. At each, I stopped and just looked around, marking expended cases and any other evidence of sustained firing. Final reports from MSF would state categorically that the RPA had fired steadily with small arms, heavy machine guns, and other heavy weapons for more than thirteen hours. I would have expected to see piles of expended brass several feet deep. Instead I was counting individual cartridges. Moving closer to the nexus of the camp, I began to see more bodies. I stepped on a piece of plywood and heard a deep groan. Looking down, I stared into the lifeless eyes of an old man pinned under the debris. My weight had compressed his lungs to produce the ghoulish groan. By the time I reached the Zambian compound, I had counted several hundred bodies, a mix of men, women, and children. I noted as I reached the point of the area that would have been inside the camp at the time of the breakout that the majority of the dead in that area had been killed by machetes.

Inside the Zambian compound, we were received with no small degree of suspicion. Mickey and I both wore BDUs and shoulder rigs; it was clear we were definitely not UNAMIR. The Zambians finally talked a bit. They focused on the displaced persons' initial surge into their compound. More than one said some of the Rwandans were armed with machetes. As for the Aussies, they told us about the casualties they had treated, confirming more than a few had been from machetes. One officer explained how they had done a casualty matrix: they had counted the dead in a certain area and then applied that density to the camp area in general. The first figure reached had been two thousand; that was judged inadequate, so they doubled it. Voila! Four thousand dead! Looking around I concluded that two thousand dead was probably pretty close.[5]

Mickey and I continued on up the hill past the MSF-run hospital. It remained surrounded by UNAMIR and RPA troops. Once past, an RPA runner came down and grabbed us and motioned us to follow. At the heel of the west prong, we found the RPA leadership surveying the mop-up of the operation. By now it was nearly 1330, but the RPA had already cleared most of the camp. A few thousand Rwandans remained huddled in a column waiting transport to receiving centers from where they would be sent home. Colonels Nyamwasa and Kaka were both there. Sam Kaka waved and said hello. Nyamwasa was never that cordial. Charles Muheri was there as well, along with Karenzi. I went up and sat down.

"So, Charles, when are you gonna do this in Goma?"

He grinned but then said, "We had some problems, but we finally completed the job."

Pointing at the MSF hospital, he said, "We have some sniper fire from there. There are a couple of hundred holdouts inside as well. We are trying to talk them out."

While we were sitting with Charles and Karenzi, not a single UNAMIR officer approached the RPA leaders. As we chatted, Karenzi came up and said, "Look!" He pointed at a line of low buildings used to hold less-cooperative males until they were loaded onto the trucks. A trap door opened on the roof, and an obvious escapee crawled out on the roof. Charles barked an order in his radio, and the officer standing in front of the building moved to the side to where he could see the roof. Bang! No more escapee. I guess they figured he'd already had one chance.

After our session on the hill, we moved down to the helipad to wait for a lift. It was on a standby basis. The helo drivers were tired; they had been shuttling serious cases all day. Finally around 1630 we boarded a bird with two casualties on board, one gunshot and one machete. We would fly them to the Butare museum and offload them. An NGO ambulance was to meet us. It had started raining, and we were soaked and tired. Landing at Butare, we dropped off the wounded, and as I reboarded I slipped in a pool of blood on the helo's deck. I had my left hand in a boarding strap and could not let go before I spun 360 degrees on the shoulder. I felt a tear and a razor-sharp pain inside the shoulder. I shook it off at the time; it would catch up with me later.

Back on the ground in Kigali, Mickey drove and listened as I talked though my observations. Then I listened and he talked. By the time we reached the embassy, we were able to walk in and brief the ambassador and Peter. The bottom line was a difficult operation had gone bad, and people had died. I put the casualties at around two thousand. I walked David through the logic. A five-thousand-man brigade had cleared a camp of 125,000 in slightly over twenty-four hours in bad weather. Several sustained bouts of firing had broken out, and a large number—maybe seven thousand—displaced persons had forced their way out under fire. The suggestion that such firing had lasted more than twelve hours was logistically and operationally not sustainable. If one uses the sustained rate of fire of an M16 (roughly the same as an AK), sixteen rounds per minute, that is 11,520 rounds per soldier in twelve hours of sustained fire or nearly *58 million* rounds for a five-thousand-man unit. I doubted there was that much ammunition in the entire country. The evidence on the ground suggested hundreds, not thousands, of rounds. The five-thousand-man brigade could not have picked up all the brass, buried all the bodies, and cleared the camp in the time allotted. That was the Kibeho massacre, already making front-page news in the United States and Europe, with an eight-thousand-dead casualty figure. I called in the same high points to the Pentagon and put a full report out the next morning.

Kibeho: Fallout

Naturally the fallout from the Kibeho massacre began even before the final shots were fired. We had notified State immediately, and we got the expected rumbles at first. The African Bureau started in again with the Gersony refrain, and so did the ambassador in Burundi. Yet the United States did not suspend foreign assistance—just barely restarted—as did the Belgians, the Dutch, and the European Union. Deputy Assistant Secretary of Defense Vince Kern passed word to me that our report had saved the day. We had put the disastrous operation in the proper perspective against protests from the African Bureau at State. The Rwandan government moved effectively in checking much of the backlash by accepting a U.N. call to conduct a special investigation committee consisting of government representatives, U.N. agencies, and selected countries. The United States was named to the commission and Ambassador Rawson tapped Maurice Nyberg, an American lawyer who had been a member of the U.N. Special Investigations Unit, the predecessor to the International Tribunal. During his month tenure with the commission, Nyberg ended up staying with us at the Lane house.

But before any commission could begin, the Kibeho camp had to be cleared completely. Since the final rush began April 22, hardliners and other DPs had taken refuge inside the building MSF used as its main hospital. Both the RPA and UNAMIR had reported taking limited fire from that direction even before the evening finale. MSF had its people in the compound while that was going on. Highly critical of UNAMIR and the RPA after the massacre, MSF sidestepped the issue of allowing armed elements to operate within the hospital. The NGO also sidestepped criticism that its staff in Kibeho had actively counseled the refugees not to leave the compound. The hardliners were still there when Mickey and I walked by the place on April 23. They were already killing each other. The SRSG of UNAMIR quickly called on the entire Kigali diplomatic leadership to convene on Kibeho on April 28 to try and talk the survivors out. Mickey and I escorted David down to the camp in a convoy of diplomatic vehicles.

All the ambassadors followed SRSG Khan inside the compound to talk to the crazies. Mickey and I stayed outside watching the proceedings. I went up to the main entrance and was greeted by the sight of a recently slain woman with her equally dead baby at her breast. She had been dead less than twelve hours. Her eyes were not yet glazed over. We learned later the killing inside the MSF hospital had begun in earnest on April 23 when the hardliners decided all members from a particular commune were RPA sympathizers. None had been back in the commune since the end of the war. But a Hutu native of the village had returned and accepted the mayoral post under the new government, a move transformed inside the hate and fear of Kibeho into commune-wide treachery by the militias. Inside the pressure cooker of that hospital, the hardliners declared that those present from the commune in question were also traitors and turned on them. Distant events could get you dead in places like Kibeho. Finally, the holdouts allowed the RPA with UNAMIR assistance to escort them out. The hardliners were led off to prison, and the RPA discovered a few rifles and plenty of machetes inside.

As for the commission, it was probably relatively fair; it angered and pleased both sides. The final report recognized the right of the Rwandan government to close the camps and added that the government had not planned the massacre. But it also offered the curious phrase that the massacre was "not an accident that could not have been prevented." It spread the blame for the killings between the RPA and the armed elements in the camp. Notably it did not place any blame on UNAMIR for the peacekeepers' failure to intervene—something the NGO community did with malice. On the other hand it did cite several NGOs for interfering in the closing of the camp. The commission members did not attempt to get into the body count business, stating there were more killed than the government's official count of 338. Finally, the commission called upon the government and the RPA to investigate their mistakes, a move already under way in the Ministry of Defense.

UNAMIR Mandate: Go Swim but Stay Dry

The immediate result of Kibeho was to increase pressure on the government of Rwanda to agree to an extension of the UNAMIR mandate. Due to expire in early June, the mandate for the U.N. peacekeepers had long since become irrelevant, especially after Kibeho. Yet the United Nations and the international community wanted some form of U.N. military mission present in the country as a sort of moral baby blanket to soothe the members in case something went seriously awry. The solution—brokered in tough negotiations with the government—was to switch the mandate to "confidence building," and conduct a gradual reduction in the size of the U.N. force. UNAMIR would drop from 5,500 to 2,330 over the next three months and to 1,800 within four. As part of the mandate, UNAMIR was to support the provision of humanitarian aid and of assistance and expertise in engineering, logistics, medical care, and demining. UNAMIR was no longer charged with the security of the Rwandan people, something it could never have done anyway. By default, the new mandate granted the government responsibility for national security, a position already stated and taken by the Rwandans. Yet the United Nations refused to lift the arms embargo on weapons into Rwanda and extended that embargo to surrounding countries against the importation of arms meant for use against Rwanda. In essence the new mandate gave UNAMIR the charter it had needed since the war ended, then agreed to reductions crippling its ability to achieve those goals. At the same time, it accepted the government's control of the country but then limited the government's ability to do so through embargo. It was a catch-22 for both sides.[6]

Kibeho: Model for Goma

The long-term results of Kibeho were readily apparent but not readily accepted. Kagame had issued a warning he would not accept the internal camps as permanent fixtures. He asked the United Nations and the international community do something to correct the problem. After months of delay and active resistance by certain NGOs, the RPA went in and did the job. Faced with the resultant criticism, the RPF remained unbowed. They reminded me of the Israelis; they did what they felt they had to do and let the results speak for themselves. With the closure of Kibeho, the rest of the camps in the southwest emptied almost overnight. Who wanted to wait for an RPA unit to show up when the results were foretold? With the internal refugee situation resolved, Kagame issued the same type of warning about the camps in Zaire. The format was the same: he asked for the countries involved, the United Nations, and the larger international community to do something to resolve the situation. Then he stated that Rwanda would not accept the refugee camps on its borders as permanent fixtures. The clock had started.

Deaf Ears and Closed Minds

I heard the ticking. The ambassador heard the ticking, as did Peter Whaley. So did the Department of Defense and USAID. Dick McCall, the AID chief of staff, made several extended visits to Rwanda during the spring and summer. I briefed him on the country, and he listened. I wish I could say the same was true for the Department of State. We—the policy group in the embassy—had the collective sinking feeling that State thinking ran along the lines it had before Kibeho: Kagame would not dare do anything outside Rwanda; he was bluffing. Or worse, we could strong-arm him into inaction or merely string him along. Unfortunately, reporting from Kinshasa continued to add to that delusion. Ambassador Simpson had taken over the mission in Kinshasa after leaving the doomed mission in Mogadishu. This was his third tour in Zaire. He had a very strong personality, and he exercised it regularly. According to those who knew him from earlier assignments, he believed in the "one mission, one view" rule when it came to reporting. That is okay if the mission got the story correct. It could be disastrous if it did not. Kinshasa did not and would not get the story right until 1997 when Kinshasa fell to Rwandan-backed rebel forces. Kinshasa's position in 1995 on the camps was no militias, no arms, no training, and no cross-border activity.[7]

That was truly a remarkable position to take. I had direct access to the RPA and Karenzi. He told me when they intercepted cross-border operations and when they did not. UNAMIR also reported numerous infiltration efforts along the eastern border. Many were economically motivated. Stealing cattle was common. One had to ask—and I did—why they would risk rustling cows if they were in the camps and getting fed already. But if they were outside the main camps and did not have complete access to the food lines, several head of cattle could feed a lot of troops. Other cross-border operations were direct actions. Ambushes, sniping, mining, and assassinations grew more frequent as the year progressed. We reported all of this, and Kinshasa refuted it. In July, 1995, Medicins Sans Frontiers issued a long report on the deadlock on the crisis. In that report, MSF catalogued cross-border attacks, including some confirmed by the CZSC, the "new" Zairian security forces around the camps. These were the soldiers Kinshasa repeatedly stated could effectively police the camps. Those same soldiers told MSF that they knew the militias were training and were impotent to do anything about it.[8]

Continuing problems in Burundi added to the murky picture State had of the situation. Tutsi equals Tutsi equals Tutsi was the line vigorously espoused by the ambassador in Bjumbura, meaning a "bad" Tutsi army in Burundi was the same as a "bad" Tutsi army in Rwanda. There were massacres at camps and continued atrocities inside Burundi that the embassy focused on, and rightly so. The ambassador there blasted the Tutsi Burundian military for not living up to its promises. But by tying the RPA to that military, he lent credence to the idea that Kagame did not *really* mean what he said.

In an effort to develop a more coherent picture of the regional problem, State dispatched Ambassador Richard Bogosian as a special envoy to the Great Lakes region. His charter was to move between Rwanda and Burundi and all bordering countries to assess their positions on the issues. Hopefully, he would be able to draw on enough common threads to weave a coherent policy aimed at stabilizing the region. I developed great respect for Ambassador Bogosian. But our initial talks were frustrating. Fresh from Washington and pumped up on the African Bureau's party line, he initially did not seem to hear what we had to say. In a matter of weeks, he began to see our way of thinking: given the host of problems the government faced, they were doing about as well as could be expected.

Consider the issue of prisons and trials. The first trial by the International Tribunal was years away, and the investigations were, in mid-1995, glacial in their pace. The government in general and the RPA in particular had been blasted more than once for "revenge killings." The Gersony report had attempted to make the case that those killings were not only sanctioned by the government but also orchestrated by the leaders of the RPA. Kibeho had led to similar charges, also somewhat disproved. NGOs like MSF blasted the government for not fostering a climate conducive to returning refugees. Yet eight hundred thousand Rwandans had died in the genocide, and most had yet to be buried. Their families were still there to recognize the killers when they returned. Those killers were soon dead themselves if the government stood by and did nothing. They could not pick up those accused and take them back to the border. Nor could they leave them in place without getting accused of sanctioning revenge killings. So they arrested them; by mid-summer, 1995, there were more than forty-nine-thousand prisoners in Rwandan jails. And there were no courts, judges, or lawyers to try them. Conditions in the prisons were bad, but once accused, life outside the prison without a trial could be brutally short. None of the choices for the government were easy; they had plenty of advice from a host of international players and NGOs on what was the "right thing to do."

I really believe Ambassador Bogosian's Armenian heritage helped him understand how deep the post-genocide trauma had wounded the country. (The Armenians still pursue the issue of genocide against the Turks after eight decades.) Bogosian never—at least in my hearing—suggested the Rwandans should just "get over" the genocide like it was the flu. Ultimately he came to recognize there was no magic wand to wave over the tragedies of the past, distant and recent. And that future tragedy, like Kibeho, was equally certain. Like David and I had come to understand in late 1994, our mission was not to stop the killing but perhaps limit its spread. The only way to do that was to emphasize clear warnings when we detected them and hope the right folks would take notice. I knew from my experience before the Gulf War how difficult that could be. Like Kagame, we began to pump up the volume about Goma before the blood at Kibeho had dried.

Influence Comes through Promises Delivered

At the same time we pounded the drums on Goma, we attempted to deliver on our promises to the struggling government. Despite his emotional reaction in the middle of the Kibeho tragedy, Ambassador Rawson continued to lead us in that struggle. I had already begun on the humanitarian side with assistance to the Rwandan medical and education sectors. We had the demining effort at the stage where I would shortly have 3rd SFG on the ground. Funds already budgeted under Expanded-International Military Education and Training (E-IMET) had been released, and we were soon to send a group of Rwandan military officers to the States for the second stage of the Naval Justice course. The first had been the seminar in January, 1994, held in the USIS conference room. The team leader for the second stage was to be Maj. Richard Sezebera, a military doctor in the RPA. Richard became the Rwandan ambassador to the United States in 1999.

I was still pushing increased military assistance to the RPA in the areas of communications, mobility, and training should we succeed in getting the U.N. embargo lifted. Parallel to my efforts as senior military representative, USAID was also pushing the envelope. Congress had restricted AID training of justice and police officials after the experiences of the 1960s Congo and Vietnam. But the birth of the post–Cold War era had eased those restrictions in places like Haiti and the former Yugoslavia. Consequently, USAID had, under the direct guidance of Chief of Staff McCall, concentrated its non-disaster relief efforts on rebuilding the Rwandan justice system. As ambassador, David not only guided our efforts but also lent his influence to NGO and international programs that meshed with our goals. To his credit, David played hardball in this area. His first question when someone or some organization asked for help with the government was always what that someone or organization intended to do for the government. Altogether we had an integrated company team and a coherent plan.

We worked hard on selling our ideas to the key players, especially in State. With Bogosian tapped as a regional representative, Assistant Secretary George Moose again came out for consultations. The topics were much the same. Reprisal killings, prisons, refugee return, and stability were all on the list. The difference was Bogosian was ready to suggest that the RPA might help us help them in the security arena through more open sharing. Aside from David, Bogosian was the first State official to even hint we might be able to help the Rwandans with security assistance. I was tabbed to go in as a scribe in the important meetings with Kagame and his inner staff. There were no real surprises in the visit but again Bogosian was coming around.

A Campaign Plan: How to "Do the Right Thing"

I was not sure that our plan was understood much less accepted outside the micro-world of U.S. embassy Kigali. I went to David and suggested the last thing we wanted to foster was a creeping evolution of commitments lacking a central policy objective. We needed, as I explained to the ambassador, a campaign plan to clarify what we were doing in Kigali. That is to say, clarify for Washington and U.S. European Command what we were doing in Rwanda. He concurred and I wrote the multipage document in a day. A campaign plan is not a tactical operations order; it is a statement on how to achieve a strategic vision. In World War II, Eisenhower's strategic marching orders were to go to England, invade Europe, and defeat the Axis powers. From that, he derived a campaign plan to achieve those lofty goals. Anything not serving the central purpose was at best wasted effort and at worst counterproductive.

In 1995, a year after the genocide and end of the war, we certainly did not have a clear strategic objective in Rwanda—at least one stated by the administration. Washington remained reactive to events. We crafted our own: we sought to limit the killing in Rwanda through offering assistance to increase internal stability and reduce external threats. That was our "conquer Europe" mission. Our selection of that basic goal was equally simple. We believed if we did not work toward that aim, the new government in Rwanda was bound to strike out at its external enemies and grow increasingly harder on its internal foes. Regional conflict was on the horizon. As a strategic tool, David and I believed getting U.S. European Command, the Joint Staff, and Defense to sign up for the plan would offer us greater leverage in dealing with State. I knew Defense was on board as was USAID. I believed—and later learned that I was correct—that U.S. European Command and the Joint Staff would sign on. We also had a patron at the National Security Council with Susan Rice. Aside from the African Bureau, our detractors were the U.S. Mission to the United Nations and the CIA. The U.S. Mission to the United Nations seemed to take every statement or action of the government toward the United Nations as a personal affront. My CIA "friends" over in Zaire were sharpening their knives for me with the active support of my replacement. Meanwhile my ambassador had angered Langley by refusing to accept a station in Kigali. Finally, midlevel management at the DIA opposed the plan simply because it implied a permanent DAO. Nevertheless, we moved forward with a clearer view of our path. I could see we had a hard road ahead, and the bridges were shaky. If we did not move quickly enough, those bridges would collapse, and Rwanda would take most of central Africa with it into war.

Demining II: Getting Started, Getting Fired

After the earlier site survey had completed its work in Rwanda, I believed we had a pretty good plan for getting on with the demining effort. We got Willy, a bright and dedicated staff sergeant from 3rd SFG, to begin the initial contracting needed to get underway. Willy had been with the SOCEUR Survey. His job was to locate housing for the teams coming, select a training base, and negotiate for vehicles for the teams and the Rwandan deminers. I gave him a long leash to work with; I did not have the time to be peeking over his shoulder every fifteen minutes. Neither did Mickey. Willy checked in with us everyday and debriefed with one or both of us. From the beginning, it was clear he would get the work done. He found housing and with my approval signed a conditional lease. He also located a Nissan dealer who had his franchise in Kampala. We initially considered leases on the vehicles but decided to go with buying the trucks at roughly twenty to thirty thousand each depending on the model. As "AID project officer," I sought and got permission to buy non-U.S. vehicles. American vehicles were not built for Africa, and parts were scarce. The Nissans fit the bill, and we signed a tentative purchase order for ten.

The training base was a bit more difficult. Clearly, we needed a school or similar building for the classroom technical instruction. Aside from basic explosives and mine detection, we had to teach first aid, information processing, and computer skills. Field instruction—lane training on mine detection—could be done almost anywhere. Willy came to me and said the Rwandans wanted to know if we could assist in renovating their staff school facilities. The school had been heavily damaged during the war. But it was ideally suited for a training base. I got on the phone to European Command and received almost immediate approval for the project. For $200,000 we would be able to renovate the school and use part of it as a permanent base for the Rwandan National Demining Office. Another quick contract and work was underway. While getting European Command's approval, the command Demining Office asked if we would be interested in a follow-on contract to bring in demining dogs and a contractor to train the Rwandans on how to use them. Naturally I jumped on that offer.

Several weeks later, we received the Special Operations Forces survey team to finalize the project with the Rwandans. Under a 3rd SFG major, the team consisted of Special Forces (S.F.), Civil Affairs, and PSYOPS planners. I gave them a full rundown on the Rwandan situation and then set up a meeting with the RPA leadership. We had the conference the next day. I introduced all the planners and explained their individual roles to the RPA leaders present, including Colonels Kaka, Muheri, and Nyamwasa. Karenzi was also present along with Major Mbaraga, the designated commander of the demining program. Things went quite cordially and after a couple of hours, I left it to the major to get on with it.

That evening around six, the major came by the house with his company sergeant major. Mickey and I offered them a beer, but the major announced he did not drink. We sat down around the table on the porch. I expected he was there to give me a progress report. I also expected it to be positive. It was not.

The major started by questioning the Rwandans' commitment to the program, remarking they had not done their share. I set my beer down and asked, "What do you mean by their share, Major?" He wanted more soldiers, something I could understand but something already agreed on by our earlier negotiations. But what was not understandable and even less acceptable was his proposal that the Rwandans pay for the vehicles and the renovations on the training building.

"Hold it right there, Major," I said, cutting him off. "We have an agreement with the Rwandans approved and funded by EUCOM. That agreement is simple. They provide fifty men and officers for the initial phase of training. We provide everything else. Period. We have contracts for vehicles and the renovations—." He cut me off with a remark that the program was unfair. I had heard enough.

"Major, listen to me carefully. You don't decide what is 'right.' I do. The ambassador does. EUCOM approves it. You execute it. I don't need or want your opinion on whether the Rwandans are doing their share. They don't have anything to offer other than the men. You got it?"

He nodded a yes. And I took it as an understanding. They had but another day or so before they returned to the States to start preparations. The major had said he would go back to Fort Bragg to finalize the plans and then deploy with the training mission. Once started he would change command with another Special Forces major and then leave. The same NCO who had served as the interim planner would stay as liaison to the RPA and the embassy. Each day I got a debrief. It appeared things were going all right. As planned, the SOF survey team left at the end of the week.

The day they departed, I got a surprise visit from Major Rusagara, our old liaison to the Ministry of Defense. Frank as usual lived up to his name. He did not mince words.

"Colonel, I am here to tell you the vice president has decided that if we are expected to meet the demands your demining trainers had laid on the table, we will have to decline the program," he said. He then continued to explain the RPA could not provide one hundred troops along with vehicles. He also added the RPA leadership had understood we were going to pay for the renovations on the staff college, an agreement he wanted to reaffirm.

"Frank, your earlier understanding is still correct. Let me find out what has happened, and I will come see you and the vice president as soon as I can."

He agreed, and we shook hands on it. I called for Mickey and told him to get Willy in the embassy as soon as possible. Our S.F. sergeant soon arrived. He told us the full story, adding he had been ordered not to say anything to me or anyone else at the embassy about what had transpired. Even though I had told the 3rd SFG major not to place demands or conditions on the RPA, he went ahead and did just that. Not only did he demand the Rwandans ante up for the training, he then said the S.F. teams would need communications with their battalion headquarters, scheduled to be in Zimbabwe on exercise. That caught the Rwandans off guard as well, as it implied they might be working on another mission—something the French would do. When they referred to the agreement with the embassy and European Command, he ignored them and then started to lecture.

"Sir, he talked down to them like they were a bunch of Haitians," Willy offered. "I honestly started getting scared. They looked at him and me like we were enemies. The senior man walked out," he finished, adding the senior man had been Colonel Muheri.

I was mentally booting myself for not chairing all the meetings. I did not know anything about an exercise. I started probing Willy, and I did not like what I found out. When Willy had returned to Fort Bragg after his initial time in country, he learned his battalion commander had gone ahead with his own planning. Essentially, he had taken a demining plan used in Cambodia and changed the country to Rwanda. That accounted for the doubling of the manpower. The battalion was due to execute its annual training mission in Africa, so they decided Rwanda was the ideal location for the central communications node.

Before going to see Kagame, I called European Command and asked point blank if the January agreement between the command and the RPA still stood. There was a new demining officer, but he was fully briefed on the earlier survey. He assured me that was still the case and then asked if there was a problem. I told him what I knew and that I was on my way to see the vice president. He knew about the Special Forces exercise in Africa but stated the demining program was to be totally separate. He said he would be checking in with SOCEUR to see what they knew about it. My meeting with Kagame was not pleasant. He went through some of the issues and then said if the new demands remained in place, the RPA would have to pull out. I told him European Command remained committed to the earlier agreement. He should ignore what the team commander had said.

"General, sometimes majors get too impressed with themselves. Let me fix this," I offered in conclusion.

That drew a smile from the man who'd been a major one day and a general the next. "Yes, I was a major once myself."

Back at the embassy, I briefed the ambassador on the entire problem. I told him I would fix it. "Let me handle it at my level, David. If I need your big guns, I'll call for fire," I said, and he agreed.

By now we had also gotten in a coordination message from 3rd SFG. There it was bigger than life. Rwanda was to serve as the exercise communications node. As such, we would also get in more troops who had nothing to do with the demining. The message demanded clearances for special communications gear as well as the unit's standard weapons load, yet another surprise not addressed while the SOF planners had been on the ground. I had Willy call Fort Bragg and deliver a message that the battalion commander should call me immediately.

Soon the phone rang with a member of the battalion staff calling for the commander. Two can play that game, and it was their long distance dime. I refused to take the phone until the commander was on the line. I was not in a mood to be gentle. I told him flat out his major had almost derailed the demining program before it got started.

"The EUCOM demining plan stands, and you will not change it, Colonel," I said. "Your major will not be returning to this country. Do you understand?"

"You don't make those decisions. I am in command," he countered.

"You're right. I don't make those decisions. The ambassador does. Guess what? Your major just had his country clearance permanently withdrawn. No further clearances will be granted to any of your personnel unless they are identified as demining trainers. That means no extra bodies for your exercise communications and no extra toys."

He did not like it, but I did not care. Ultimately we agreed the teams could bring in their weapons packages and store them in the embassy. It was a rocky start to what should have been an easy mission. I thought I had avoided other problems. A few weeks later the teams arrived via a C141. I pulled all officers and key NCOs into the embassy conference room. Just as I had before, I ran down the Rwandan situation for them. I also added a warning.

"I understand many of you have just come out of Haiti. I understand how frustrating that mission was. I have been to Haiti, and I should have been there by now as the defense attaché. I chose to stay here because I can do more here. Part of that is this program. I warn you now, and make sure you get this. The RPA is not the Haitian military. The RPA just won a war. They did it on their own. They have also just come out of genocide. They are broke and they want our help. But they are proud. I repeat they are not Haitians. If I hear of anyone showing any disrespect to any of them, I will come down on you like a ton of bricks—and so will the ambassador," I said, looking at all of them but focusing on the new major.

"Now go make it happen. Welcome to Kigali. We are happy to have you," I finished.

And they did start making it happen. The A-teams divided the schoolhouse and lane training between themselves. One team set up in the school to teach the more technical skills. The other set up in a local RPA garrison and roughed it with the "Boys." The PSYOP and Civil Affairs teams concentrated on the National Demining Office (NDO). The NDO would be the center for the mine awareness effort. It would also serve as the operations office for the demining teams once they became operational. The Rwandans under Major Mbaraga also turned out to be willing learners. After the pressure to field one hundred trainees, the RPA bumped their numbers up to seventy. Things began to click, and I was pleased.

But once burned, twice wise, so I kept an eye on things, especially the new major. He had to know why his predecessor had not returned. I made sure he did. I told him. I also told him I believed soldiers should get a mission and be given the latitude to carry it out. Mistakes made in ignorance could be fixed. Mistakes generated by stupidity were not acceptable.

"That means if you run into a problem, deal with it but keep me informed. If I give you a different solution to implement, I have a reason. Not listening is classed as stupidity."

"Yes, Sir."

Though he seemed to understand, I detected warning signs as the weeks passed. First was the relationship between him as the B-team commander and the two A-teams. The A-team out with the boys was sort of like a redheaded stepchild. Willy was part of that team, and the team commander, Capt. Scott Suites, had been on the original SO-CEUR demining survey. Willy had told me Suites had argued against the 3rd SFG's changes to the plan. Willy was viewed as something of a traitor because he had told me what had happened at the last major's meeting with the RPA. The new major seemed to regard the entire team as suspect, something the team reveled in behind his back. It was not my problem, but I watched it carefully.

The other warning sign flashed even brighter, and it was my problem. The new major started in with me one day about the RPA's commitment to the program. I cut him off at the knees and told him it was his final warning. He seemed to get the message. The teams had given all the Rwandan trainees a physical fitness test as a screening tool. Many had failed. They lacked upper body and abdominal strength; pushups and sit-ups killed them. They did okay on the run, but they walked the Rwandan mountains like goats. When a suggestion surfaced to cull the trainees on the basis of the fitness test, the major stopped it. He told me about it at the club one evening.

"Congratulations, Major! You might just make colonel after all, " I said both as a joke and a caution.

"Sir, I am absolutely sure I will make lieutenant colonel," he announced.

At the time I thought, "I'm sure you are."

One Friday evening at happy hour, Scott Suites came up to me at the bar, full of enthusiasm. I liked the young officer. He had been in Goma at the end, and he had a clearer picture of the Rwandan scene than most. His team liked him. And he boasted about them—exactly what you want in an A-team.

"We done good today, Colonel," he announced, almost wagging his tail like a puppy. I motioned for more and he continued.

"The RPA found a dud mortar round alongside the road we run on every morning. A kid had actually picked it up, but they stopped him. They told Master Sergeant Duffy about it and he grabbed the engineer sergeant to go take a look. The Rwandan trainees aren't ready yet for this so Duffy talked them through it as the engineer sergeant blew it in place. We made some real points for that. It was all over in thirty minutes," he said, beaming.

"Tell Duff good job!" I answered. Duffy was the team "Daddy" and a steady man. I thought no more of it until the next day when I walked into the front office to find Duffy and the team engineer sitting on the sofa.

"Sir, can we speak to you?" Duffy asked.

"Sure, come on in. What's up?"

"Sir, the major read me my rights this morning along with the captain and the engineer. He said we had knowingly violated the Rules of Engagement and is going for at least an Article 15," he said without emotion.

Then he continued, "He ordered us not to speak to anyone about this, especially you."

I told him I would look into it but to keep a low profile until he heard from me. He did tell me the Rwandans knew about it and did not understand what the problem was. Neither did I. I knew what the ROE were; at no time were U.S. soldiers to enter a mined or UXO area to conduct actual demining. But what about when they were already in a UXO area before they found out? The Rwandans had found the mortar round adjacent to the main road into the military compound. A child had been handling it. The A-team ran by that round every morning with their Rwandan trainees. The trainees might have been able to blow it. Then again they might have blown themselves sky high. What was Duffy to do? Ask for help and then wait? No, he did what a U.S. non-commissioned officer is supposed to do. He weighed his options and then did what was needed.

I called Charles at RPA headquarters. Of course, he knew about the incident. Training had halted, and the RPA was scratching its collective head wondering why. He asked if he should call in the major and ask for an explanation. I approved and then after dismissing Duffy, briefed the ambassador. He rolled his eyes in disbelief before offering his assistance. "No, Boss, let me see if I can fix this one as well," was my answer.

Later I tracked down the major. I told him I had heard through the RPA there had been some incident involving an unexploded mortar round. He described what had happened and then said he was pressing charges against the soldiers involved as well as the team leader. He indicated he was already in contact with his commander, now in Zimbabwe. According to him, the battalion commander fully concurred in the charges. Thus far, the soldiers had not indicated they would accept an Article 15—I knew that already as Duffy had told me in my office. That meant a 15-6 investigative officer would be coming out to see if there were grounds for courts-martial. I listened to all of this before speaking.

"Major, I do not agree with your assessment of the incident. I have read the ROE, and I do not believe they were violated. Neither does the ambassador. Your command is your command, and I will not interfere. But I will tell the 15-6 investigator what I think and so will the ambassador. Judge wisely before you act," I finished.

He blinked and walked off.

As fate would have it, we were expecting the visit of the SOCEUR commander that week. I was in a delicate position here. European Command had accepted me as a de facto senior military representative for Rwanda because I was there. Officially, I was still a TDY "Kelly girl" filling for Jim Cobb in Cameroon. The DIA—meaning my supervisor at headquarters—would not back me if I got into a pig wrestle with 3d SFG over the mortar round incident. Still, ethically and morally, I could not allow a suspect field-grade officer to destroy a good officer and two excellent NCOs. Finesse was called for, and I went to see Colonel Charles, the G3.

Charles, as an ex-civilian lawyer, handled many of the RPA's discipline cases. He understood as I explained what was going on. I could not jump inside what was a legal matter internal to the chain of command of 3d SFG. I would have to wait—along with the 3d SFG chain of command—for the 15-6 officer to complete his report. That officer was due in with the visit of the SOCEUR. Charles, on the other hand, could raise the question of why the American soldiers had been charged for saving Rwandan lives. He could also point to the disrupted training schedule as a tragic loss of valuable training time. Charles grinned as he listened. Then he added his own ideas. He would be at the training site along with other senior officers. They would all praise the trainers, then question what was happening.

So that is what we did. The SOCEUR commander had to cancel but sent the 3d SFG commander in his stead. A full colonel with a long career in Special Forces, he immediately took to the RPA. We laid on a full demonstration of the training, both at the school and the NDO. Major Mbaraga briefed him at every station, and the RPA trainees demonstrated their growing proficiency. We finished at the field-training site under Captain Suites and Master Sergeant Duffy. Everyone, including the RPA soldiers, executed with crackling efficiency. The site reeked of happy trainers and happier trainees. Charles was there, and I introduced the two colonels. They talked about the mission and then Charles eased the S.F. colonel away for a private conversation. I watched and sweated. Charles looked like he was back in a courtroom. In a way he was, and the A-team leaders nearby were on trial. He waved his arms and pointed at the S.F. troops and then the RPA. The S.F. colonel listened and then the two smiled and shook hands. Walking toward me, Charles shook hands with our visitor and winked at me before walking to his vehicle. It was time for us to leave, and I headed to my truck as the visitors climbed into one of the NDO vehicles.

"Colonel Odom, ride with me, please," commanded my visitor. I complied and got in the shotgun seat. After warning me about interfering in 3d SFG's chain of command, he offered that he wanted the program to work. I acknowledged the warning and accepted his intent to get on with the program.

From that point on we chatted about the training. I also brought up that the ambassador hoped for more training in the future. I suggested a Joint-Combined Exercise for Training (JCET) in the future. I emphasized how well his Special Forces troopers had done with the RPA. He smiled at that, and I knew Charles and I had not fooled this guy for one minute. I also felt he understood why we had tried. With the 15-6 officer on the ground, the investigation was done in less than a week. He delivered his verdict to the ambassador and me: there were no grounds for the charges specified. Master Sergeant Duffy had done what an S.F. team sergeant is trained to do. Charges dismissed. I bought Duffy and the others a round at the bar that evening.

The matter was closed, and I wanted it kept that way. I remained cordially correct with the major, but I kept my ear to the ground. The ambassador and I had agreed it was in the best interest of the program to handle all the gaffes as low-key as possible. I had, however, kept an ever-evolving message to SOCEUR on my computer. The message cataloged all the problems we had encountered; it was a bomb I did not want to send. Thus far, no one had been hurt, physically or professionally. The first major had gone home without a detectable blemish. I just did not let him come back. I hoped that with the charges dropped 3d SFG would make sure Suites and his team sergeants did not suffer on their next report cards. I believed that with the 3d SFG commander's visit and the negative results of the 15-6 the major would allow the matter to die gracefully. The major, however, was not so inclined; instead he declared a public vendetta against the entire A-team at formation in front of the Rwandan National Demining Office. Those present included the other A-team, the Civil Affairs team, and the PSYOP detachment, along with a group of curious RPA officers. Major Mbaraga was one of the latter.

It was the wrong thing to say and the wrong audience to say it to. The other A-team commander and another officer made it their mission to find me. Joseph Mbaraga and Charles Muheri did the same the next day. I pulled up the message "bomb" and completed it. The ambassador reviewed it, as did Mickey. Addressed to SOCEUR and Fort Bragg, it was on the way as I got the deputy commander for SOCEUR on the line. A full captain Navy SEAL, he listened as I briefed him. At first there was general silence, but as I relayed all the problems, he started cussing. Navy SEALs have amazing vocabularies, and he used most of the cusswords in his kitbag.

Three hours later, I heard Mickey enter my office holding a fax. He handed it to me. It recalled the major to Fort Bragg immediately, replacing him with the executive officer of 3d SFG. A lieutenant colonel, the executive officer would brief the ambassador and the defense attaché upon arrival. I walked the fax into the ambassador's office and showed it to David. "Well, maybe a colonel can get the job done," was all he said. Later that day, I handed the fax to the major. I told him Mickey was making travel arrangements as I watched his face pale.

The new colonel did get the job done. We opened the National Demining Office on schedule. Vice President Kagame gave the address and shook each new deminer's hand. Then he asked that the U.S. trainers stand and lead the assemblage in a round of applause in their honor. He thanked me personally, and I felt like a woman who has just delivered an eleven-pound baby. It was painful, but I was proud of the results. By the way, it had been nine months since the SOCEUR survey team had said yes to its conception. In May, 1998, an inspector general team looked at the NDO and gave it top marks, making it the standard by which all other demining operations would be judged.

Rumbles in the West

All the while I was birthing the National Demining Office, the Rwandan security situation grew more serious. The camps in Goma were the most notorious, but there were problems to the south as well. Kibumba as the main Goma camp had become a UNHCR plastic city. There were bars, brothels, video stores, and nightclubs—all making money lining someone's pockets. With thirteen million dollars from the UNHCR, the Zairians had created the Contingent Zairois pour la Securité des Camps (CZSC) from elements of the Special Presidential Division (DSP) after the international community had refused to create a special U.N. peacekeeping force for the mission. The CZSC came with arms; the UNHCR provided communications and uniforms. No doubt most of the thirteen million went into the ever-greedy pockets of the Zairian leadership. It is highly likely my contact Yigal had sold the idea of using SOZAIS as a security force on a larger scale since the troops came out of the DSP—just like the thugs in his security business. The CZSC operated nominally under the direction—but not command—of an internationally recruited Civilian Security Liaison Group. There were one thousand CZSC troops in the Goma camps and another five hundred in Bukavu. NGOs reported that the CZSC had made some improvements in security related to foreign workers during daylight. Part of that was due to the resurrection of Rwandan political structures that had facilitated the genocide. The Commission Sociale was organized around fifteen principals, most tied to the old MRND, deceased President Habyarimana's old apparatus. It rebuilt the cell and commune structure around leaders willing to carry out its policies. The Commission linked itself to the "government-in-exile" as well as the former military. Though it cleaned up its image by reasserting control over the refugees, key NGOs like MSF labeled the changes as cosmetic. The emergence of the Commission did allow the UNHCR to finally conduct a census and adjust food distribution. But before that happened, thousands of tons had disappeared over a six-month period, probably into caches for the ex-FAR and the militias. The bottom line policy goal for the Commission remained keeping the refugees in place while it sponsored unrest inside Rwanda.

Another key element of the improved security was the disappearance of the ex-FAR from its camp south of Goma. In late 1994, the former army took off its uniforms and headed south to the Bukavu area. Kate Crawford first tipped me to this, and we started tracking the soldiers. They reassembled in various locations near the Rwandan border. In one rather blatant act, they established a new base camp in Bukavu directly across from RPA positions on the heights above Cyangugu. The RPA largely left them alone until there was an exchange of fire; heavy fire from the Rwandan side convinced them to displace farther from the border. Back in Goma, the groups of sullen soldiers I was used to had disappeared. That did not mean the militias were gone. CZSC sources reported they were still in place. Their training activities had, however, been shifted to less conspicuous areas, out of sight of prying eyes.

I was pleased to see some of what I had been reporting had eventually surfaced via the world press. We had had several reports that arms were coming into the region from a variety of sources. Earlier Stan and I had tracked the same thing into Angola: open an arms market and "they will come." The arms seized from the ex-FAR, we knew from Saleem, our airlift operator, had been shipped to Kinshasa. It was entirely probable the Zairians were selling the arms back to the ex-FAR. There were other reports that the Zairians were actively assisting the Rwandans rearm; I am sure they were, as long as they made money on the deals. International press also broke a story we had been tracking: there was a series of arms flights into Goma beginning in early April, 1995. Each landed at 11 P.M. On one occasion the so-called prime minister for the exiled Rwandans and the former head of the Interahamwe met the flights.[9] Of course my counterpart in Kinshasa dismissed all this activity as media hype. Her favorite technique was to ask the Defense Ministry if the Zairian leadership was involved in rearming the Rwandans in and around the camps. Being good *citoyens* all, they denied any arms trafficking or training was occurring. Rather, the arms were intended for the CZSC, a curious statement given that the CZSC had been in place for several months and had its own arms.

They even went so far as to stage a public relations event to prove their nobility. For months the Zairians had been saying the former Rwandan military had been completely disarmed, a claim echoed by the embassy in Kinshasa. I knew that was not the case: I had been in the middle of them and had seen the heavy weapons trucks and armored cars. Suddenly the Zairians said they would give back the Panhards as a gesture of goodwill toward Kigali. We went up to the border to watch the exchange as arranged through the United Nations. The handful of Panhards clattered and choked their way back into Rwanda. Largely useless in the war, they were of even less interest to the RPA or the ex-FAR and militias across the border. My comment to a CIA representative who snuck across the border to talk with me was, "If the ex-FAR had been disarmed, then how come they drove these things past me in July, 1994?" Though sympathetic, he merely shrugged and smiled.

Meanwhile events at Kibeho had shut down all repatriation. The radicals in the camps used the news to their advantage. I believed then and still do believe that the international community had never got ahead of the radical leadership in the information war. The bottom line was the situation was stalemated; the refugees were not going back, and the new government inside Rwanda was limited in its ability to change that fact. More accurately the new government in Rwanda had limited choices in dealing with the status quo: it could wait and do nothing, perhaps in the hope someone else might take action. Or it could repeat the Kibeho clearing action in Goma. Choosing to wait initially did not eliminate the possibility of final action. The situation was a like a boiler with the release valve shut off. Nothing appeared to be happening. But when it did, the results would be noticeable.

Pushing the Envelope: Arms for the RPA?

Consequently, as we beat the drums warning another war was coming, we sought more security assistance for the RPA. The ambassador and I shared the belief that the only way to stop the RPA from going after the radicals in the camps was to increase the military's ability to control the border. North to south, Rwanda is some one hundred miles along its western border as the crow flies. But no border is that straight. Some sixty miles of that border includes Lake Kivu, with hundreds of small inlets and small islands along its coast. Mountains and ravines coupled with heavy vegetation make the entire frontier a smuggler's playground.

The RPA lacked the manpower and the technology to establish a barrier defense along this border. Doing so would have required three or four times the manpower and would strip the rest of the military from other areas in the country. At this time the RPA lacked the mobility to establish a reactive defense based on a series of outposts. They also lacked the surveillance gear necessary to make such a defense work. As for Lake Kivu, the RPA had no patrol boats worthy of the name. In total, they were in a holding action. They could and did patrol the border areas and occasionally ambushed infiltrators. I had no doubt they also sent patrols ranging inside Zaire. But catching potential infiltrators was as much a matter of luck as it was martial skills. Their only solution to resolving the escalating infiltration was to take out the source by attacking and clearing the camps a la Kibeho.

We had strong support in the Pentagon, USAID, and Susan Rice at the NSC, along with growing support from Ambassador Bogosian on a more proactive program. Lt. Col. Greg Saunders and Mike Johnson at OSD-ISA had us draw up a "wish list" for security assistance to the RPA. The ambassador, Mickey, and I all worked on the list. We deliberately chose to keep it as "non-lethal" as possible in the hopes that might help it past the inevitable opposition in D.C. The focus remained mobility, communications, and surveillance to include maritime surveillance. Frankly, I did not have high hopes for our prospects. But we did get a major shot in the arm when the assistant secretary of defense for international security affairs, Dr. Joseph Nye, announced he was coming to see us. Vince Kern as his deputy for Africa would also be coming, along with Mike Johnson and a colonel from the Joint Staff. The suggested itinerary said Nye would be with us for several days and Kern would stay on for another week. Because Nye and Kern were visiting other countries as well, they would fly into Entebbe, Uganda, and we would meet up with them for the trip back down to Kigali.

Armed with the news Nye was coming, we went to see the RPA. I met with Col. Charles Muheri first as the G3 and my main operational contact. He was happy with the news and arranged follow-on meetings with Colonels Kaka and Nyamwasa. Kaka was skeptical about what actual assistance might be offered but turned us back over to Colonel Muheri as the main coordinator for the visit.

The Nye and Kern Visit

With Colonel Charles and Lieutenant Colonel Karenzi as action officers, we had no problems getting ready for the assistant secretary's visit in mid-August. We had already talked long hours about the needs of the RPA. My independent suggestions to D.C. matched almost word for word Muheri's needs list. That in itself was gratifying. I had seen the Sudanese come in with a "dream" list way back in 1984 when I was in Khartoum. The Zairians were always looking for new toys to break. You could summarize the RPA request as the operator's triad: "move, shoot, and communicate." As for shooting, they wanted weapons, but they were more interested in U.S. training. The move and communicate related to vehicles and radios. The most exotic item on the list was riverine patrol "Swift" boats for Lake Kivu.

The itinerary was a bit different since we had to go up to Entebbe and meet the party. Kampala was Kampala—sort of like an upscale Khartoum without mosques. Nevertheless the Kampala Sheraton was nice and had a nicer bar. Called the "Rhino Pub," they sold T-shirts showing a slightly drunk rhino leaning backwards against the bar having a beer. This was the same bar to which my air force friend had taken his crews after the Goma airdrop fiasco. We proceeded to buy our own T-shirts and imitate the rhino. Two days later we moved out to Entebbe to meet the VIPs. The day before our visitors arrived, I fully dislocated my left shoulder diving off the three-meter board at the pool and then put it back in while paddling like a wounded frog. It was a terrible way to start an important week, and the road trip south the next day was grueling. Fortunately, Mike Johnson was with Vince Kern as his action officer for the trip. I asked Mike to drive as he had the experience to dodge Uganda's Mad Max bus drivers. The trip went without a hitch, but we had a reception to attend as soon as we arrived in Kigali. The ambassador had invited the senior RPA leadership to a cocktail hour to meet the visiting delegation.

Such gatherings are the real essence of diplomacy. More gets done at a cocktail than at formal negotiations. The invitation list is a game. The ambassador was behind us on this effort, and he invited the military leadership up through Major General Kagame. He also invited the UNAMIR force commander. The gamesmanship comes in with who accepts. Kagame and Ambassador Rawson had a correct but not cordial relationship. So we were not surprised by Kagame's absence at the party. But he did send a representative from his office along with virtually all the senior RPA officers. Notably, Dr. Col. Joe Karamera, the health minister, was in attendance. Joe was the designated messenger for the RPF. When they had something to run by us, Joe always called me to his office for a talk. General Tousignant and his senior staff attended as well. That added a different dynamic to the equation but a necessary one. We had told the RPA that allowing UNAMIR to remain in country for another six months would reduce opposition to security assistance to the Rwandan military.

In several earlier meetings that included Assistant Secretary of State for African Affairs George Moose and Ambassador Richard Bogosian, the U.S. delegation had raised the question of RPA accountability for killing civilians. Kagame had in each meeting acknowledged the killings were happening but stated that the RPA was arresting those responsible. I believed Kagame—one of my contacts was arrested the next month. But the RPA was a just-emerged guerrilla movement, not inclined to open up to outsiders. Yet we needed some kind of documentation on those arrests. It was a sore subject with Kagame: he was being pressured to punish soldiers for post-war killings when not a single genocide trial had taken place. Plus he was getting blasted for arresting those associated with the genocide versus leaving them free to be killed, most of the time by soldiers. The message Secretary Nye sought to press on the RPA was that we understood their problems and were hoping to help. To do that, we needed Kagame to help us by being more forthcoming. Specifically, we needed names and dates on those RPA soldiers arrested for killings. At the meeting with Kagame, the vice president indicated he would meet our request.

The rest of the visit was standard. We did fly the secretary and DASD Kern to Ntarama Church. The government had cleaned it up somewhat. They had removed all the skulls and bones from the killing zone surrounding the hilltop church. The skulls were all placed on a platform table outside the church; the rest of the bones were underneath. The dead inside the church, however, remained undisturbed. Nye and Kern got to meet with a woman who had survived the massacre by playing dead until she could sneak off. She told the tale of the protracted killings and rapes. It put the issue of revenge killings and prisons into perspective for our visitors.

Secretary Nye and all but DASD Kern departed the next day.[10] Vince stayed with us for several more days, and we did the Rwanda tour. The ambassador went all out to support us as he had done before. David applied the rule, "If they are coming to tell the Rwandans what to do, they have to be willing to do something for the Rwandans." Those who just came to make pronouncements got less support. We had too many of those. Nye and Kern wanted to help so we did our best. I had asked the force commander at UNAMIR to help out. General Tousignant knew full well my reports on Kibcho had cast doubt on some of UNAMIR's claims. He told me that but remarked, "I know we both have our roles." We were able to get an aerial tour of western Rwanda via a UNAMIR helicopter thanks to the General.

A Canadian friend of mine, Joel, flew the bird. Mickey took left seat and videoed much of the trip. Vince, Colonel Karenzi, and I sat in the back. Joel started with the junction of the Rwanda-Zaire border south of Bukavu and then flew north to Gisenyi. We stopped for a visit to UNAMIR headquarters at Gisenyi and also met the local RPA commander, Colonel William. While taking off, we circled the local prison, offering Vince a birds-eye view of the overcrowding. From there we went to have lunch with my favorite American lady, Roz Carr. Vince of course had heard of her, but they had never met. As always, Roz was charmingly hard-nosed in talking about the new government. The presence of Karenzi at the table had no effect.

Our return landing was not without its bit of drama. The international airport had an inbound commercial flight on final, so we could not land straight away. Joel diverted to an alternate helipad adjacent to the force commander's house. He told us on the intercom we would hold there until cleared for the airport as he sat the U.N. Huey on the ground. The pad itself was on a downhill slope overlooked by General Tousignant's back porch. I looked up at the house in time to see several soldiers running down the steps and assuming firing positions—aimed at us. I tapped Joel on the shoulder and pointed. He shut the bird down and we "surrendered" to the force commander's bodyguard before they got too nervous. We got out of the helicopter, covered by the Canadian Special Forces guys—all of whom we knew from the club. The team leader sheepishly explained they were required by their procedures to react to unannounced visitors in a protective manner, even when the visitors were in a U.N. helo. He invited us in, and General Tousignant joined us for a Coke.

Upcountry with the RPA's Best: Colonel William

Shortly after Vince Kern headed back to the States, Sgt. 1st Class Ron Carr joined us from the USDAO in Chad. Ron's arrival marked the countdown to Mickey's departure near the end of September. The Mick had already left once and then decided to return with his new bride, thus offering her an opportunity to see a bit of Africa. They did the standard gorilla tour and took a short trip up to Queen Elizabeth Park in Uganda. But in doing so, Mickey had already extended his retirement date once. It was time for him to get on with his life, so Ron had volunteered to come down from Chad to overlap with him. Once again, I got lucky. Ron was another class act. I could always count on him to get the job done. Just after Ron got in country, Colonel William summoned us from Gisenyi. He had approval to offer us almost carte blanche access to his brigade area adjacent to Goma. If we were ever going to get a better feel for how the RPA operated, this trip was going to be it.

Off we went to Gisenyi to meet with the colonel. He took us up to the heights overlooking Kibumba camp and gave us a walking talk on the main militia infiltration routes into the country. It was the classic defensive dilemma: too much border and too few troops. Active patrolling helped attenuate but did not eliminate the cross-border operations. The terrain itself favored the infiltrator. Heavy vegetation and compartmented terrain offered countless passages into Rwanda. William explained they used hunter-killer teams to intimidate the crossers with ambushes and snipers. Platoons backed up the teams along the main infiltration routes. Still it was an imperfect system: there were just too many ways to cross the border.

Outside Gisenyi, William took us to the old Rwandan navy base at the northern end of Lake Kivu. Once the base for lake patrol boats, the facility still had its wharfs and boatsheds. All the boats had disappeared in the flight to Zaire. William had already established a scout swimmer program and hoped to add patrol boats in the future. Though it was measurably chilly for a September morning, he had two "candidates" doing dog-paddle laps alongside the main wharf. We had lunch at his house on the hill overlooking Gisenyi. While chatting we talked about what had happened in July, 1994. It was in this conversation I learned about William's failed attempts to hit Mount Goma with mortar fire. He was most amused by my description of being on the receiving end of the fire that past summer. We returned to Kigali the next day.

In the Woodshed with the RPA

It was not always hugs and kisses with the RPA. With the departure of the Nye and Kern party, we hoped we would be able to overcome resistance in Washington to actually helping the fledgling army. But part of that help had to come from the RPA, especially on the issue of reprisal killings. Kagame had indicated they would provide names and sentences of military personnel found guilty of vengeance killings. The vice president had said he had more than four hundred officers under arrest. Sad to say we needed the names and sentences to offset increasingly hyper voices against the increasing number of prisoners held under suspicion of being involved in the genocide.

The stench of death at the massacre sites was but a shadow of the cruel smell I had encountered in the fall of 1994. Yes, in 1995 there were still skulls and bones, but time had somehow muted the savagery. In contrast, the prisons were full, and the "victims" therein could tell each visitor how unfairly they had been imprisoned. The classic case of naiveté was on a swan-song visit of a retiring U.S. senator and a couple of staffers. They started at Goma and were upset by the degradation of the camps, according to Peter Whaley, who was their Kigali handler. Then they crossed into Rwanda and were "horrified" by the conditions in the prisons. Immediately they criticized all contacts with the new government and especially the RPA. As far as I know, they never went to see a genocide site.

One evening at the bar, Mickey, well lubricated and not at all shy about offering a chief's viewpoint, was talking with Philip Gourevitch about this syndrome. Mickey remarked that the word "genocide" had about as much emotional impact as the words "cheese sandwich." I had heard the comparison before and agreed fully. Mickey made his point with Phillip, who recorded the conversation quite accurately in his book.[11] It was easy to trivialize the genocide if you had not seen the results first hand.

After Nye and Kern left I had to follow up on the issue of the reprisals. Ironically one of the first arrests I could confirm was that of Colonel William. The "best of the RPA" had a company go berserk in the middle of an openly hostile Hutu village, and nearly a hundred civilians were slaughtered. William was relieved of his command and arrested. I ended up sending the vice president a written demarche asking for his direct assistance in getting the promised information. Just two days after sending the note, I was summoned to the Defense Ministry.

I was often over at the Ministry of Defense, many times more than once a week. My summons had come from Frank Rusagara, the original RPA liaison officer to the embassy. Even when I was there to see the vice president and defense minister, the reception was always relaxed. This case was different: a secretary had me wait in a small receiving room before I was ushered in to see Frank, dressed in a formal suit.

"Hello, Frank, we haven't seen you over at the embassy for weeks."

"Good afternoon, Colonel Odom. Be seated, please," was all I got in return. Notably, Frank did not offer to shake hands, and he stayed seated behind his desk.

I decided to keep up the casual approach. "What's on your mind, Frank?"

"Colonel Odom, the defense minister received your letter requesting more information about RPA officers and men under arrest. He has directed I inform you we consider this an intrusion on our national sovereignty. He also said he felt the tone of the letter was inappropriate—"

"Frank, if the letter's tone offended, I apologize. I wrote the letter as one soldier writes another. Please convey my apologies to the general if that somehow offended—"

Frank cut me off and continued reading, "We do not accept your demand for information concerning a matter internal to our military—"

"Wait a minute, Frank. That letter as it stated in the text was a follow-up to promises made by the defense minister to provide the information—"

Our verbal tennis continued with, "As I was saying, Colonel, we do not accept this demand for information. Do you understand?"

"I acknowledge the statement, Frank. But understand you are reversing what was promised in meetings with the United States assistant secretary of defense. General Kagame made those promises."

"Do you understand we do not accept the demands?"

"I said I acknowledge your statement. Do you understand I will relay this reversal to the U.S. government? Do you understand this will not help us help you?"

"I am not here to acknowledge what you say, Colonel. Do you understand our position on this?"

"Frank, I get this message, and Washington will also get it within the next few hours. Again, please convey that to the defense minister. Anything else?"

"No, Colonel. Thank you for coming over," Frank said as he stood. Then he came around the desk and said, "It's nothing personal, Tom."

"No, Frank, I know. And that's too bad because Washington will take it personally."

It's hard to say how much impact that reversal had on what we were trying to do. Certainly the naysayers in Washington pointed to it as proof the RPA was not to be trusted. The more thoughtful saw it as the maturing of the military-led government. Ambassador Bogosian commented on it when he next saw me. "You did well. You held the line without antagonizing them. They wanted to let us know they would not be pushed." I knew Bogosian was right, and I appreciated that he had in fact read the report. Still it put a major wrench into the works on security assistance.

Back to the States

With the end of September nearing, we were also drawing near to sea change in staffing. Mickey was—this time for real—going home to retire. The demining training team was also headed back, their work well done despite the hiccups in leadership. To my surprise, the support folks back at D.C. recognized I too might need a break.

So I was issued funded travel orders back to Washington for consultations and then a couple of weeks leave. Ron Carr would handle the office while I was away. DIA had finally agreed to establish an office. Headquarters told us to look for a DAO house, and Ron had to find one before I got back.

We gave Mickey and the deminers the send-off they deserved at the club. The entire international community turned out—well, at least the ones who mattered. I put five hundred dollars on the bar, and Peter kicked in another couple of hundred. The club laid out a special BBQ and we turned up the music enough to draw complaints from the neighbors. The seven hundred dollars was gone in under an hour, but the party did not stop till the wee hours. I flew out the next day. Mickey flew with the deminers back to Fort Bragg. We met in Washington, and I stayed with him at his apartment until my consultations were done.

Dogs for Deminers and the Doghouse for Me

My first priority was to see the folks at the Pentagon. I spent a couple of days with them, and it was the "bad news, good news" routine. Despite the efforts of Assistant Secretary Nye and Deputy Kern, it looked like expanded security assistance for the RPA was dead in the water. My session in the woodshed with Rusagara had been enough to kill immediate hopes for direct military assistance. So we looked to the next year for better luck—if our time did not run out. So much for the bad news, the good news was welcome. DIA had notified the Pentagon they would be standing up a permanent DAO in Kigali. Even better, Maj. Rick Orth would be the first official occupant of the office. The good news kept coming. Bill McCoy at Defense humanitarian affairs, working with the European Command demining office, had secured additional monies for the Rwandan program, funds Dick McCall at AID had matched. We were going to get a contractor to train the RPA deminers on the use of demining dogs. To get the funds set aside, AID named me the program manager just before the fiscal year ended. The initial survey team would meet me in Kigali when I got back.

With that success under my belt I went over to headquarters for consultations. Talk about a less-than-welcome reception; I was clearly the black sheep of the bureau. Rick Moore was his usual cheerful self. He had a morning debrief set up, and I met with the analytical community from D.C. I beat the usual drums, warning that an expanded war was likely unless the Zaire camps were closed or moved. Some listened. Some did not. The split was along the usual lines. Afterwards Rick told me my bureau director wanted to see me, so I reported to the boss.

"Good to see you, Tom," he opened. "You have had a busy year, and you have done well. I heard that you had gotten hurt out there."

I told him of the arm dislocation, saying, "I slipped in blood."

He did not even blink before quipping, "I hate it when that happens." That told me more than anything else that this crew would never ever get a good picture of life on the fringe. I kept my visit as short as possible. I was about to leave the building when Rick told me that the DIA inspector general's office wanted to see me. I was leaving the next day and wanted to get the lose ends tied up.

"Colonel Odom, the embassy in Kinshasa filed a complaint with our regional inspector when he was out there this summer. They state you are not coordinating message traffic with them. What can you tell us about that?" opened my interrogator in the IG office.

"In a word, that is bullshit and they know it," I answered. I continued, "The director of our bureau ordered us via special message this summer to offer all reports concerning neighboring countries to the appropriate office for comment before going final. I have done that on several messages. Kinshasa had never reciprocated. In fact when we—the ambassador and I—sent them a comment on one of their reports, they refused to include it in a message retransmission. Check my reports. Check Kinshasa's reports. Check with my reports officer. Check with Major Orth, the Rwanda analyst at DIA."

By now I was thoroughly angered. These two were just doing their jobs, but they had not done their homework. First step on the reporting complaint should have been to pull the appropriate reports. That would have ended any concerns on my reporting. But someone in the embassy in Kinshasa had filed a false complaint. Again the two inquisitors in front of me had not even caught that one. Or if they had, they did not intend to pursue it. I got up and walked out.

I went downstairs and asked Rick what he had been told. He had not been made privy to the IG's interest in me. I told Rick what had happened and asked him to pull my reports Kinshasa had commented on. I phoned Rick Orth and let him know what had happened. Then I left for leave and then back to Kigali. There was nothing good likely to happen for me by staying around headquarters. I was glad to be retiring.

CHAPTER 8

War Clouds Gather

Once again it seemed strange to be going back to Rwanda. I had been there a year on a ninety-day assignment. I mulled over the changes in my life. I had lost a marriage, and I was looking at retiring in six months. The latter sparked the realization that this was my last trip overseas as a soldier. In October, 1995, I could remember the excitement I had felt in August, 1982, on my way to my first overseas assignment. Where had the time gone? A glance in a mirror told me the time had gone to the same place as my once-brown hair. It also seemed strange to be going back without Mickey, in a way worse than saying goodbye to Stan. Mickey and I had lived together for almost a year like brothers. He watched my back. His last words to me were "Remember, machetes don't click on empty."

Iwawa Island

Not long after I got back, Karenzi called me. "Have you heard about the fighting in the west?" he asked. "We are just finishing up clearing an island. You are invited to take a look tomorrow."

He then provided the details. On November 11, the RPA had seized Iwawa Island inside Rwandan territorial waters and cleared it in a day's fight. With his tip-off, I headed straight to UNAMIR headquarters and the intelligence section. The Canadians had provided a professional intelligence officer and a warrant officer to staff the section. We cooperated whenever possible, and I told him what was going on. I also stopped in and briefed the force commander on the situation. It was news to him, and he agreed to provide a helicopter to Gisenyi the next day. I later found out the UNMOs in the sector—under the same Russian I had known in Sinai—already knew of the operation and had briefly visited the island. They had not notified UNAMIR headquarters, saving the information for the weekly brief. Tousignant was a gentleman, but he was also a soldier. He blistered the UNMO commander for incompetence. His closing shot was something to the effect of, "It says something about our abilities when the U.S. defense attaché has to come tell me what is happening out there when we should be telling him."

The next morning Ron and I headed out to the airport to rendezvous with our group. The UNAMIR intelligence officer and his warrant officer were coming. Karenzi and Muheri were due to meet us as well. The vice president's office sent Charles Dusaidy as a special representative to go along on the mission. The flight to Gisenyi went quickly and a small convoy of RPA and U.N. vehicles drove us to the Meridien Hotel. The RPA colonel who had replaced Colonel William as the sector commander met us on the terrace. He gave us a thumbnail brief of what had gone down over the past couple of days.

Ex-FAR and militia cross-border operations had increased steadily over the past six months all along the western border with Zaire. The greatest number of those incidents had taken place in the middle of the border where Lake Kivu was at its widest points. Just as Colonel William had said, the RPA was justifiably concerned with security operations to control the lake. Unbeknownst to us, the RPA had turned to its erstwhile supporter to partially answer the problem. We had heard but not confirmed that something had come down from Uganda as part of Museveni's visit that August. The something had been two high-speed patrol boats built in Canada. Powered by nearly seven hundred horsepower present in twin outboards, the boats were nearly twenty-five feet in length. Long and pencil-shaped for speed, the boats had an inflatable stability ring around the hull for hauling troops. The front decks and sides were rail-lined to hold fourteen soldiers. A tub-mounted machine gun turret was mounted one-third back from the bow with the boat commander's position just aft. The boats had GPS and radar for direction and tracking.

Later General Tousignant tried to pin the delivery on me. After I returned from Iwawa, he mentioned he had heard the RPA really liked the boats the United States had provided. I laughed as I replied, "General, those boats were built in Canada." That ended that line of questioning.

The RPA had figured the ex-FAR and the militias were not making the nearly thirty-kilometer trip across the lake for every one of those raids. Idjwi Island was a known stronghold for the hardliners, and the RPA could have attacked it in the past. But Idjwi was Zairian territory and an invasion was not yet an option to the government in Kigali. The RPA fought and died by the human intelligence developed by Karenzi's department. They had discovered the hardliners had established an intermediate staging base on tiny Iwawa Island inside Rwandan territorial waters. Iwawa was less than five kilometers from the northern tip of Idjwi, and more than twenty kilometers due west of the Rwandan mainland. It was over thirty kilometers south-southwest of Gisenyi. Just under three kilometers north to south and a kilometer wide east to west, the island was actually two small islets connected by a narrow peninsula less than one hundred meters wide. The northern islet was one kilometer long angled from northwest to southeast, perhaps four hundred meters at its widest. Of the two islets, the northern was the dominant. The central ridge overlooked the waters to the northeast and east as well as the lower islet to the south. It both guarded and provided the best natural defensive structure against attack from the Rwandan mainland. The connecting peninsula ran from the westernmost side of the northern islet to the southern islet some five hundred to six hundred meters away. The southern islet was shaped like an eggplant on its side along a north-south axis. It was roughly two kilometers long and just under a kilometer wide. Unlike the northern islet, the southern extension was not dominated by a single ridgeline. It had a central plateau with rolling forested contours. Except for a narrow landing point at the connecting peninsula, there were no beaches. One stepped from water to rocky shore that generally rose at least ten feet above the waterline.

The ex-FAR and the militias had gradually built their forces on the island, easy to do from nearby Idjwi Island. By that November, there were some three hundred to four hundred hardliners on Iwawa. They were armed with small arms and crew-served weapons including heavy machine guns, RPGs, and recoilless rifles. But four hundred troops are not enough to defend an island, even one as small as Iwawa. The hardliners compounded their own defensive problems. In pure military terms, the key terrain on Iwawa was the dominant high ground on the northern islet. It guarded all lake approaches except that directly from the south, which was choked off somewhat by the southern islet. At the same time, it controlled the southern approach across the narrow peninsula from the south. Dominant terrain, however, is only dominant if it has the necessary forces properly set in to defend it. The ex-FAR had those forces. They did not have the defensive plan to go with them.

Whoever the ex-FAR leader was, he had made the classic defensive mistake. He had attempted to defend all, thereby defending nothing. The main defenses on the northern islet were oriented toward the lake. None covered the approaches from the south. The peninsula itself was largely undefended, dependent on a handful of troops in aging huts along the shore. The southern islet's defense depended absolutely on a ring of bunkers around the water's edge. Each was isolated, and only a few had any alternate positions in depth to support them. Although there were food stores and training facilities inside that outer ring, there were no defenses in depth. The outer shell defense was just that: an eggshell that would crack easily.

The RPA's forte was the indirect approach. They used a feinting frontal attack repeatedly in the war, followed quickly by a looping-around to flank or envelop the ex-FAR. They did not even have to fake the main attack against Iwawa. Thirty-six hours before I set foot on the island, the RPA used their two high-speed patrol boats to tow two large fishing boats out to the southern side of the southern islet. The boats held close to 100 troops, and this initial force cracked the defensive egg. Meanwhile, the boats made another run bringing in more troops. Ultimately 250 RPA troops stormed up the center of the southern islet, simultaneously rolling up the flanks on either side of them. With the gunboats in support, they pushed on across the peninsula and then seized the high ground from the south where there were no defensive positions. Those ex-FAR and militia who succeeded in retreating to the northern ridge had two choices: swim for it or die. Most tried to swim and died anyway. Their route across the lake to Idjwi was part of the killing zone they themselves had planned to use against the RPA. There were fewer than fifty survivors from the three hundred to four hundred who had been on the island. The RPA lost fewer than fifty killed or wounded.[1]

With the colonel finished we boarded the boats under Colonel Charles' direction. He stopped me and asked, "Tom, can you swim?"

"Yes, Charles, I swim almost an hour every day."

"Good, because I need your life jacket," he said, grinning.

I looked at all the senior RPA officers. Naval tradition be hanged; they all had lifejackets. No way were these "captains" going down with the ship—or boat in this case. I started laughing. Faced with the possibility of a ten-mile swim if the boat sank, I might as well have

Landing at Iwawa Island. RPA troops are in foreground. Note the prisoners clustered near the building. **Courtesy of the Canadian Department of Defense.**

worn weights. The boat started off slow until the coxswain let loose those seven hundred horses. We had a rooster tail tracking us across the lake, and we made the fifteen miles in less than thirty minutes, not at all bad for a patrol boat with twenty-plus passengers and crew. At the northern tip we passed to the west of the island and made a complete circuit. I could see bunkers along the edge of the southern islet. Not only were they obvious, they were isolated from each other by the natural curve of the vegetated island. At the RPA's landing site in the south, one of the two wooden fishing boats was beached on the rocks.

Coming back around the northern side, we made for the landing beach on the western side of the peninsula. We could see two small buildings that constituted the only village on the island. RPA troopers guarded some twenty prisoners who crouched alongside one of the buildings out of the sun. As we approached the beach, we spotted a body floating against the rocks. We learned shortly that he had been in hiding and then made a break for the water that morning. The RPA opened up while a Belgian TV crew filmed the event. On shore, RPA handlers waited for the boat to beach and then steadied it as we jumped off and waded the last few feet to dry land.

The RPA had collected most of the small arms, crew-served weapons, and explosives for our inspection. The Canadian warrant officer videoed as the major and I cataloged the weapons. It was a mixed bag of small arms from AKs to G3s to R4s. The machine guns ranged from heavy 14-mm to platoon general-purpose machine guns. There were modern U.S. M240 machine gun parts that had been sold to Saudi Arabia. They had probably found their way into Rwanda through Sudan. Explosives included various makes of plastique and detonation cord. There were mines from the nastily stealthy Italian plastic anti-personnel mines to U.S.-made anti-tank mines. All in all it was quite a cache for a small irregular force. Getting all the numbers and descriptions took us nearly an hour. The Belgian reporters attempted to talk to me, and I ignored them. An American Associated Press stringer who was with them told me later they had put me on Belgian TV as the "U.S. advisor" to the RPA. VdW would have been proud, at least if the old boy were still kicking.

Inventory complete, we started out to the north. Our path ran along the spine of the peninsula, and we passed a couple of stiffs. Although they had been dead less than twenty-four hours, the tropical heat and humidity had already started the decomposition process. The bodies were swelling, and occasionally one would "moan" as gas released. I

One of the assault boats on the beach at Iwawa Island. **Courtesy of the Canadian Department of Defense.**

Some of the captured weaponry. A land mine implanted near the tripod of the middle machine gun exploded later that day, severely wounding an RPA soldier. Lt. Col. Karake Karenzi, the G2 of the RPA, is at right. **Courtesy of the Canadian Department of Defense.**

I count and catalog the captured weapons and explosives used by the ex-FAR. **Courtesy of the Canadian Department of Defense.**

Case of Italian-manufactured plastic anti-personnel mines. **Courtesy of the Canadian Department of Defense.**

had heard it before, but it was still unpleasant, especially the smells. As we walked along I scanned the ground around us. All those mines back at the beach had gotten my attention. It was just like Lebanon: you did what you could to be careful and left the rest to luck. We soon reached the base of the northern ridge and began the climb. It was not really that high, perhaps 300 to 350 meters, but it did dominate the area, both north and south. Yet fighting positions were noticeably absent along the south slope. I saw a couple of hasty defensive positions complete with stiffening corpses. They had obviously been too hasty to be effective.

As we neared the top, I saw sleeping huts and cooking pits. The main defensive line was on the northern military crest of the ridge looking down on the lake toward Gisenyi. Charles and I walked through the area as our bodyguards fanned out around us. Most of the positions were primitive and lacked sufficient cover. One was especially interesting: it had good cover and fields of fire to the north and northeast. But the RPA had hit it from the south, and the occupant had attempted to go out his northern firing port. He had apparently forgotten planting anti-personnel mines along the forward slope of his bunker. Low crawling over a mine is a tough way to go. Charles found an administrative and supply order intended for the main base over on Idjwi Island and showed it to me. All told there were twenty to thirty bodies on the ridge and more down the face of the ridgeline to the water. That was where most of the ex-FAR and militiamen had fled. They had died in the water, and Charles was trying to figure out a way to recover their weapons.

Finished on the northern islet, we backtracked down the peninsula to the southern islet. Just south of the "village" we found a physical training field where the ex-FAR and militias had trained. Less than a third of a mile in length, the "track" had three parallel trails around its edge, worn by formation running. Another ten to fifteen bodies decorated the scene here. On the southern edge of the training field, we found the cooking and storage area with a small hut filled with USAID donor beans. From there the walk was trickier as the terrain became rocky, broken, and heavily forested. We passed a number of bodies.

The Rwandan fall weather had changed again, and the sun was out. The Canadians in their heavy gabardine battle dress suffered in the heat and humidity. Others did as well, especially the civilian from the vice president's office. Colonel Charles called a break alongside the lake next to the beached boat. I was in an upbeat mood, and the Canadian warrant officer captured me grinning on film. A friend later said I scared him. I guess with my shaved head I did look like Brando's version of Colonel Kurtz.

After a few minutes, we headed back to the village, and as we entered, a large *boom* greeted us. We turned the corner to see the RPA carrying an obviously wounded soldier out to one of the boats. Karenzi pointed at where the captured machine guns still stood in a row. The RPA soldier had trod on an anti-personnel mine planted almost exactly where I had knelt that morning. The Canadian major and I looked at each other and simultaneously swore. He had been standing on the other side of the gun as I called out the numbers. A fraction of an inch the wrong way and both of us would have taken the blast. That evening we shared a couple of drinks at the club to toast our luck. Over the next two days, anti-personnel mines wounded six more people. My deminers deployed to the island, and they found an anti-tank mine on the beach where we had landed. Our luck had been doubly strong. The pesky anti-personnel mines plagued the deminers. The only way to find them was by probing, a difficult and dangerous technique.

The Iwawa operation captured the differences between the RPA and their enemies in Zaire. Kagame's army had used a smaller force, stealth, deception, and audacity to wrest Iwawa from a larger but incompetent foe. From the moment their initial landing cracked the eggshell defense, the RPA had the battle won. I had tried repeatedly to get across to doubters in Washington and in neighboring countries the RPA could fight and beat any infantry-based army on the continent. One would have to go to South Africa, Egypt, or perhaps Ethiopia to find a worthy opponent. Zaire in contrast would be a walkover; the real challenge would be crossing more than a thousand miles of bush to reach Kinshasa. Although I knew I had gotten that message across to a select audience in D.C, I also realized others would never get it. The RPA was the new "bull" in central Africa, and like the saying goes, "you mess with the bull, you get the horns." Iwawa should have been a clear warning, but the bull's next target was not listening.

Another Stab at Repatriation

Just a few days later, I got a call from the head of the UNHCR's Rwanda office. Mr. W. R. Urasa asked me to come over to discuss a sensitive issue. I met with him that afternoon, and he explained that after the Iwawa island raid, some two hundred to three hundred ex-FAR soldiers had expressed a desire to repatriate to Rwanda. He was quite up-front; the UNHCR maintained the position that refugees had the right to decide when to return. He could offer no more than a conduit for discussions between the ex-FAR and the RPA. Urasa said that given my special status with the RPA he had decided I was the best conduit to deliver the ex-FAR's message of interest.

I notified Karenzi and told him what had been said. I also went over and briefed the force commander. Both Karenzi and the force commander were willing to support an honest request for repatriation. Neither wanted to get involved in a ploy for concessions by the exiled soldiers. There had already been such instances: ex-FAR leaders said they wanted to come home, but once back, they began a campaign of demands and pleas to erase the genocide. Karenzi, Urasa, and I actually went down to Cyangugu to meet with the exiles. It failed for the same reasons as the previous attempts had failed. The failure also hardened the RPA's resolve to end the refugee camp dilemma.

A New Ambassador

In January, we got a new chief of mission. Ambassador Robert Gribbin and his family arrived from the Central African Republic. Gribbin and I hit it off. We never got as close as David and I had become, but we only served three months together. David and I had shared some of the worst Rwanda had to offer. Gribbin, on the other hand, did not share the same baggage David had carried with him. Gribbin knew Kagame from his days in the embassy in Uganda when the vice president was head of Museveni's military intelligence wing. Shortly after Gribbin's arrival, Kagame's office called him. The ambassador told me he was going over to meet with the vice president.

"Expect him to raise the camps issue. He is going to demand something be done. He will follow that demand with a warning that he will not wait forever. Take the warning seriously," I warned the ambassador.

Gribbin went, and I saw him the next morning. "You called it exactly. He said just what you said he would," Gribbin said. I was soon to leave, but I could see the new ambassador would make a good team with Rick Orth when he arrived in a few months.

Winding Down

David Rawson's departure opened the final act of my strange sojourn in Rwanda. Parallel to my own ending, UNAMIR began to draw down its elements. I had a few more hoops to go through before leaving. The first was the visit of the U.S. ambassador to the United Nations, Madeline Albright. She came in via a special mission Boeing 737 out of Europe with an entourage that included Susan Rice. It was almost a non-event. We had arranged a reception that evening with the government. But when Albright arrived, her executive assistant announced Albright was ill and would forgo the event, a refusal sure to insult the government.

The evening before my departure the RPA said goodbye to me in a small gathering at their officers club. Karenzi, Muheri, Mbaraga, Rusagara, and the health minister, fighting Dr. Col. Joe Karamera, honored me with their presence and friendship. It was emotional for me, and I headed back to the house for my final night in Kigali. The next evening a friend dropped me at the airport, and as I passed into the diplomatic waiting room, I wondered where life would next take me. I had traveled many miles and many lands to look over the edge into the darkness of man. That darkness had proven more intense than the brightest of lights. I wondered how badly my soul had been burned.

Epilogue

wo weeks later dressed in my greens I sat in my truck outside the personnel office at Fort Meade. It was my retirement day and the final time to wear my greens. Since my return the last day of March, I had out-processed DIA and then the army. Rick Moore at headquarters handed me a retirement award, and we shook hands. That was my goodbye from DIA. I took a retirement physical, and the doctor noted my blood pressure was high. He asked what was going on in my life, and I said, "I just came back from thirty months in Zaire and Rwanda. I am facing a divorce. And I am retiring from the army next week." At 0900 on the sixteenth of April, 1996, I walked in, signed the papers, and walked out. The only band playing was the music inside my head. My twenty years of active duty were done. I was now a civilian. I headed back to Texas.

It was all very surreal to be back in the States and out of the army. I found myself very restless but at the same time almost listless. I worked out and walked. I jumped on the Internet in a big way. One day I was headed to Dallas to see a friend, and once done there I just kept going. I called home and told my mother I had "gone walkabout." I stopped in Leavenworth to see Roger Spiller and the guys. I shared some of my experiences but not all. The next morning I headed west to Mickey's place in Idaho.

The Mick looked happy. But I think his wife thought I was there to recruit him for some overseas work. She relaxed when she realized I was just saying hello. Mickey and I went to his local shooting club, and I watched him in a Western black powder shoot. He had gotten his dream bike but lacked the money to get the insurance. He had saved his spare cash to pay me back for a phone bill I had covered. I just told him to put the money on his insurance and to take the wife for a ride. Again, the restless urge made me leave, and I drove out. Three weeks and seven thousand miles later I was back in southeast Texas.

It was then I met "the Beast," as I came to refer to my bouts with depression. The Beast could come at anytime day or night and take me from myself. After Goma, General Hughes had praised me for helping save thousands of lives. But did they really deserve salvation? Would I have been happier to see that volcano blow and eliminate them? It is easy to say such questions were not mine to decide. It is harder to remove those questions and the associated images from one's mind. Things would just sort of slide into a dark pit and take me with them. Sometimes I would just start crying and not know why; the nighttime version of this was to wake up screaming. Then the kaleidoscope of horrors would play before my eyes. I would see the bodies stacked along the roads in Goma. I replayed time and time again the little girl dying under that vehicle in Kibumba camp. I watched the machete disembowel the suspected spy in front of our truck. I could smell the coppery blood and the stench of decay at Ntarama Church. I heard the flies swarm around my head as I looked inside that first time. I walked Kibeho camp, stepping on the old man whose corpse gasped at my tread. I crossed Iwawa Island again, this time expecting to feel a mine rip me apart. Then usually I would go back to sleep.

The Beast stayed with me for months, and I stayed to myself. Finally I broke free, resumed skydiving as a hobby after a seventeen-year hiatus, and moved to Florida. The next year my shoulder injury from Kibeho caught up with me in freefall at nine thousand feet. It dislocated and sent me into a spin until seven thousand feet when I put it back in and deployed my chute. I had two operations on the shoulder and a third on an ankle injured in my 82d days. My skydiving days were again over, this time for good.

Events did not stop in Rwanda. In late 1996 with Rick Orth on the scene as the defense attaché, Kagame kept his word. The RPA moved into Zaire and forcefully closed the camps where the former government had recreated an army of 110,000. When stability problems continued in the region, the Rwandans created an allied army of Tutsi exiles in Zaire and ultimately conquered the country. That bold maneuver lead unfortunately to an expanded war that is ongoing. Zaire is now the Congo once again, the scene of uneasy peace and periodic fighting between the armies of Uganda, Zimbabwe, Zambia, the Congo, and Rwanda. Analysts call it the African World War. As of 2003, the estimated casualties exceed three million.

Events did not stop elsewhere in the world either. The Balkans drew us further into that morass with the war in Kosovo. The Middle East erupted, once more drawing back from the precipice of possible peace, prompted again by hate and stubbornness on both sides by the same people. I saw the clips of the bombing of the U.S. embassies in

Kenya and Tanzania. I realized had I had my way, I probably would have been inside the Nairobi embassy when the bomb went off. A couple of years later, the USS *Cole* lost nearly twenty sailors to a terrorist bomb while at anchor off Yemen. Americans expressed outrage over that attack or perhaps just indignation because it disturbed their morning coffee. But regardless of feelings, the episode passed quickly. The "danger of shark attacks" off Florida's beaches sustained media attention longer. Then I sat at my desk early on September 11, 2001, watching one tower of the World Trade Center burn when the live broadcast showed a second airliner hit the sister tower. America had been attacked. We had been surprised. We were at war.

Looking back at my career as a scout and analyst, I can now say I was right most of the times I had to make a difficult assessment. But experience has taught me that being right is often irrelevant. In the wake of the 9-11 attacks, I told friends and coworkers when it was all boiled down, the American public would learn that someone, somewhere had attempted to warn key leaders a threat was afoot. First let me say that, historically, what are commonly referred to as intelligence failures are usually failures to heed intelligence. Two examples spring to mind: Pearl Harbor and its immediate aftermath, and then the Chinese Intervention in Korea. On the Japanese attack at Pearl, it is clear that intelligence did in fact provide consistent and relatively clear warnings a Japanese attack was coming. But as I will show later and as occurred in the case of 9-11, the best intelligence is useless unless it is heeded. The U.S. senior leaders, military and civilian, misread the threat from the Japanese, choosing to believe infiltration and sabotage were the key threats against U.S. military installations in the Pacific. Hence aircraft at Pearl were bunched together, which made them easier to guard. The same measures remained in effect in the Philippines hours after the attack on Pearl. Much has been made in the movies about the late arrival of a war warning after the Japanese had hit battleship row. True, but the same fleet had already sunk a Japanese sub outside the mouth of the harbor. As for Korea, the Chinese had made it clear they regarded U.S. and U.N. forces' movements into North Korea as a *cassus belli.* And U.S. intelligence had echoed that warning. Still the U.S. forces under MacArthur had ignored both warnings.

I was involved personally in six separate but similar episodes. The first was in Turkey when I tried to tighten security only to be told I was "talking about pretty sophisticated terrorists," whose friends soon blew up the Marine Barracks in Beirut. In July, 1987, I warned my commander and friend, Lt. Col. Rich Higgins, he could not do his job as he intended without severe personal risk. In February, 1988, just six weeks after assuming that job, Rich was taken hostage and later murdered. In June, 1990, I warned that war clouds were forming on the horizon in the Middle East. A senior intelligence officer berated me and concluded he "could not envision any scenario that might mean war in the Middle East." In July that year, I warned Saddam would indeed invade Kuwait and pose a serious threat to Saudi Arabia, only to have the senior intelligence officer of the U.S. Army dismiss that threat as a bluff. I had warned repeatedly since 1994 that the Rwandan War was not over and was likely to spread. I was not alone in issuing those warnings, and I know they went to the top. I learned later the same cast of characters who ignored the genocide would be surprised when those warnings proved true.

So what does this all mean? Understand first that intelligence is not like Tom Clancy might have you believe. You do not get the golden nugget telling you everything that is going to happen. Even if you did uncover such a truth, you and all above you would suspect the veracity of the intelligence. What you do get is fleeting and typically disjointed bits and pieces that have to be analyzed in context. And that analysis often entails instinct and pure guesswork. The Chicken Little complex plays large in all of this. Warn too many times and no one listens. Not warn, and we have endless investigations. In all the examples I offered above, the common thread is that heeding the warnings did not match the agenda or interests of those being warned. Rich Higgins said he had to do the job to his best ability. My general told me after the 1990 Iraqi invasion I had "failed to convince" him; he would have had to reverse earlier pronouncements about the lack of an Iraqi threat. State and CIA said the Rwandans would never consider invading another country, a stance easier to maintain than actually considering and preparing if such an invasion occurred. It was inconvenient to put the fleet on a war footing at Pearl, easier to guard aircraft if you parked them in the middle of the apron. And if you were Douglas MacArthur, you never doubted your own pronouncements on the Chinese.

Bottom line: 9-11 warnings were probably ignored. People died as a result, because the people who dismissed the warnings were human. As humans, it is easier to offer the words "intelligence failure" than accept your own mistakes.

There is also a great deal of talk these days about "fixing intelligence." Assuming such a fix would affect the aforementioned tendency to ignore valid intelligence warnings, one has to ask, how do you "fix" intelligence? One school of thought is to fix human intelligence by adding more bodies to the collection effort. That has merit but does not offer immediate relief from the problem at hand. Robert Baer in his memoir *See Know Evil* documents the decline in case officer qualifications and expertise in the Central Intelligence Agency.[1] He also echoes my comments on the tendency to only hear what you want to hear exhibited by policy makers. Baer was a foot soldier in clandestine intelligence collection for twenty years. I was a foot soldier in overt intelligence collection for nearly the same length of time. It takes time and experience to develop the expertise and the art necessary to be effective in human intelligence. And if you do develop that degree of effectiveness, it does not mean your warnings will be heeded when they are inconvenient.

Another school of thought falls back on organizational upheaval as the answer. We have an alphabet soup of intelligence and intelligence-related agencies, all driven by agendas and, to a large degree, budgets. I do not believe we will ever streamline intelligence under one controlling headquarters, despite some calls to do so. Nor do I believe such a course of action would be wise. Agendas are there, but agendas tend to reflect needs of the organization. Army intelligence reflects the culture imbedded in the U.S. Army. The army concentrates on decisive victory through winning on the ground, hopefully as part of a grand strategy. That is the reason the army developed the foreign area officer program ahead of the other services. Air force intelligence reflects the air force cultural bent toward targeting and air combat. Naval intelligence does the same but by concentrating on sea control as espoused by Mahan in the last century. Joint military intelligence agencies attempting to fuse those varied cultures into a comprehensive picture do so with varying degrees of success. But without the investment in service intelligence expertise, chances of building an effective joint military intelligence structure would be nonexistent.

The same holds true in other intelligence fields. The State Department is, despite all pronouncements to the contrary, a primary collector of foreign human intelligence. It needs to embrace that role. So is the CIA. The latter, however, wears a secondary hat that grew out of the original mission of its father, the Office of Strategic Studies (OSS) in

World War II. The OSS was established to offer the president a second view of all intelligence-related matters. And under Donovan's hand, it did so quite effectively. It was also used to do those special tasks the president and the services did not want to tackle. The modern CIA struggles with the same mandate. Because it has no vested interest like the army does, in preserving combat power through effective intelligence, the CIA's agenda often translates into justifying its existence. That means building shadow armies and promoting itself as the doyen of all foreign intelligence, regardless of its expertise in either field.

Domestically we see the same role taken on by the Federal Bureau of Investigation. The FBI has a proud history of counter-espionage and crime fighting. Does that mean the FBI should control all domestic intelligence issues? Probably not. The Drug Enforcement Administration; the Treasury Department with the Secret Service and Bureau of Alcohol, Tobacco, and Firearms; Interior with Customs, Border Patrol, and Immigration; Transportation with the Federal Aviation Administration; and others all compete, cooperate, and sometimes collide in domestic intelligence. And none of that friction accounts for the underlying state and local agencies with intelligence-related functions. With 9-11 we now see the new Homeland Security Agency attempting to pull all domestic terrorist and security-related intelligence affairs into a single agency. Chances of its success in that endeavor, remembering that all things in government relate to political affairs, are dismal.

I do believe, on the other hand, there is a chance to normalize intelligence at the top. And that means formalizing the roles of the director of central intelligence, the national security advisor, the director of the defense intelligence agency, and other key players. Establish them as a separate coordinating board whose main function is information management, give them the power to enforce that role, and hold them accountable when they fail to do so. That means fire them and, in a case like 9-11, prosecute them for negligence the same way any military commander may be charged and court-martialed. As I stated earlier, intelligence is a human endeavor and mistakes will be made; humans learn from experience and sometimes that experience involves responsibility. We need to err on the side of pushing analysis up and sharing information. It may sound strange, but we have to get out of the mentality that keeping secrets from our own intelligence system is the preferred method of doing business.

I will go one step further before ending this journey and add that overall we as a nation and as the remaining superpower are pretty damn good at intelligence-gathering and using that intelligence effectively. The source of that strength is our freethinking society. If you want an example of the opposite, look at the now-defunct USSR. The KGB and its military partner the GRU were also damn good, but their leadership was forced to report intelligence molded by the Communist model. There were any number of KGB intelligence victories during the Cold War; the USSR still lost the war because its leadership could only see the world through a distorted prism that did not allow freethinking analysis. We should look with similar caution on those who seek to control or spin intelligence to pursue a policy.

I remain proud of my record as a foreign area officer. I was a strategic scout for the army for nearly fifteen years. I served in two war zones, and I lost some dear friends. In my own way, I helped achieve and record our victory in the desert in 1991. I salute all fellow FAOs who are out on the fringe today.

Finally, I would offer what the army chief of staff had to say about FAOs in 1994:

> I had two very important encounters with FAOs during my recent trip to Africa and Europe . . . :
>
> First, in Africa, I saw how important LTC Marley and LTC Odom are to their respective Ambassadors and to the CINC. They are both out in harm's way using their unique skills to be invaluable eyes and ears in this crisis . . .
>
> As I go around the Army today, I find that the Marleys [sic] and the Odoms [sic] are as important as ever—maybe even more important when [you] consider the role they could play in many of the crises we are facing almost daily.
> Gordon R. Sullivan
> General, United States Army
> Chief of Staff[2]

Notes

Foreword

1. General Reimer is referring to an incident that took place during World War II and that he highlights in his memoirs as follows:

> In September 1944, on the Crozon Peninsula, German MG Hermann Ramcke asked to discuss surrender terms with the American Army. General Ramcke was in his bunker. His staff brought the 8th Infantry Division's Assistant Division Commander, BG Charles Canham, down the concrete stairway to the underground headquarters. Ramcke addressed Canham through his interpreter. He said, "I am to surrender to you. Let me see your credentials." Pointing to the American infantrymen crowding the dugout entrance, Canham replied, "These are my credentials."

That sentiment is true today. Soldiers are our credentials. The quote is taken from Gen. Dennis J. Reimer and James Jay Carafano, *Soldiers Are Our Credentials: The Collected Works and Selected Papers of the Thirty-third Chief of Staff, United States Army* (Washington, D.C.: Center of Military History, U.S. Army, 2000).

Chapter 1

1. Donald R. Morris, *The Washing of the Spears, The Rise and Fall of the Zulu Nation* (New York, New York: Simon and Schuster, 1958).

Chapter 2

1. Fred E. Wagoner, *Dragon Rouge: The Rescue of Hostages in the Congo* (Washington, D.C.: National Defense University, 1980).
2. David Reed, *111 Days in Stanleyville* (New York: Harper & Row, 1965).
3. Frederic J. L. A. Vandewalle, *L'Ommengang: Odysée et Reconquête du Stanleyville, 1964* (Brussels, Belgium: Le Livre Africain, Collection Temoinage Africain, 1970). Vandewalle describes in detail his return to the Congo in 1964 and the ultimate recapture of Stanleyville.

4. Maj. Thomas P. Odom, *Leavenworth Paper #14: The Dragon Operations, Hostage Rescues in the Congo, 1964–1965* (Fort Leavenworth, Kans.: Combat Studies Institute, 1988).

5. The tragedy of Peter's death was captured by the simultaneous publication of his death notice and an article by Sue McCarthy, his wife, and Debra Kempe on making the most of a tour in the Middle East with UNTSO. The article ends with the admonition, "We trust you will appreciate YOUR EVERY MOMENT." Debra Kempe and Sue McCarthy, "Just a moment . . . in the Middle East," *U.N.T.S.O. News,* vol. 9, no.1, Feb., 1988.

6. Robin Higgins, *Patriot Dreams: The Murder of Colonel Rich Higgins* (Quantico, Va.: Marine Corps Association, 1999), pp. 1–19. Robin quotes some letters that Rich sent her after he had taken command. In them he confirms what I thought at the time. Rich was indeed out to prove that an American could do the job.

7. United Nations Information Centre, Washington, D.C., press release, "Secretary-General, Accepting Nobel Peace Prize, Says Award is 'Tribute' to Those Who Made United Nations Peace-Keeping a Reality," Dec. 9, 1988.

8. Lt. Col. Thomas P. Odom, *Shaba II: The French and Belgian Intervention in Zaire in 1978* (Fort Leavenworth, Kans.: Combat Studies Institute, 1993).

9. As quoted in Gen. Robert H. Scales, *Certain Victory: The U.S. Army in the Gulf War* (Washington, D.C. : Office of the Chief of Staff, U.S. Army, 1993), p. 51. The author was a principal researcher and writer for *Certain Victory.*

10. Higgins, *Patriot Dreams,* pp. 192, 198.

11. Scales, *Certain Victory.*

Chapter 3

1. The 31st Para regiment had been formed in the late 1970s under French advisors. The 1977 Shaba I War both shocked and embarrassed Mobutu. The Paras were supposed to be the backbone of a spineless FAZ. The Shaba II War in 1978 caught them only partially trained with one marginally effective battalion under then Major Mahele. At Mobutu's direct orders, Mahele jumped one untrained company on Kolwezi before the French or Belgians could get there. That resulted in the loss of the company and the death of a number of hostages. Other units soon eclipsed the 31st as the star in Mobutu's military crown. See Odom, *Shaba II.*

2. Devlin was the CIA station chief throughout the 1960s. He is regarded as the man who created Mobutu, a description supported by the fact that he went to work for Mo after he retired. For an excellent account of early 1960s shenanigans, see Madelaine G. Kalb, *The Congo Cables:*

The Cold War in Africa—From Eisenhower to Kennedy (New York: Macmillan Publishing Co., 1982).

Chapter 4

1. Shaharyar M. Khan, *The Shallow Graves of Rwanda* (New York: I. B. Tauris, 2000), pp. 32–49. Mr. Khan was the special representative for the secretary general of the United Nations assigned to UNAMIR. His account is quite useful, providing an insider's story to what happened in UNAMIR II's decision making. He takes a balanced viewpoint in dealing with the new Rwandan government and the impact of the genocide. But he virtually ignores the U.S. role in getting UNAMIR II into Rwanda.
2. Lt. Col. Frank Fields, USAF, email to author, May 16, 2001.
3. Maj. Ben McMullen, USAF, email to author, May 18, 2001.
4. Fields email; McMullen email.
5. Col. (P) Dave Scott, telephone interview with author, May 20, 2001.
6. Mario Fioriti, *"L'armée zairoise de noveau mise en cause,"* AFP 121048 GMT AUG 94; *"le premier ministre zairois annonce que les militaires doivent etre retires de Goma,"* Le Monde, 13 Aug 1994.
7. Kahn, *Shallow Graves of Rwanda*, pp. 41–48. The JTF's idea to coax the refugees back was hardly a unique solution. The SRSG and the UNAMIR force commander thought along these same lines.
8. Later, after a U.N. bid for another peacekeeping operation was killed in the Security Council, the UNHCR funded the fielding of the Contingent Zairios pour la Securité des Camps (CZSC). The CZSC was drawn from the ranks of the DSP, the same source for Yigal's troops in SOZAIS.

Chapter 5

1. Lieutenant-Colonel Hogard, Commandant le Groupement Sud de L'Operation Turquoise. *"Rapport: Objet: Activities du DL U.S., A Cyangugu, le 4 Aout 1994."* August 4, 1994.
2. The official word was "do not eat local food." See U.S. Army MED-COM, "Staying Alive in Uganda, Zaire, and Rwanda," July 27, 1994, Thomas P. Odom Collected Papers.
3. In early September, USEUCOM and the JTF had to dance by a UN-HCR request that the JTF mission be extended by six months, a red flag to those who saw Support Hope as "Restore Hope II." What made it difficult was that National Security Advisor Tony Lake was prepared to accept the UNHCR request. See Deputy Commander in Chief, U.S. AEUR, Memorandum for Commander in Chief Europe, Subject: U.N.H.C.R. Request for Six-Month Extension of Military Support, [date obscured]; Joint Task Force Support Hope, Entebbe Uganda,

Memorandum for DCINCEUR, Subject: DoD Phaseout From Rwanda Relief Operations: U.N.H.C.R. Response to U.S.G Inquiry, 8 September 1994; U.S. Air Force Europe, Operation Support Hope Briefing Slides; complete packet in Thomas P. Odom Collected Papers.

4. Khan, *Shallow Graves of Rwanda*, p. 40. Again, the SRSG completely ignores the U.S. role in getting UNAMIR II on the ground. He gives all credit for getting the Kigali airport back into operation to UNAMIR elements. Ironically, the UNHCR and the British ODA complained mightily when the JTF began returning the ALCE to Entebbe every evening, effectively making the airport daylight operations only. Joint Force Support Hope, Entebbe Uganda Memorandum for CINCEUR, subject Joint Task Force SUPPORT HOPE Operational Concept Update Number 8, 8 September 1994; DART@REDSO.FFP@NAIROBI email to Regina Tooley@FHA.OFDA@AIDW dated 9 September 1994; Entebbe Field Notes—September 4 1994; LTC Bruce Bartolain, J5 MEAF, Southern Africa U.S.EUCOM, FAX to Director MEAF, J5 Africa Branch Chief, dated 081842LSEP94; packet in Thomas P. Odom Collected Papers.

Chapter 6

1. As stated earlier, the heart of the RPA was its twenty-thousand-man core. As the war progressed, additional troops joined, and its numbers grew. Many came in the final months when young men and boys were added as they were gathered up in the countryside.

2. Khan, *Shallow Graves of Rwanda*, pp. 50–56. The former SRSG does an excellent job relating how the Gersony episode went down. His doubts regarding the alleged atrocities match my own; there were too many eyes on the ground to miss large-scale reprisals. Plus those making the claims were most practiced in the art of the "Big Lie."

3. Ibid. The former SRSG points out that the RPA/RPF had been remarkably restrained in its actions after the genocide. I tried to make the same point many times when dealing with Washington, especially the State Department.

4. Muheri is now the commander of the Rwandan Air Force.

5. Karamera is now the Rwandan ambassador to South Africa.

6. Khan, *Shallow Graves of Rwanda*, p. 15. One might expect that the former SRSG of UNAMIR II would take a dim few of the RPA after the frustrations of dealing with them in Rwanda. Yet that is hardly the case. Mr. Khan was a diplomat of more than thirty years experience. He says repeatedly that the RPA was an extremely well-disciplined force, especially given the context of genocide.

7. Michela Wrong, *In the Footsteps of Mr. Kurtz: Living on the Brink of Disaster in Mobutu's Congo* (New York: HarperCollins, 2001), pp. 251–309. She also had an ambassador who was a self-declared expert

on Zaire. Simpson was in his third tour there. He believed until the end that the rebels would never reach Kinshasa. Wrong lists his bad calls on that. He made similar bad calls through his defense attaché. He was not alone. I ran into old hands from the U.S. Security Assistance Mission in Zaire who just refused to believe that the Zairian military was indeed a broken machine.

8. The CZSC probably grew out of Yigal's trip to look for a potential contract for SOZAIS in policing the camps. Nzimbi was the main man for the DSP, and he landed the CZSC contract, the same way he would have had SOZAIS taken on the mission. Later NGO reports stated that there were "mercenaries" with the CZSC. I suspect the mercenaries in question were Israelis with connections to Yigal and SOZAIS.

9. Copies of messages, memos, and letters in Thomas P. Odom Collected Papers. Jim Pardew, the reader will recall, was the colonel who headed my section in the Pentagon during the Gulf War and is now the ambassador in Bulgaria.

10. See Khan, *Shallow Graves of Rwanda*, pp. 97–100 for a full discussion of UNAMIR–Rwandan government relations. Khan's greatest frustration was the same as that expressed by General Kagame. UNAMIR consumed millions of dollars, as did the refugee support operations exterior to Rwanda. But with all that money, neither Khan as the SRSG nor Kagame as the Rwandan vice president could get the United Nations to spend money actually helping his government. Khan states up front that a souring of relations was inevitable under that dynamic.

Chapter 7

1. Rosamond Halsey Carr with Ann Howard Halsey, *Land of a Thousand Hills: My Life in Rwanda* (New York: Penguin Putnam, 1999), pp. 205–35.

2. "Deadlock in the Rwandan Refugee Crisis: Virtual Standstill on Repatriation," Medicins Sans Frontieres, July, 1995, p.33.

3. Khan, *Shallow Graves of Rwanda*, pp. 70–71, 104–19.

4. Ibid., pp. 104–19.

5. Ibid. Nearly six years later I was pleased to read the SRSG's account of Kibeho and find that it generally tracked with my reporting, aside from his claim of an attempted RPA coup.

6. Ibid., pp. 35, 43, 94. The SRSG spells out his frustration in great detail on this matter. Of the $2 billion spent on the Rwandan crisis by 1995, $1.4 billion went to supporting external refugees. Fully $2 million per day was spent keeping the camps in operation. Inside Rwanda, UNAMIR spent $500,000 per day on itself. Yet all efforts to get money into the hands of the new government got snarled in U.N. and other international red tape. The classic was the extant World Bank account

for Rwanda, which held nearly $160 million. The World Bank directed that $20 million be diverted into the bulging Rwanda accounts for the UNHCR, UNICEF, WFP, and WHO—all directed at supporting the refugees. Inside Rwanda, the new government would be required to put up $9 million in back interest owed by the government now in exile before it could tap the main World Bank accounts. See also John Erickson, et al., "The International Response to Conflict and Genocide: Lessons from the Rwanda Experience," Joint Evaluation of Emergency Assistance to Rwanda (JEAR), *Journal of Humanitarian Assistance,* http://www.jha.sps.cam.ac.uk/a/a752.htm, posted 12 June 1998.
7. Wrong, *Mr. Kurtz,* pp. 251–309.
8. "Deadlock in the Rwandan Refugee Crisis," Medicins Sans Frontiers, pp.12–18.
9. Khan, *Shallow Graves of Rwanda,* pp. 142–43. The SRSG provides an extract of a press report that provided some of the detail we had been getting from our sources.
10. Nye apparently sent DHS a similar note, noting my support for the visit because I received a laudatory message from the DHS deputy director thanking me for a job well done. Message DIA Washington DC//DH-D to AMEMBASSY Kigali R DTG 152301Z SEP 95, Personal for LTC Odom from Mr. Jerry Magoulas, Subject: Congratulations, Thomas P. Odom Collected Papers. Note the date as mid-September as it relates to my reception in DH6 just a couple of weeks later.
11. Philip Gourevitch, *We Wish to Inform You that Tomorrow We Will Be Killed with Our Families* (New York: Farrar, Straus, and Giroux, 1998), pp. 170–71.

Chapter 8

1. Khan, *Shallow Graves of Rwanda,* pp. 168–69. Khan describes the attack fairly accurately except he says the RPA used two boats they had "converted." The boats I rode to the island were specifically designed for the mission including the machine gun "tubs."

Epilogue

1. Robert Baer, *See No Evil: The True Story of a Ground Soldier in the C.I.A.'s War on Global Terrorism* (New York: Crown Publishers, 2002).
2. Memorandum for DCSOPS, SUBJECT FAO Program, 15 August 1994, signed Gordon R. Sullivan, General, United States Army, Thomas P. Odom Collected Papers.

Bibliography

Baer, Robert. *See No Evil: The True Story of a Ground Soldier in the C.I.A.'s War on Global Terrorism.* New York: Crown Publishers, 2002.

Bowden, Mark. *Black Hawk Down.* Maine: G.K. Hall and Company, 2000.

Carr, Rosamond Halsey, with Ann Howard Halsey. *Land of a Thousand Hills: My Life in Rwanda.* New York: Penguin Putnam, 1999.

Des Forges, Alison. *Leave None to Tell the Story: Genocide in Rwanda.* Washington, D.C.: Human Rights Watch, 1999.

Erickson, John, et al, "The International Response to Conflict and Genocide: Lessons from the Rwanda Experience," Joint Evaluation of Emergency Assistance to Rwanda (JEAR), *Journal of Humanitarian Assistance,* http://www.jha.sps.cam.ac.uk/a/a752.htm, posted June 12, 1988.

Gourevitch, Philip. *We Wish to Inform You that Tomorrow We Will Be Killed with Our Families.* New York: Farrar, Straus, and Giroux, 1998.

Higgins, Robin, Lt. Col. (ret.). *Patriot Dreams: The Murder of Colonel Rich Higgins.* Quantico, Va.: Marine Corps Association, 1999.

Hochschild, Adam. *King Leopold's Ghost.* New York: Houghton Mifflin Company, 1998.

Hoyt, Michael P. E. *Captive in the Congo: A Consul's Return to the Heart of Darkness.* Annapolis, Md.: Naval Institute Press, 2000.

Kalb, Madelaine G. *The Congo Cables: The Cold War in Africa—From Eisenhower to Kennedy.* New York: McMillan Publishing Co., 1982.

Khan, Shaharyar M. *The Shallow Graves of Rwanda.* New York: I. B. Tauris Publishers, 2000.

Larose-Edwards, Paul. *The Rwandan Crisis of April 1994: The Lessons Learned.* Ottawa, Canada: International Human Rights, Democracy, and Conflict Resolution, November 30, 1994.

Odom, Maj. Thomas P. *Leavenworth Paper #14, Dragon Operations: Hostage Rescues in the Congo, 1964–1965.* Fort Leavenworth, Kans.: Combat Studies Institute, 1988.

Odom, Lt. Col. Thomas P. *Shaba II: The French and Belgian Intervention in Zaire in 1978.* Fort Leavenworth, Kans.: Combat Studies Institute, 1993.

Orth, Rick. "Four Variables in Preventive Diplomacy: Their Application in the Rwanda Case," *The Journal of Conflict Studies, Spring 1997* (University of New Brunswick): 79–100.

———. "African Operational Experiences in Peacekeeping." *Small Wars and Insurgencies* (London), vol.7, no. 3 (winter, 1996): 308–23.

———. "Rwanda's Hutu Extremist Genocidal Insurgency: An Eyewitness Perspective," draft, copy in Thomas P. Odom Collected Papers.

Scales, Brig. Gen. Robert H., Jr. *Certain Victory: The U.S. Army in the Gulf War.* Washington, D.C. : Office of the Chief of Staff, U.S. Army, 1993.

Vandewalle, Frederic J. L. A. *L'Ommengang: Odysée et Reconquête de Stanleyville, 1964.* Brussels, Belgium: Le Livre Africain, Collection Temoinage Africain, 1970.

Wrong, Michela. *In the Footsteps of Mr. Kurtz: Living on the Brink of Disaster in Mobutu's Congo.* New York: Harper Collins, 2001.

Index

U.S. Defense Attaché Brazzaville, Congo, 101–103, 108–109, 135–38

U.S. Defense Attaché Office (USDAO) Kigali, 202–207

U.S. Defense Attaché Office (USDAO) Kinshasa. *See* U.S. Embassy Kinshasa

U.S. Defense Attaché Office (USDAO) Yaoundé, 157, 206, 207. *See also* Cobb, James (Jim)

U.S. Defense Attaché Kinshasa (new), 158, 181, 183, 196–97, 237, 259. *See also* U.S. Embassy Kinshasa

U.S. Defense Attaché Liberia, 156

U.S. Department of Defense: Central African War, 202; FAOs as representatives of, xii; security assistance, support for, 233, 250, 256. *See also* Office of the Secretary of Defense for International Security Affairs (OSD-ISA); Office of the Secretary of Defense-Special Operations and Low Intensity Conflict (OSD-SOLIC)

U.S. Department of State: Africa Bureau, policy toward, 164, 174; Central African War, 202; Gersony report, 174, 176; Goma, 233; as intelligence collector, 275; Kibeho, reaction to, 230; Mobutu and FAZ, policy toward, 59; Rwandan genocide, stance on, 76, 164; Zairian Military Attaché, 64

U.S. Embassy Kigali: actions during war and genocide, 164–66; campaign planning, 236–37; manning, 165; military justice training, 192; U.S. Embassy Kinshasa, conflicts with, 197–98

U.S. Embassy Kinshasa: DIA Inspector General, 259; Goma col-

lection, 81–82, 139–40; military and political violence reporting, 78–79; organization, 54–61; reporting on Zairian military, 197–98

U.S. European Command (USEU-COM): acceptance of campaign plan, 236–37; demining program, approval of, 237, 239; demining programs, 196, 237–41, 256; Goma, reaction to, 82, 101, 109, 111, 116, 133, 134; Lt. Col. Odom, 64, 216–17, 245

USS *Higgins DDG76*, 50

U.S. Special Operations Command Europe (USSOCEUR or SOCEUR): B Team Commander demining training, relief of, 246–47; demining program, 237, 240, 245–47; survey team Goma, 107–108, 131 216–20, 242

Vandewalle, Frederic J. L. A. (VdW), 19, 37, 73, 207, 265

Vukovic, Charles (Chuck), 157

Vuono, Carl, 41–44, 46–51

Wagoner, Fred, 118

Walken, Christopher, *The Dogs of War*, 93

Warner, Volney J. Jr. (Jim), 8

Weaver, Sigourney, *Gorrillas in the Mist*, 145, 222

Whaley, Peter: arrival Rwanda, 223; escorts U.S. senator, 255; reaction to Kibeho, 223, 225–26, 229; reporting U.S. Embassy Kinshasa, 73, 84, 139; warnings to Washington, 233

Whitehead, Robert, 192–93

White House: air show in Goma, 108, 110, 112–13, 115–16; Central African War, 202

William, Col.: mortar attack Mount Goma, 91–92; relieved

DATE DUE
